Financial Futures and Options

Recent Titles from Quorum Books

Behavioral Accounting: The Research and Practical Issues
Ahmed Belkaoui

Personnel Policies and Procedures for Health Care Facilities: A Manager's Manual and Guide
Eugene P. Buccini and Charles P. Mullaney

Designing the Cost-Effective Office: A Guide for Facilities Planners and Managers
Jack M. Fredrickson

The Employment Contract: Rights and Duties of Employers and Employees
Warren Freedman

Lobbying and Government Relations: A Guide for Executives
Charles S. Mack

U.S. Protectionism and the World Debt Crisis
Edward John Ray

The Social and Economic Consequences of Deregulation: The Transportation Industry in Transition
Paul Stephen Dempsey

The Accountant's Guide to Corporation, Partnership, and Agency Law
Sidney M. Wolf

Human Information Processing in Accounting
Ahmed Belkaoui

Alternative Transportation Fuels
Daniel Sperling

The Design and Implementation of Administrative Controls: A Guide for Financial Executives
John P. Fertakis

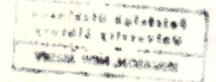

FINANCIAL FUTURES AND OPTIONS

A Guide to Markets, Applications, and Strategies

Todd E. Petzel

QUORUM BOOKS

NEW YORK · WESTPORT, CONNECTICUT · LONDON

Library of Congress Cataloging-in-Publication Data

Petzel, Todd E.
　　Financial futures and options : a guide to markets, applications,
and strategies / Todd E. Petzel.
　　　　p.　　cm.
　　Bibliography: p.
　　Includes index.
　　ISBN 0-89930-152-5 (alk. paper)
　　1. Financial futures.　2. Options (Finance).　I. Title.
　　HG6024.A3P48　1989
　　332.64′52—dc19　　　　　89-3775

British Library Cataloguing in Publication Data is available.

Library of Congress Catalog Card Number: 89-3775
ISBN: 0-89930-152-5

First published in 1989 by Quorum Books

Greenwood Press, Inc.
88 Post Road West, Westport, Connecticut 06881

Printed in the United States of America

The paper used in this book complies with the
Permanent Paper Standard issued by the National
Information Standards Organization (Z39.48-1984).
10 9 8 7 6 5

Contents

Figures and Tables

FIGURES

TABLES

Preface

Many of today's participants in financial futures and options do not know the genesis of these markets, despite the fact that their entire history has occurred since 1972. Some participants are too young to have experienced the early events, and others came to the markets only after they reached active trading levels. For these traders, seeing a steady stream of prices come across a quote screen is as natural and automatic as watching a light come on when the switch is flipped.

Members of a smaller group recall, or have studied carefully, the nurturing of financial futures and options. Having more than just a collection of interesting war stories, they have a historical perspective that provides insights into the basic functioning of the markets. The purpose of this book is to build upon this historical perspective in providing an explanation of how financial futures and options work. The intended audience consists of those new to the markets, whose numbers continue to grow, and those who by their vocation or avocation have already had some exposure, but in a limited way.

This work will not offer particular trading advice or tout any system of trading. What it provides is a description of how the contracts are constructed and how they might be used. If you are a trader who is looking at these contracts for commercial uses, there will be many general examples provided. If you are a speculator, the commercial emphasis may seem overdone, but a word of caution. Contrary to some popular opinion, the speculative tail does not wag the commercial dog. Financial futures, like all other futures markets, are dominated by professionals constantly involved with the fundamentals of the marketplace. These commercial users are well capitalized, usually are very well informed, and have motives for trading that are different from those of the noncommercial trader. The speculator who ignores the basic composition and working of the markets because they are too complicated does so at his or her own peril.

The organization is designed to facilitate a reader's particular needs. The first chapter provides an overview of the first 15 years of financial futures examining both successes and failures. The basic hypothesis of what components are necessary for success is developed. The second and third chapters present the fundamentals of futures and options and may be skipped without loss of continuity by anyone with an understanding of this material. Chapters 4, 5, and 6 deal with the equity index, interest rate, and foreign currency futures and options markets, respectively. In each of these chapters the forms of the dominant contracts are described and trading examples provided. Finally, chapter 7 is an overview of accounting, tax, and regulatory issues that affect the development and trading of financial futures and options.

Several colleagues have contributed to the form and content of this work. Members of the trade, too numerous to name, have always shown an enthusiasm for the subject. Rarely will you find an industry where its members share so willingly of their knowledge, and my debt to this group is great. Deborah Bosi, Dick McDonald, Matt Moran, Jerry Salzman, and Steve Youngren all made valuable suggestions about the manuscript that are greatly appreciated. Finally, I would like to thank my wife, Susan, for her many patient contributions.

Abbreviations

CBOE	Chicago Board Options Exchange
CBOT	Chicago Board of Trade
CEA	Commodity Exchange Act
CFTC	Commodity Futures Trading Commission
CME	Chicago Mercantile Exchange
CPI	Consumer Price Index
CSCE	Coffee, Sugar & Cocoa Exchange, Inc.
DIFF	Eurorate Differential Contract
ERISA	Employee Retirement Income Security Act
FASB	Financial Accounting Standards Board
FCM	Futures Commission Merchant
FHLBB	Federal Home Loan Bank Board
FIA	Futures Industry Association
FSLIC	Federal Savings and Loan Insurance Corporation
GFA	Grain Futures Administration
GIC	Guaranteed Investment Contract
GNMA	Government National Mortgage Association
HFC	Hershey Foods Corporation
IMM	International Monetary Market

IO	Interest Only
KCBT	Kansas City Board of Trade
LIBOR	London Interbank Offer Rate
MOC	Market on Close Order
NFA	National Futures Association
OCC	Option Clearing Corporation
OSE	Osaka Stock Exchange
OTC	Over the Counter
PO	Principal Only
RIC	Regulated Investment Company
SEC	Securities and Exchange Commission
SFAS	Statement of Financial Accounting Standards
S&P	Standard and Poors
TAA	Tactical Asset Allocation
TSE	Tokyo Stock Exchange
USDA	United States Department of Agriculture

CHAPTER 1

Introduction

On May 16, 1972, financial futures came into being with the introduction of foreign exchange futures at the International Monetary Market (IMM), a division of the Chicago Mercantile Exchange (CME). As with most genuine innovations, acceptance was not immediate. Bankers active in the area noted that there was a well-functioning foreign market in forward exchange (which they ran) and viewed the new futures as redundant at best. At worst, the claims were that futures would only introduce a gambling element that would subvert the legitimate function of the market. By year's end in 1972, 145,000 lots changed hands in seven different currency contacts, accounting for 3.1 percent of the total CME volume.[1] Japanese yen, the most actively traded currency contract that first year, had an average daily volume near 250 lots.

By 1976 very little had changed. Total IMM volume was 192,000, still 3.1 percent of the CME 6.2 million total. The Japanese yen contract had tumbled to an average daily volume of six lots, and the prime contract that year was for Mexican pesos with just over 51,000 contracts traded. More than four years' experience saw the jury still out on the long-term benefits of foreign currency futures, but the most extreme predictions of speculative-induced volatility had been shown to be baseless.

In ten more years, the landscape changed dramatically. Foreign currency futures trading at the IMM in 1986 totaled almost 19 million contracts, or nearly 32 percent of the CME's total futures volume, and currencies were only part of the story. Consider the following for 1986 at the CME:

1. Interest rate products (Eurodollars and T-bills) accounted for 12.6 million lots of volume.

2. One stock index contract, the Standard and Poors (S&P) 500 futures, traded 19.5 million lots.

3. More than 8 million options on financial futures were traded.

Taken together, financial instruments at the CME accounted for more than 86 percent of the year's total trading activity.

Although the CME's success is dramatic, it is not unique. In 1972 total industry volume was just over 18 million lots. The total in 1986 was 216 million, two-thirds of which was from financial instruments that did not exist 15 years earlier. The events since 1976 constitute a major restructuring of the futures industry. In terms of exchange and member-firm revenues, the traditional areas of agricultural and industrial commodities that once shouldered the entire burden now carry a minority share. With that shift has come a much broader representation of membership governing exchange policy and plotting the course for future industry development. But it will be argued here that the fundamentals of futures have not changed. Instead, new industries have discovered the benefits offered by traditional forms and have developed the markets to meet their own needs. In doing so, investment opportunities have been created beyond the imagination of just a few years ago.

One might expect that with the explosive growth in these markets there would have evolved a theory of futures trading to explain the behavior of the markets. In fact, there are several models that have been applied to these markets over the years, but none has proved to be completely satisfactory. Each model is built upon assumptions of how a typical trader behaves, and unfortunately, there are many types of traders. A theory built upon the behavior of any one of them is bound to be deficient. There will be no attempt here to provide a single, easy answer to the question of how financial futures and options work. What will be provided is a foundation common to all successful markets on which the specific contract features can be built.

A clear understanding comes from knowing the participants in the market and their motivations. A government bond dealer will likely behave differently from a speculating economist looking at a statistical model of interest rates, but the interaction of their orders with those of a thousand other traders on the floor of an exchange is key to the dynamics of interest rate determination. The following list includes some of the more typical trading behaviors that will be described in detail in the next chapter:

Inventory hedging

Commercial buying and selling

Performing dealer functions

Arbitraging

Speculating

For a market to be successful it must be useful to traders from different groups. No market has ever had long-term prosperity appealing exclusively to speculators, and similarly, very narrow trade-oriented contracts that have limited speculative appeal go through illiquid periods when it is very difficult to transact business. Utility comes from different contract aspects for various traders, and in developing and maintaining successful contracts there are five criteria that can be identified as important.

1.   There is a sizable pool of assets or income at risk.

Markets flourish when the number of potential traders is large, but nothing will induce them to produce a steady stream of bids and offers unless that pool of capital is subject to an identifiable, systematic risk. Had interest rate or foreign exchange futures been invented in the 1950s, they almost certainly would have failed in a world of pegged rates. There was no systematic risk and little reason to trade.

2.   The instrument or index underlying the futures contract is an accurate reflection of that risk.

A term that will be used throughout this book is *basis,* which is widely used to mean the relationship between two prices. For futures traders the key basis is the difference between the price of the futures contract and the price of the cash market good they are trading against. In the simplest case, suppose that an importer has a stock of French francs and is worried about fluctuating exchange rates over the next few months. The CME French franc contract calls for delivery of a certain quantity of francs on the delivery day. There is a very high probability that any movements in the cash, or spot, market for francs will be closely matched by movements in the CME franc futures contract. For this importer the CME contract is a very good reflection of the cash market value; the risk of the basis changing is low. As the number of potential participants that face low basis risk grows, so does the chance of a market's success.

3.   The instrument or index underlying the futures contract is not subject to manipulation or distortion.

Manipulation of a futures or options market is a federal crime, but more importantly, it is very bad for business. A fundamental fact is that no one is conscripted to trade. If shocks or distortions can drive the futures price away from the cash market values, traders will view this uncertainty as a cost of doing business, and at some point these costs can become prohibitive. The members of futures exchanges have a very strong motivation to establish self-regulatory procedures to minimize the chance of market manipulations and distortions, since a contract that is prone to manipulation has little chance of success.

4.   There must be a regular source of information about the instrument or index so that
     participants may trade knowledgeably.

People trade on information that they believe has economic value. For the
interest rate markets, people look to data on the money supply, government and
consumer spending, foreign exchange rates, unemployment figures, and scores
of other statistics that are believed to be meaningful in divining the course of
future events. For the oat market, there are probably fewer than 100 people who
carefully monitor data on crop size and demand. It is not surprising that the
average daily volume on the Chicago Board of Trade (CBOT) T-bond contract in
1986 exceeded the annual volume of their oat futures contract, which has been
trading for more than 100 years.

5.   The successful futures market must meet the requirements of the different participants
     more efficiently than do the competing markets.

Markets have many attributes that will be discussed in detail below, but one of
the most important is liquidity. The importer holding French francs might look at
the CME contract and see that on average the basis risk is low, but it will also be
noted that there is very little trading activity on the contract, producing a relatively wide spread between the prevailing bid and offer. This importer may
decide that whatever needs are to be met can best be handled by the interbank
forward market or perhaps even another foreign currency future that is more
actively traded. For a contract to succeed it must offer something unique at a
price, in terms of transaction costs, that is reasonable to the participants. The
decade beginning in 1975 is full of examples of exchanges trying to launch
duplicative contracts that offer very few unique features. The universal experience has been one of disappointment.

Contracts that meet these criteria appeal to many traders. Some investors are
attracted to volatile markets by the prospects of significant profits, whereas
commercial firms see futures as an important tool among their risk management
instruments. By understanding the basic behavior of the various key groups of
traders, insights into the overall working of the market may be obtained. The
next two chapters provide these fundamentals for futures and options and lay the
foundation for exploring how individual contracts are traded.

NOTE

1. All trading volume and open interest data are from Futures Industry Association
(FIA) sources.

================= CHAPTER 2 =================

Basics of Futures

2.1   WHAT IS A FUTURES CONTRACT?

Futures contracts are standardized legal agreements to transact in either physical or financial assets at some designated future time. They represent a step in an evolutionary chain that begins with cash, or "spot" transactions, and progresses to forward contracts. In a *forward contract* a particular buyer and seller agree to exchange goods or cash for goods at some later date. Descriptively called "to arrive" contracts, such forward transactions allow both parties to extend their business-planning horizons. Shipments of wheat expected to arrive at eastern terminal markets were the basis of some of the first clearly documented forward transactions in the United States, although there are records of similar markets dating from the tenth century.[1]

Although the advantages of forward contracts over spot transactions are many, there are still numerous drawbacks that have prompted the development of the standardized futures contract. The primary drawbacks are that forward contracts can be too specific, cumbersome, and insecure.

Specificity may appear to be a virtue in a contract, but if either party's circumstances should change, contract specificity becomes a cost associated with the overall transaction. The remedies available to the parties in question are limited. The contract may be fulfilled in its original terms at a higher expense, or one participant may approach the other and seek a renegotiation. In most cases of this type, the disadvantaged party is readily identified in the bargaining process.

Forward contracts bind the two parties in question, but rarely are markets that simplistic. Producer A contracts with Dealer B, who in turn trades forward with

Dealer C and so on. In each instance the individual forward contract is an inviolate link in the chain. Rights and obligations of a party are not transferable without the consent of the counterparty, making the complete structure of forward transactions cumbersome.

In this system of transactions the risks of nonperformance fall only on the contracting parties. Folklore tells of the midwestern grain farmer in the mid-1800s who had sold his crop forward to a merchant in Chicago. At harvest there was an abundance of grain and prices had fallen well below the agreed-upon price. When the farmer arrived in Chicago with his grain, ready to carry out his half of the bargain, he found the merchant unwilling to honor his commitment. The story goes that the farmer said, "I have a wagon of grain and a shotgun with me. Which should I unload?" Whether true or apocryphal, the story describes the environment of the risky forward contract that spawned the Chicago Board of Trade and organized grain futures trading in the United States.

Futures contracts overcome these problems by being general in design and easy to work with. Subsequent refinements throughout the years have extended the coverage and safety of futures contracts considerably. Of particular importance has been the clear definition of the standard elements and the relatively modern development of the clearing association, which provides a strong measure of protection for both parties to the transaction.

2.2   STANDARD ELEMENTS OF FUTURES CONTRACTS

Successful futures contracts have enough standard elements to insure that both the buyer and the seller have a clear understanding about what performance is expected. Care is taken not to favor one side of the transaction over the other. Ironically, a well-functioning futures contract will represent an imperfect transaction for both parties, being general enough to apply to a broad range of buyers and sellers. The standard elements include the definition of the commodity or index on which the contract is based, the size of the contract, the form of price quotation, and the method of final settlement, which may or may not include a formal delivery. Each characteristic will be described in detail. Once the standard features are defined, the only subject open to negotiation is price.

2.2.1   Definition of the Commodity or Index

Defining what commodity or index forms the basis for trading may seem to be obvious or trivial, but it is, in fact, the most important part of the equation. For traditional agricultural commodities like sugar it is necessary to define the minimum quality specifications and what, if any, premiums are to be paid for deliveries that exceed the minimum. It is also critical to define where the product must be delivered. No. 2 yellow corn may appear to be a fairly standard commodity, but it makes a great deal of difference to Kelloggs whether the product is located in Chicago or in an elevator in Battle Creek, Michigan.

For financial futures the problem is in many ways less complicated. Foreign exchange futures call for the delivery of a specific currency, and barring the possibility of counterfeit money, the product is widely accepted in all of its denominations. Interest rate products pose somewhat greater difficulties but are still easier than most agricultural goods. For CBOT Treasury bond futures, a wide array of existing instruments are potentially deliverable at any time, and there has developed an extensive literature discussing the identification of the "cheapest-to-deliver" bond. This literature recognizes that within the generalized definition of the product, the seller has the option of what good is actually to be delivered and will always choose instruments that have the lowest alternative value in the cash or "spot" market. The buyers on the contract understand that they should expect to receive the cheapest allowable product, and they form their bids accordingly. It is the exchange's obligation to define a high enough standard so that the minimum represents a desirable good to the buyer, without making the standards so rigid that it is difficult for the sellers to obtain a sufficient deliverable supply.

One of the most significant innovations of the 1980s was the development of stock index futures. In addition to opening futures-style trading to the equities population, these products popularized cash settlement. Instead of actually transferring a physical product between seller and buyer, futures contracts could be settled by transferring funds, the amount of which was determined by the value of an index number. The Kansas City Board of Trade (KCBT) first introduced the Value Line Stock Index in 1982, and very quickly thereafter the CME brought out its own contract based on the S&P 500 Index. The definitions of both indices were widely known throughout the equities industry, so there was little confusion about what the contracts represented.

Final settlement of such index contracts was originally designed to be based on the closing value of the index on the expiration date.[2] If you had gone long at an index level lower than the ultimate settlement value and had held the contract to maturity, at expiration you would implicitly be selling at the higher value and would collect the difference. Conversely, you would lose with a long position and declining index values. In either event, the precision of the definition of a stock index contract and its final settlement is such that it can be clearly understood by both buyers and sellers and is fair to both sides.

2.2.2   Size of Contract; Form of Price Quotation

Once the foundation of the contract is defined, the size of the basic trading unit must be established. This is a balancing act between the wishes of large commercial interests and those of floor traders and public speculators. A government bond dealer with a modest portfolio of $100 million might argue that a $1 million T-bond contract size would be appropriate since it would allow flexibility in hedging strategies while providing complete coverage with only 100 contracts (and only 100 lots worth of commissions). Such a trading unit would imply that a

$\frac{1}{32}$ of a percentage point change in price (the minimum "tick" size) would change the value of the contract by $312.50 (0.01 × $\frac{1}{32}$ × $1 million). That minimum fluctuation might discourage floor traders trying to "scalp" the market or small speculators trying to outguess the course of interest rates. In their view, the optimal contract might be smaller.

The CBOT chose $100,000 as the size of the contract with the hope that it would be large enough to be useful to commercials, yet not so large as to discourage the floor and public customers who provide essential liquidity to the market. An average day on the CBOT in the mid-1980s saw more than 200,000 T-bond contracts change hands, representing more than $20 billion dollars. This is one contract size that has proven most effective.

Volatility is a key element in the decision making concerning contract size. T-bills, which have a short maturity, face considerably less dollar risk from a given change in interest rates than do T-bonds. Recognizing this, the CME designed its T-bill and Eurodollar contracts with $1 million as the basic size, and they have both proven effective. In general, the smaller the relative volatility, the larger the dollar value of the contract should be.

Some contracts pose great difficulty in this regard as a contract size can become outmoded. The original Mexican peso contract at the CME called for the delivery of 1 million pesos, a reasonable value in 1972. By 1986 and the experience of a decade and a half of steady devaluations, the value of 1 million pesos had fallen to below $1,000, and trading had completely stopped. In such cases, if the trading community believes there is a viable market at some appropriate size, modifications could be introduced in an attempt to salvage the basic product.[3]

Related to the contract-size problem is the issue of price-quotation form. Typically, the goal is to copy standard cash market practice. If bond dealers trade in multiples of $\frac{1}{32}$ of a point representing a percentage of par, futures contracts identically specified will give those dealers maximum flexibility in establishing countertrades. In areas where there is no tradition of cash practice (e.g., stock index contracts) the rules are guided by the principle of making the minimum price change small enough to encourage liquidity without being an annoyingly small value. If errors are to be made in this design, however, it is better to make the tick size too small, since the traders can always cluster their trades around the popular intervals.

2.2.3 Time of Final Settlement

In the era before financial futures, this section would have been known as time of delivery. The contract months determining when the corn or wheat deliveries take place is as important an element as any. With the invention of cash settlement, which is discussed in detail in the next section, actual physical deliveries were eliminated. In a cash settlement market there is merely a time of final settlement when the contracts cease to exist, eliminating any further obligation on the part of either the buyer or the seller.

Setting of the contract months is guided by the wishes of the market participants. Offering too many months in an attempt to provide a wide menu of choices to potential customers has risks because trading interest may be spread too thinly across the various contracts to allow for liquid trading in any. By offering a cycle of staggered months, attention is focused on the available instruments, and both volume and open interest prosper. The number of maturities is also subject to experimentation. If individuals do not believe they have unique information about a distant maturity, they will not trade it. For agricultural markets it is usual to have contracts extending over a year. In that way traders may establish positions affecting both this year's crop and the crop not yet harvested. Contracts do not typically extend further because there is not enough information in the marketplace about the prospects for production that is not yet planted and consumption that could be subject to considerable shocks.

In financial futures there are no seasonal factors comparable to the harvesting of a crop. If a central bank wants to enter into an open market transaction, it is as likely to do so next week as next year, and there should be no discernible pattern of performance over the year. With no physical crop to be allocated across years and no seasonal pattern of production, financial futures have discovered that fewer maturities are needed to meet the traders' needs. Typically, well over 90 percent of the total open position in a stock index contract is concentrated in the nearby month, and an extremely high fraction of activity in stock index, interest rate, and currency futures is found in the first one or two contracts, which are usually separated by a calendar quarter. The only major exception to this rule is the CME Eurodollar contract, which has developed significant open interest spanning several years. This is due to some unique trading practices that are described in detail in Section 5.4.2.

2.2.4   Method of Final Settlement

Final settlement describes the mechanism by which the obligations of both parties to the contract are released. Traditional contracts all provided for the potential for delivery, although most contracts were offset before that time. In fact, for many years Illinois state law specifically banned contracts lacking delivery provisions, because they were viewed to be gambling devices. For storable agricultural products and metals, the delivery specifications call for the product to be located in exchange-licensed warehouses. Settlement occurs when the deliverer gives the receiver the warehouse receipt in exchange for full payment. If the deliverer does not have the commodity "in location," it is necessary to transport, store, sample, and grade the product before any delivery can be made. The associated expenses discourage most sellers on these futures contracts from actually delivering on their commitments. In most instances it is far more economical to find a buyer for the cash good away from the exchange and then buy back the short futures position to close out the position.

It might appear that buyers have an advantage in such a system, since by standing firm in their position they could "squeeze" the shorts to bid higher prices to liquidate their contracts. In well-designed contracts there are compensating elements that impose costs as well on the buyers who stand for delivery. For agricultural commodity contracts there is frequently a choice of a number of delivery locations and, as previously mentioned, a range of grades deliverable, all at the seller's option. For the buyer taking delivery it is a matter of pot luck, since the specifics of the delivery are not known until it is made. The one certainty is that there is little chance of getting the highest quality good. The seller holding all of the delivery options will be sure to offer what is cheapest to deliver.

Many financial contracts have fairly traditional delivery mechanisms. The CBOT T-bond and T-note contracts call for the wire transfer of instruments meeting the minimum delivery specifications. There is an extensive literature that has evolved in the 1980s exploring what bonds or notes are cheapest to deliver on the respective contracts, but the problem is fundamentally no different from that faced by the grain merchant. A key advantage held by the bond trader is the vast pool of instruments continuously available for delivery. Ironically, because of this supply, sellers find it easier to buy back their position, and the longs in the market have little incentive to try to squeeze the market, since there is virtually no chance of success. The result is that there are very few ultimate deliveries against most financial futures. Those that do occur happen because it is extremely cost effective to do so.

In 1981 a major innovation occurred with the introduction of cash settlement for the CME Eurodollar contract. Instead of delivering a bundle of three-month Eurodollar time-deposit funds to settle the contract, on the last trading date a final settlement price is constructed by polling London banks as to their current LIBOR (London Interbank Offer Rate). The exact procedure is finely defined and constructed to minimize any chance of manipulation. After the average rate is determined, the final settlement price is used as a standard for all outstanding contracts. Buyers who had purchased futures at prices below final settlement receive the value of the difference. But the sellers of those contracts pay. The converse is true for those who bought above the final settlement price.[4]

Cash settlement made it possible to have liquid futures trading in contracts for which actual delivery would be difficult, if not impossible. The most prominent examples of cash-settled contracts are the stock index futures, where it would be almost absurd to try to deliver an appropriately weighted portfolio containing each of the stocks in the index. Cash settlement is not, however, the answer for all contracts. It is essential that an unmanipulable, definite source of information be available on which to base the final settlement value. If for any reason the final barometer of value is not perceived to be fair and accurate, traders will shy away from the market.

2.2.5   The Nonstandard Component

Once the commodity or index has been defined, the maturities and the size- and price-quotation mechanism set, and the method of final settlement determined, there is only one thing left open to question: the price.

Traders place bids or offers into the market with confidence, knowing that everyone is operating under the same set of rules and that these terms will not vary over the life of the contract. There is no assurance that they will trade with success, but by bidding and offering they transmit important information to all market participants. As buyers aggressively bid for a contract, it sends a clear signal to potential suppliers that the product can be brought to market more profitably. It further tells speculative shorts that others do not share their view and that it may be a good time to reevaluate one's trading strategy.

For a strictly defined good or index like the S&P 500, the price in the marketplace will reflect the consensus of how the future value relates to the current spot price. For contracts that offer a variety of deliverable grades, the market will price the ''cheapest-to-deliver'' since it is the seller's decision of what is actually offered if delivery occurs. In either case both the buyers and sellers will bring to the market all of the information they believe is relevant in determining future value.

2.3   WHERE AND HOW FUTURES ARE TRADED

Futures contracts in the United States, as distinguished from forward, or ''to-arrive'' contracts, are legally traded exclusively on exchanges designated by the Commodity Futures Trading Commission (CFTC). It has only been since the passage of the Commodity Exchange Act (CEA) of 1974, creating the CFTC, that all U.S. futures contracts have been under the federal regulatory umbrella. Before that year many contracts including metals and foreign soft commodities (coffee, sugar, and cocoa, for example) were outside the jurisdiction of any federal regulator.

The history of futures regulation dates from the passage of the Grain Futures Act of 1922, which arose out of a perception that grain speculation was a major contributor to the depressed post–Great War farm economy. Aiming to curb manipulation and fraud in the trading of grain and cotton futures, the Grain Futures Administration (GFA) operated within the United States Department of Agriculture (USDA). The GFA evolved into the Commodity Exchange Authority, but until 1974 the scope of futures regulation was limited to domestic agriculture.

Many events combined in the early 1970s to prompt legislative change. The introduction of currency futures at the International Monetary Market, a division of the CME, focused attention on the disparity of regulation for commodities trading even under the same roof. Philip Johnson reported that around this time the CBOT strongly considered trading futures on individual companies' stock.[5]

In part because options on equities could approximate the risk characteristics of futures, however, and because the regulatory picture contained many open questions, the CBOT formed a new exchange in 1973 to trade options. The Chicago Board Options Exchange fell under the domain of the Securities and Exchange Commission, avoiding immediate regulatory problems, but the episode suggested that the prevailing federal legislation covering futures needed reworking.

The CFTC is a direct descendant of the Commodity Exchange Authority, but with the expanded array of contracts to be covered, it was decided that the CFTC should be an independent agency outside the USDA. Making the CFTC independent and charging it with oversight of all futures has not eliminated jurisdictional issues. Now, instead of having contracts outside any agency's view, the problem can be which of the competing regulators should have jurisdiction over newly developed instruments that look like futures but are based on products traditionally the domain of another regulator.[6]

Some might wonder how a futures industry that had its origins in this country in the midnineteenth century fared before the comprehensive federal oversight that was designed to prevent manipulation and fraud. "Very well," would be the answer of many in the industry. Manipulation and fraud are not activities common to successful markets, and this was true for grains before 1922 and for all of the other markets before 1974. It was, and continues to be, primarily up to the exchanges to regulate their own market participants. By maintaining fair markets, exchanges prosper by attracting a wide variety of traders who have confidence in the institutions. It can be argued that federal regulation provides a second line of defense, the proverbial suspenders and a belt, that gives assurance to public customers that are outside of the commercial memberships of the exchanges, but there have never been any studies demonstrating benefits associated with the considerable costs.

2.3.1   The Traders

The exchanges are not-for-profit membership organizations whose members are very much for profit. Typically, every major competitor in an industry served by a futures contract will be active in the contract and in exchange governance. The motive can be seen as a high-minded desire to promote an efficient institution, but as a practical matter, each participating member does so to protect his own interest against possible conflicts with competitors. An exchange fosters this by having representatives of various interest groups on its board. Each has its own constituent groups and objectives that insures the contracts will not become biased. In the short run such a bias would confer an advantage to one side, but in the long run the contract would ultimately fail, to the detriment of all.

Some erroneously hold the belief that exchanges actually participate in the transactions, either buying or selling directly or by acting as an agent bringing parties together. If such activities were permitted, impartiality would be impossible. Exchanges pay their bills by collecting fees on every transaction, typically less than a dollar per side. Both the buyer and the seller pay the fees, and as volume increases exchanges can provide more services to improve and expand the markets.

To become a member one merely needs to buy a seat and meet minimum financial requirements.[7] The number of seats are fixed at any given time, although growing exchanges do provide new issues to build both membership and capital for further expansion. Seats are traded competitively, and the price of a seat reflects the market perception of the income stream available to members. Small exchanges that have initially issued more seats than their level of business would support have seen seat prices below $1,000. At the other end of the spectrum are the full-membership seats at the Chicago Board of Trade and Chicago Mercantile Exchange that give their owners the right to trade any of the respective exchange's futures or options, and which have traded in the late 1980s around $500,000 each.[8]

It is useful to know the participants in the futures markets and to understand their motives to appreciate how the contracts may best be employed. There are four general categories of members: commercial traders, futures commission merchants (FCMs), floor brokers, and public customers. The activities of each are not always distinct, but the divisions are still meaningful.

Commercial traders. Anyone who would transact in a financial instrument as part of his or her normal business, *independent of whether or not a related futures contract exists,* can be called a commercial trader. Government securities dealers, foreign exchange brokers, and portfolio managers are all included under this heading. Traditional theory contends that commercial traders are active in futures because they hold asset positions that are subject to price risk, and by taking on opposite positions in futures they can transfer that risk to others willing to assume it. The desire for insurance is frequently mentioned as the primary motivation for these traders, but this is a naive view that underestimates the sophisticated strategies of the commercial traders.

Futures markets offer various opportunities for different commercial traders. For the bond dealer holding an inventory of new issues, interest rate futures can provide a temporary resting place for the bonds until actual buyers can be found. For the manufacturer selling a product abroad in British pounds, foreign exchange futures provide the opportunity to fix profit margins in dollar terms. For the portfolio manager, stock index futures allow the quick transformation to a larger cash position without actually liquidating the particular equities.

Each of these activities has the effect of reducing the risk of the assets being held, but this would not be considered the primary motivation behind the transactions. Financial futures are another tool in the array of instruments available to the commercial trader to achieve the firm's objectives.

Commercial firms make up key parts of the membership and the governing bodies of an exchange. They want to see that the contracts are a good reflection of cash market practice and that rules designed to provide fair trading are being observed.

Futures Commission Merchants perform the activity that their name obliquely implies. They act as agents soliciting business and funneling orders to the floor of the exchange. For this service they charge a commission that is competitively determined and varies with the services provided. Major wire houses have many services, including research for their customers, and consequently charge higher commissions than the so-called discount brokers who merely offer order execution. Even within firms, different customers can be charged different commissions with the most active traders receiving a lower per-contract rate of commission than the less active trader.

Customers of the FCMs include public investors and commercial accounts with widely differing strategies and understanding of the market. Care is taken in the FCM to make sure that customer orders are processed efficiently and that the appropriate level of funds are maintained in each account. The FCM usually will not have a trading position of its own, except as a depository for erroneously made trades for which it has a financial responsibility. There are standards of conduct to insure that the broker handles the customer's account properly, and these standards are monitored first by the FCM and then by the exchanges, the CFTC, and, most recently, the National Futures Association (NFA). Fines, suspensions, and other sanctions can result from a finding of improper FCM behavior.

The objectives of FCM members of an exchange are to see that contract terms are not skewed toward large commercial interests at the expense of the public customer. They also take a strong interest in education and marketing efforts of the exchanges that contribute to the development of more public business.

Floor traders can be thought of as the front-line troops in the marketplace. Orders to buy and sell originate from many quarters, but they all come together on the floor of the exchange. Floor traders operate within a system known as open outcry (described in more detail below), whereby every individual is a potential buyer or seller and transactions are completed in staccato fashion around the trading pit or ring.

These traders hold the exclusive right to transact business at the exhanges but this right conveys little in the way of monopoly power. The number of floor traders is large at most exchanges, and unlike stock market specialists, they are not bound to any particular contract. The competition in the actively traded contracts is keen, and there is no guarantee of success.

A floor trader may be representing a buyer or seller from off the floor, providing this brokerage service at a modest fee. Some members specialize in this activity when their income is dependent only on the volume of business and the accuracy of their executions.[9]

At most futures exchanges there is no prohibition on traders both brokering customer business and trading for their own accounts.[10] Members who trade for themselves and execute customer orders are engaged in "dual trading," a practice that has generated considerable misunderstanding and suspicion. Securities markets have traditionally addressed dual trading by placing restrictions on the activities of different floor members. Futures exchanges have approached the issue by constructing extensive rules to prohibit abuses that could arise from the sometimes conflicting roles of trader and broker. In general, however, the market itself polices the behavior of the floor brokers in that customers who receive poor trade execution (either through incompetence or mischief) are prone to take their business elsewhere.

Floor brokers want liquidity to improve their brokerage and to improve the short-term trading opportunities for themselves. They work to insure that the minimum price change, the "tick" size, is not so large as to discourage active participation by the floor or public customers. Floor traders also tend to encourage expansion into new contracts as a method of generating new business, which increases both commission income and the expected value of the exchange seat. New products have the further advantage of diversifying a floor broker's risk. If trading in existing markets should be curtailed or discontinued for any reason, there will be other active markets to trade.

Public customers. The "outsiders" of the market, public customers, are the only category of traders that do not directly rely on the futures or the related cash markets for their livelihood. They come to the market as speculators, some willing to take on great risk for the chance of considerable profit. Others employ more risk-controlled strategies. Although they may bring considerable capital to the market, they are frequently dependent on their FCM for accurate information about current market conditions. Their desire is to have markets where all orders, irrespective of source, are treated equally, and where price reflects supply and demand, rather than artificial forces. Most public customers trading financial futures understand that they do not have all of the resources available to them that government securities or foreign exchange dealers have, but they have a right to expect that their order will be treated fairly and that the market is not subject to distortion from the trading activities of others.

2.3.2 Open Outcry System

The various members trade at the exchange in a system known as *open outcry*. In this process every buy and sell order is brought to the floor of the exchange and announced to the ring or pit. Each floor member in attendance is a potential counterparty, and the individual trying to buy or sell is supposed to trade with the first member to meet the bid or offer. In this way all actual and potential trades are known to the entire community, and market information is quickly disseminated. Unlike securities trading, in futures there are no block trades or other transactions off the floor. The Commodity Exchange Act specifically prohibits the trading of futures away from designated marketplaces, and one of the big adjustments that has had to be made by financial futures traders is recognizing the differing methods between the cash and futures sides of the business.

An advantage of the open outcry system is the keen competition that exists on the floor of the exchanges. Members trading a given contract do not have assigned roles, nor are they bound to make a market in any specific index or commodity. Instead, floor traders can move from pit to pit seeking out the best opportunities. For the trader off the floor, this system gives assurance that any order is executed competitively and is reflective of market conditions. One disadvantage stems, however, from this freewheeling approach. As more floor traders are attracted to an active market, it becomes less likely that each broker will be cognizant of all of the activity in the market. If this occurs to an extreme measure, the chance of two different prices occurring simultaneously in the same market grows, and efficiency of order execution is diminished.

For markets like the S&P 500 futures at the CME and T-bonds at the CBOT, success has meant the presence at any given time of more than 200 brokers all trading by open outcry. To the untrained observer such markets are seas of mass confusion, but there is an organizational structure. The brokers and exchange employees are trying to make sure that there is only one highest bid and one lowest offer in the pit at a time. But given the physical limitations of individuals, it is inevitable that not all bids and offers are heard by each trader. There have been many discussions in the 1980s about ways of automating some of this process, but to date there has been little progress in futures to alter the fundamental open outcry system for all orders.

One frequently mentioned potential improvement is an automatic small-order execution system similar to that used in some securities and options markets. Large orders would still be brought to the floor and traded by open outcry, but small orders would be matched automatically at the prevailing price. Although this makes intuitive sense, there is a question as to what is a small order in futures when a single contract may be valued above $100,000. Working out such details and overcoming the objections of floor-trading members who make their living executing trades are two important steps that must be overcome before open outcry is modified significantly.

The most dramatic step in the evolution of the open outcry system are automated trading systems. Instead of having a physical presence in a pit, a trader has an electronic presence on a network connecting geographically dispersed members. The system automatically shows the best bid and offer, and there is no chance of a transaction occurring that "does not hear" a better opportunity.

Traditionalists argue that no electronic system can emulate the dynamics of a futures trading pit. There is important information to be learned by listening to the inflection in a voice or by looking at a trader's expression or the amount of sweat on his brow. For these people, trading is a personal, intimate activity.

The counterpoint to this asks the question why basic institutions of trading have changed little in over 100 years, despite the rapid changes that have radically altered the cash markets. Trading pits that once contained a dozen people speaking in conversational tones now contain hundreds shouting strenuously. There is little doubt that the current system has costs at that level of activity. There are further limitations due to the timing of trades through the day. Cash currency markets are literally open 24 hours a day. No open outcry system has demonstrated an ability to serve its markets continuously with a consistent level of performance.

The early experiments with automated trading systems, or "electronic open outcry," have had mixed success. Intex, a Bermuda-based exchange, had good software but failed in large part because it tried to duplicate well-established products. Whatever mechanical advantage the system might have enjoyed could not outweigh its disadvantages in low initial liquidity. But there have been successes. The Tokyo Stock Exchange (TSE) and the Osaka Stock Exchange (OSE) have automated trading systems for many of their individual stocks and their stock index futures contracts. In London white sugar is similarly traded successfully.

The first major U.S. exchange to move into this area has been the CME with its joint project with Reuters to create "GLOBEX." By far the most ambitious system yet conceived, it would combine the worldwide network of Reuters with the trading features of the CME to provide the potential for continuous 24-hour trading. Initially, GLOBEX is planned to complement the open outcry session at the CME, operating only outside of the regular trading hours. In that way the trading day is extended while floor trading is maintained. Expected to become operational in 1989, GLOBEX will provide a great opportunity to demonstrate the virtues of automated trading without detracting from the existing, liquid markets.

2.4   CLEARING ASSOCIATION FUNCTIONS

Security and transaction efficiency have been mentioned as key advantages of futures trading over forward contracting, and both of these features arise from the organization of the clearing association. In the United States some exchanges maintain clearing associations as divisions of their overall administrations, whereas others have close relationships with separate corporations. The form of the enterprise is of lesser importance than the functions performed: processing and matching trades.

Members of a clearing association can be thought of as "supermembers" of an exchange. In addition to holding exchange membership, the firms must meet considerably more stringent financial requirements.[11] For this extra burden, the clearing member receives the right to process business through the exchange. Just as each futures transaction must be made in the pit by a floor broker, it must also be "cleared" through an exchange clearing member. Similar to the floor broker, the clearing member performs this service for a small fee.

There are several advantages of being a clearing member. Many FCMs maintain such operations as a source of commission income, whereas trade firms might see clearing memberships as a way to save on commissions and to keep their business activities known only to those within the firm.

Once a transaction is completed on the floor, both the buyer and the seller notify the clearing members acting on their behalf of the trade's particulars. Importantly, in addition to stating the commodity, the contract month, and the price, the traders identify the opposite broker and clearing member. At the end of the day, or sooner in more modern systems, the clearing members submit this trade data to the clearing association for matching. If the data supplied by the buyer and seller match, the trade clears. Otherwise, a "break" occurs, and the discrepancies have to be resolved between the brokers. An important piece of data that is *not* supplied is the identity of the ultimate accountholder, an item that is a matter of confidence between the individual and the clearing member.

At the point of clearance, the initial bond between buyer and seller is broken. If clearing member A is the original seller, and B is the buyer, each account will be properly credited. Member A will be listed as "Short one September Eurodollar contract at 93.25," and B will have a similar, though opposite, entry. On neither account will the counterparty be identified since the clearing association has taken over that role once the trade has cleared. The association interposes itself into each transaction, becoming the buyer to every original seller and the seller to each initial buyer. In this way, if either the long or the short makes a subsequent offsetting trade with a third party, it is unnecessary to maintain a chain of financial responsibility. An example will highlight this feature of the clearing process.

Member A sells one March Eurodollar contract to B at a price of 94.50. Each member's account is credited properly, and subsequently, B sells one of the same contracts to C for 94.60. When this trade clears, B's account will be "flat," the long and short position having cancelled out, but it will be credited with $250, the profit on the trade.[12] In a system of forward contracts, both of these transactions would be maintained, and although B would still have a certain profit of $250, it could not be realized until both obligations to A and C were met. The ability to eliminate offsetting positions is an important feature, since the ultimate chains that would result from maintaining them could be large. More importantly, they could be fragile in that if any one party failed to perform, it would have a ripple effect across the remaining trades in the chain.

Two important concepts relating to the clearing mechanism are *volume* and *open interest*. Every time someone buys a futures contract from another party, a unit of volume has been created. Open interest is the number of outstanding positions at any given time, although typically, it is measured and reported on a daily-close-of-business basis. Net impact of any trade on open interest depends on the initial position of the participants. In the example above, if A and B had entered into the first ever transaction for a particular contract, their act would have created one lot of volume and one lot of open interest.[13] At the point at which B sells to C, another lot of volume occurs, but the open position remains unchanged. All that happens is that the long part of the original trade moves from B to C. The entire position can be closed when C sells to A, creating one more lot of volume but eliminating the one contract of open interest.

In a system that does not recognize ongoing offset, the open interest would be the running total of all volume. The system of position reporting in many British markets contains some of these ongoing elements, allowing accounts to hold open simultaneously both long and short positions in the same contract. The U.S. system is governed by precise CFTC regulations that were drawn up from long-standing exchange practice that emphasizes the net position of each account. By and large, U.S. open interest reports are direct and present no problems to their users. There are no questions about which positions are real and which are artifacts of accounting practices that sometimes ignore offsets.

Accounting for the open position is done at two levels. First, each clearing member maintains detailed records on each of its accounts. Some customers may be long while others are short. The clearing member in turn reports to the clearing association its *gross* position held on behalf of its customers and, separately, any position it has in its house account.

It is important if a clearing member has, for example, 1,000 lots long in customer accounts for a certain contract and 1,500 customer lots short in the same contract that its report to the clearing association shows the total position. It might appear that the member has an exposure of 500 lots short and that internally the balance of the position is offsetting. From a risk standpoint this is true and will be discussed in the next section, but from the perspective of making sure that the exchange rules and protection apply to all positions, it is necessary to identify all of the contracts. Firms that match customer buy and sell orders outside the exchange are engaged in "bucketing" orders, which is explicitly prohibited by the Commodity Exchange Act.

Unless a customer order is executed by open outcry on the floor of the exchange and is cleared through the clearing association, it is not a legal futures transaction and enjoys none of the rights and protection afforded by exchange rules. Some of the most egregious fraudulent commodity schemes have involved bucket shops that misrepresented to their clients that they were trading exchange futures or options when in fact the positions were not executed on the floor or cleared. When ultimately there was nonperformance on a contract, the customers discovered they had no protection from an organized market. As active as the CFTC Enforcement Division is in trying to limit this kind of activity, it is the customer who ultimately has the best defense against fraud. By dealing only with reputable FCMs, whose history and registration may be checked with the National Futures Association and the CFTC, a customer has taken the first major step in insuring the legitimacy of the transaction.

The role of the clearing association is much broader than that of merely order matching and accounting for open interest. Its primary job is to provide financial safeguards in the event of nonperformance on an obligation to pay. A system of margins, discussed in the next section, provides the foundation for this security, but there are many more safeguards. Each clearing member must deposit funds into a clearing house account, which provides the first reserve in case a clearing member fails to pay. Beyond that, if a firm should fail, the remaining clearing members have the financial responsibility of making up any shortfall, from their own capital if necessary. Being a clearing member carries with its privileges many responsibilities, which are never taken lightly. Because there is no desire on the part of any clearing member to dip into its own reserves to cover the mistakes of others, there is great emphasis placed on margins. Appropriately set and collected, futures margins offer considerable protection against the risks of nonperformance.

2.5   MARGINS

The principle of futures margin is simple, although much confusion has resulted throughout the years because similar terminology has been used in the securities and futures industries for very dissimilar concepts. In the stock market you can buy a stock "on margin" by paying a fraction of the value of the stock and borrowing the remainder from your broker. This makes margin look like a down payment since if the stock is held for an appreciable time, the balance of the stock's value will have to be repaid (with interest). Futures margins have no such connection to the idea of down payments.

In futures markets, both the buyer and the seller deposit margins with their clearing member as a performance bond. In that way, if either account loses money because of a price change (and one certainly will) there will be funds on hand to insure the position's financial integrity. Just as the clearing member collects margins from its customers to insure performance, the clearing house needs similar assurances from its members. Each clearing member is required to deposit margin, in an account related to the total position carried by the firm, with the clearing association to guarantee performance at that level. The two basic types of margin are original margin and variation margin. A third related concept for customers is maintenance margin. Each is integral to the overall financial stability of the market.

Looking at a typical purchaser of a single March S&P 500 futures contract, the first step is the deposit of *original margin* in the amount of, say, $5,000.[14] If the purchase was made at 305.00 the account would be credited as holding a long March S&P 500 contract at 305.00 and as maintaining a balance of $5,000.

If on day two this contract settles at 306.00, the account will be credited with *variation margin* of $500, representing the difference between the purchase price and the second day's settlement.[15] The account would now show a long March S&P 500 contract at 306.00 and a financial balance of $5,500. Implicitly, there is a squaring up of the accounts each night and a reinitiation of the position at the current price. This process is known as *marking to the market* daily.

The source of the $500 is from shorts who lost money between the two days. Their accounts would be debited, and funds would pass to the accounts that had profits. However, it is not necessary, and from a practical matter it would be undesirable, for the long accountholder to receive the funds from the particular account that made the original sale. Since futures are a zero-sum arrangement, the sum of all profits must equal the total of all losses. Although each account is fully credited or debited based on the day's price change, the funds that actually move represent only the net exposure of the clearing members.

Let day three bring about a drop in the stock market so that the S&P 500 index drops to 302.00. Each holder of a long position at 306.00 (the previous settlement) would have his or her account debited by $2,000, the contract equivalent of four full points. In the example account, the new position would be long one March S&P 500 future at 302.00 and a balance of $3,500. At this point a figurative warning buzzer goes off for the clearing member carrying this position.

Maintenance margin is the minimum amount necessary in a customer's margin account to maintain the position. A representative, though certainly not universal, maintenance margin is 75 percent of original margin. In the example, with a $5,000 original margin, the maintenance amount would be $3,750, and the long customer at the end of day three is below this key level.

When this happens, the customer receives a "margin call." To maintain the long position, the customer must deposit more funds demonstrating continued willingness to perform. It is not sufficient to remit $250 to bring the account to the minimum level. It is necessary to deposit an additional $1,500 to bring the account back to the original level. The alternative to answering the margin call is to liquidate the position.

In a well-functioning system of margins, one is always covering one's position with one's own funds. No one should be playing "on someone else's money." There are many stories about fortunes won without risking any of the traders' own capital, but they are not true. At some point capital was provided to the system to insure performance. It is possible that a small amount of funds can grow to be a large sum on the basis of a rapidly, and favorably, shifting market, but the seed has to be planted first.

Clearing houses set margins to reflect the volatility of the underlying market. Most exchanges perform sophisticated analysis on the recent price-change history to provide guidance about appropriate levels. The dual objective in setting margins is to set them high enough to guarantee performance in the vast majority of cases, while not setting them at levels that would tie up capital needlessly. Traditionally, since clearing members have to make up any shortages out of their own pockets, the tendency has been toward conservatism in setting margins. Margins that may appear low as a fraction of the total value of the contract are usually still high enough to provide an extremely safe level of protection.

2.6 BASICS OF TRADING

The fundamentals of futures trading are captured in one phrase, "buy low, sell high." As trite as that may seem, it is the entire story for speculators. The picture is more complicated for hedgers, but once the concept of *basis* is appreciated, the adage applies equally well.

A tool that will be used extensively throughout the discussion of trading applications is a chart showing profits and losses that result from a range of possible price outcomes. Such charts are relatively direct for futures or cash

positions but can become more complicated as options and combinations of
positions are added.

Figure 2.1 shows the possible outcomes from holding a cash position in
Japanese yen. The horizontal axis is the price in terms of dollars per 1,000 yen.
The vertical axis is the profit or loss measured in the same scale. Today's price is
labeled P_o. The upward sloping line shows the outcomes if prices change.
Advances above P_o produce point-for-point profits, and symmetrically, declines
below P_o generate losses. This chart depicts the risk profile of a *long* position,
and in this example the trader is long the cash commodity.

If the position had been long Japanese yen futures, the risk profile would have
been identical, except that the horizontal axis would be the futures price. The
chart does not show the percentage return to a margined position, but since losses
are not bounded on the chart, it emphasizes that losses are not limited to the
amount of original margin posted. These figures merely display an answer to
the question "if price ultimately becomes X, what is the total gain or loss to the
position?"

Figure 2.1
Risk from a Long Position

profit/loss

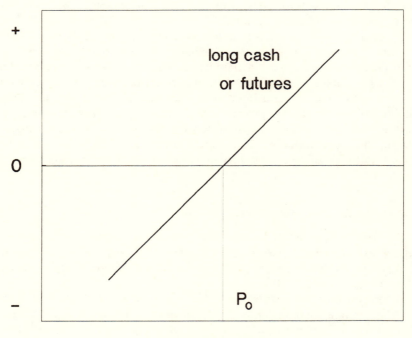

underlying price

A *short* position occurs when a trader sells futures contracts, and it has the reverse characteristics of the long position. Figure 2.2 shows how price declines produce profits for the short, and losses occur when the price moves up. It is incorrect to think of being short futures as selling something you do not have. Instead, it is a contractual obligation to sell something in the future. That obligation may be met by delivery of the good, which you may or may not own today, or by offsetting the position with a long futures in the same contract. The key is that there is no logical necessity to buy before selling; it is merely necessary to perform on the contractual obligation.

Starting with a long cash position in Japanese yen and then combining it with a short futures position creates the situation illustrated in Figure 2.3. The net position is called *flat*, neither long nor short, and as long as the cash and futures prices move together there is no risk in the position. Profits from one-half of the total position exactly offset losses accruing to the other for all market outcomes. This chart captures the most naive view of hedging, which is usually presented in most introductions to futures. The world, however, is never this simple. The act

Figure 2.2
Risk from a Short Position

profit/loss

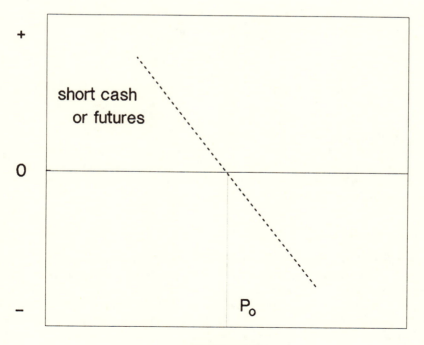

underlying price

Figure 2.3
Combining Long and Short Positions

profit/loss

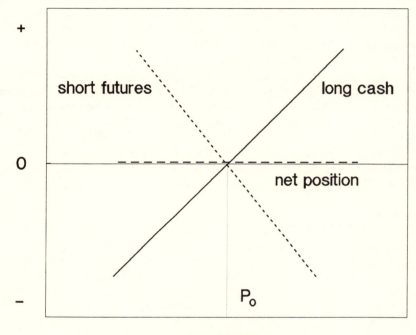

underlying price

of combining opposite cash and futures positions can significantly reduce the risk of an outright position, but because of *basis risk,* there will still be some residual profit or loss. The profit/loss charts' main weakness is their inability to capture shifts between the cash and futures prices, but they will still prove instructive in describing a wide variety of combinations.

2.7   BASIS

The *basis* is any differential between two prices. The most important basis for hedgers is the difference between cash and futures prices. As an example, a portfolio manager could hold a diversified basket of stocks and, fearing a market reversal, might take on a short position in the CME S&P 500 futures. Unless the portfolio is an exact mimic of the S&P 500, there is the likelihood that changes in the value of the stocks will not be perfectly offset by opposite changes in the futures. Depending on the degree of correlation, there is greater or lesser *basis risk,* but the portfolio manager knows that by taking on the short position, basis risk has been substituted for the outright risk of the market.

Basis can be defined for any two pairs of prices, cash versus futures, March futures versus June futures, London versus New York, and so on. As long as the two instruments are not identical, being differentiated by quality, time, or geography, there will be basis risk to be accounted for in the trading strategy.

The importance of basis cannot be overstated. For a commercial firm that has the opportunity to transact in many potential markets to achieve its objectives, the basis provides the key signal as to what action to take. The price difference gives information on the implicit market to transform the product from one state to another. Only by evaluating the basis compared to the costs it represents can the correct decisions be made.

Suppose that an importer of watches expects to need Swiss francs in three months to pay for a shipment. Also assume that the current exchange rate is acceptable to the overall business plan. The options available to the importer are buying francs now and holding them, buying in the forward market for delivery at the exact time and location needed, or buying a futures contract to secure the general price level and then later offsetting the future and buying the francs in the spot market. The basis between any pair of these markets reflects the costs of transformation from one state to another. Between spot and futures is the implicit cost of holding francs for the period before delivery, which is a function of the franc and dollar interest rates. If the cash market in Swiss francs seems cheap relative to the future or forward markets, purchases will be made there and held until needed.

The basis between some agricultural markets points out this transformation function very well. There are active soybean and soybean oil markets. A margarine manufacturer requiring soybean oil has the choice of buying this product directly or buying soybeans, crushing them, keeping the oil, and selling the meal. Unless there is a sufficient return to this activity, that is, unless the basis is sufficiently wide, the manufacturer will buy the oil and implicitly pay for all of the *transformation services.* If, however, beans are very cheap relative to oil, there is a signal to the manufacturer to go through these steps himself. The basis has indicated a shortage of transformation services by pricing oil high relative to beans, and the market signal brings about a reallocation of capital and labor to correct the imbalance.

For commercial firms the basis signals where and what kind of trades should occur. By their actions these price differences are held in line because resources will flow to the expensive market and withdraw from the cheaper arena. Although basis trading is the foundation of all commercial activity, it should not be ignored by speculators as being too difficult, or possibly even irrelevant, for their purposes. Basis is an indicator of relative value, and the speculator who ignores it is throwing away economic information that could make the difference between profit and loss.

2.8   TYPES OF TRADING

Every futures transaction plays a role in the overall strategy of the trader. Some represent the position entirely, with the trade speculating on the outcome of the market. Others are merely parts of combinations comprised of futures and cash exposures (and increasingly, as shown in the next chapter, options). Although each market has its unique features, which are described in detail in subsequent chapters, there are generic types of trading that can be usefully identified. Ranging from hedging inventories against changes in value to outright position speculation, these classifications cover a broad spectrum of trading profiles.

2.8.1   Hedging

The legal definition of *hedging* is provided in the general regulations under the Commodity Exchange Act.[16] Regulation 1.3(z) states that futures positions taken on as a temporary substitute for cash market transactions are hedges if they are economically appropriate to the reduction of risks of a commercial enterprise and can be established and liquidated in an orderly fashion. A trader who expects the Japanese yen to rally and buys a yen futures contract is not hedging, even if that trader represents a commercial firm. The definition focuses on the nature of the activity and not on the normal business of the trader. The other requirement of orderly establishment and liquidation automatically classifies trades that have the effect of squeezing or distorting a market as speculative, even if they are held by commercial firms with opposite cash market positions.

This hedging definition grew from the traditional commodity futures world that includes grain-elevator operators selling futures against their inventory and candy manufacturers buying cocoa futures to establish the price of an important factor of production. The current world of financial futures places many strains on this definition, and regulatory work is progressing to establish a more reflective standard. The motivations for using stock index and interest rate futures are in many ways remarkably similar to those of the traditional hedger, but there are identifiable cases in which commercial firms using these instruments for risk management fall outside the legal definition.

The inadequacy of the definition stems from relying on risk reduction as the primary motivation for commercials trading the market. Almost every book on futures trading highlights this argument, and it is certainly the spirit behind the 1.3(z) definition. However, in reality, there are few commercial traders who behave that way. Although it is true that a long cash position in T-bonds combined with short T-bond futures has less risk than either position individually, the combination is not held because of this feature but because the total position efficiently creates the desired exposure in the market.

In the section on basis, it was said that a person long cash and taking an offsetting position in futures substitutes basis risk for outright risk. What was not said was that there are many other alternatives to the short futures position that also eliminate outright risk. The long cash position could be sold spot, or it could be sold on a forward basis. The person could have originally entered into a repurchase agreement in which the original acquisition was coupled with a contract to reverse the trade at some later date. Avoiding outright risk can be done in many ways, and relying on risk avoidance to explain why commercials trade futures confuses the outcome with the cause.

The advantages of liquidity, security, and minimal costs combine to attract commercial firms to futures. These firms may be trading against their inventories, performing anticipatory purchases or sales, or creating synthetic cash positions out of futures, but it is certain that their objective in using these contracts is to achieve financial results unobtainable at the same cost without futures.

Inventory hedging. Dealers in financial instruments maintain inventories for the same reasons that wholesalers and retailers of merchandise do. Although storage costs are minimized if the product is sought out from source every time a buyer appears, inventories allow dealers to transact quickly and to satisfy their customers. These inventories are expensive to maintain, tying up capital and posing the risk that their value could change before sales are made. Bond dealers, for example, suffer significant losses on their inventories any time interest rates rise.

The motivation of dealers in holding inventories is that they desire accessibility to the product. In an ideal world, buy and sell orders would enter simultaneously, and dealers would match the sides for a fee. Since this rarely happens, they must maintain ready access to the product to fill any orders that may arise. Inventories serve this function, and by selling futures against them, the dealer has secured this temporary access without running the risk that the asset should change adversely while it is held.[17]

The basis is the key factor in the inventory hedge decision. By buying in the spot market, knowing the cost of financing the inventory, and then selling the appropriate futures, the dealer knows how much the act of holding an inventory will cost and can price his services accordingly. The benefit to the dealer is the ability to perform a key service in a controlled environment.

Long before the existence of financial futures there were dealers in bonds, currencies, and equities, and they priced their services according to the costs, which included a margin for the volatility of the asset being held. Since the total costs of the inventory activity were not known with certainty, smaller inventories were likely held and the bid/ask spreads of the dealers were wider. The introduction of futures made the entire process more efficient, and competition across dealers made certain those efficiencies were also enjoyed by the customers.

Anticipatory trades. A second class of commercial hedge involves the anticipatory purchase or sale of future assets or liabilities. A pension-fund manager might expect with virtual certainty an injection of cash as future annuitants make their scheduled contributions. If he or she also expects the stock market to rally significantly between now and the receipt of the cash, a purchase of stock index futures would be one way to act on these beliefs.

This behavior might be viewed as speculative since the fund manager could be wrong, but it is no different than a candy manufacturer buying cocoa and sugar at perceived favorable prices in anticipation of future needs. The hedging decision in either case has nothing to do with avoiding risk but instead provides an opportunity to execute a business decision. The pension-fund manager, if allowed by regulation, could accomplish the same end by borrowing the funds necessary to build the portfolio now while repaying the loan once the cash is received. By employing futures in an anticipatory hedge, a quick, low-cost alternative is provided.

Synthetic positions. The final category of commercial hedging can be called *synthetic-position* construction. These trades occur frequently in financial markets as low-cost alternatives to obtaining the desired position in the cash market. For example, a fixed-income fund manager holding a portfolio of long-term bonds may fear a rise in interest rates and a consequential decline in the value of the portfolio. One alternative is to liquidate a portion of the portfolio and put the proceeds into short-term paper. If the position is large, however, there may not be sufficient liquidity to sell the desired quantity without having a detrimental market impact. The fund manager can instead sell T-bond futures and synthetically achieve the desired exposure. The simultaneous combination of long cash and short futures produces the flat-risk profile shown in Figure 2.3. The pricing of the bond futures, described in chapter 5, insures that the net position generates a T-bill return with little risk.

Because of arbitrage relationships that will be described in the respective contract chapters, the act of selling futures against a portion of the portfolio is equivalent to shifting a fraction into short-term interest instruments. If the fund manager is correct, profits in the short bond position will offset the capital loss in the long bond and preserve the total asset value.

2.8.2   Arbitrage and Spread Trading

Arbitrage is the simultaneous buying and selling of related instruments for the purpose of profiting from price discrepancies. Many types of trading are loosely called arbitrage, and it is useful to distinguish between true arbitrage and the pretenders. An example from the physical gold market will demonstrate the key difference.

Suppose that you observe the spot price of gold in New York to be significantly higher than the London spot. You calculate that given the current exchange rate, the opportunity cost of capital, and the cost of freight, bullion could be bought in London, transported to New York, and sold profitably. If you engage in this activity, you are arbitraging the geographic basis in gold, and if this activity is carried on for very long the prices will converge to the point that it is no longer profitable to do so.

Mock-arbitrage in the same situation would occur if you bought London and sold New York gold futures in the anticipation that someone else would perform the actual arbitrage, causing the prices to move favorably. If your calculations are correct this *spread trade* should have a high chance of success, but it is not a certainty. There is the chance that no one will actually move gold from London to New York, and whatever distortion exists could get wider before prompting an arbitrageur into action.

This may seem like a very rigid distinction, but it is important. Many trading programs are developed that are called arbitrage and are sold to the public as low-risk investment vehicles. In general these systems are much less risky than outright position speculation, but unless there is the actual forcing of prices together, there can be significant risk while waiting for someone else to do the job. Speculating on the basis is a more accurate description of this type of trading, and it is up to the investor to explore thoroughly the claims of the fund manager before deciding whether the level of risk is acceptable.

The analysis of arbitrage would be easy if the differences in trading were always as clear as portrayed above. In fact, there is a significant grey area between the extremes. A Eurodollar arbitrageur might buy what is perceived to be an underpriced instrument and sell a corresponding futures contract. The Eurodollar future ultimately has cash settlement against an average of quotes taken from banks on the last trading day. The arbitrageur has a very strong expectation that the value of the deposit will converge to the settlement price of the future, but there is no delivery mechanism to insure this. The preference in this book is to use the term *arbitrage* narrowly to emphasize whatever residual risks exist in other types of trades.

Many commercial firms engage in arbitrage as an activity related to their main function. Around large, growing markets like T-bonds and stock index futures several specialty firms have been started that specialize in this kind of trading. All that is necessary is a source of capital and a demonstration that there are price discrepancies that when traded on provide a superior return. The risk manager of these firms must always be diligent to monitor the firm's traders in order to control the degree of exposure that comes as pure arbitrage moves toward speculating on the basis.

Anywhere there is a definable basis there is the chance for speculative spread trading. In many such cases the opportunities exist also for true arbitrage. The role of spread and arbitrage traders is to keep related markets in line. The benefits accrue to all users who know that because of arbitrage activity they do not have to search over all possible markets to find the best price. In fact, in well-arbitraged markets, search is a wasted effort since it duplicates the activity of the specialist. Without arbitrage, much more time would be spent searching for the best trading opportunity, which would be to the detriment of the entire investment return.

2.8.3   Speculation

The distinction between investing and speculating is frequently blurred. Someone who buys IBM stock is usually said to be investing. When one buys Eurodollar futures, it's called speculating. In fact, in both instances the purchases were made in anticipation of profiting from rising values, and there is no investment motive to improve the productivity of the nations' capital at all. Possibly the only consistent, though hardly satisfactory, approach is that when you trade in stocks or futures, you are investing, but when someone else does it, they are speculating.

A common perception of speculation has one or more well-capitalized traders coming to the market, and from the sheer weight of their activity they drive prices above or below the "true value." Speculators have been blamed for low grain and livestock prices, as well as for volatility in foreign exchange, interest rates, and stock markets.[18] In fact, the role speculators play is important but not nearly as dramatic as the popular press reports.

Speculators provide liquidity to the marketplace, and they are an important source of market information. Futures exchanges, far from being overrun by speculators, usually find that there are times when they wish they had more speculative activity. An example highlights the problem.

Suppose that you are the treasurer of a corporation anticipating a new issue of long-term debt in a few weeks. You look at the T-bond futures market as an indicator of current rates and find the level satisfactory. If you expect rising rates (falling prices) during the time before your issue, you could sell T-bond futures now to secure the approximate interest rate. When your corporate debt issue is ready to be sold, you buy back the T-bond position. Any profit or loss should offset to a degree the change in selling price from the original target value. This is a classic hedge as described in the section above.

A company performing this hedge may enter the market only twice over the course of several weeks, and it is willing to do so only if there is a ready market for its offers and bids. What is the likelihood of such a market existing if the only participants are other hedgers? What is the chance that another commercial firm would be willing to buy the same contract month at the same time the firm in the example is willing to sell? Neither are high probabilities. The speculator enters as an important holder of positions, either long or short, who, unintentionally through his profit motive, ends up providing liquidity to the market.

Speculating most often is thought of as the activity of floor traders and public customers but is frequently an activity of some commercial traders. Among foreign exchange and bond dealers the ability to trade around one's book is a highly prized skill, and when trying to classify a type of trade, it is much more important to look at the motivation of the trader than the identity.

There are a variety of approaches and techniques to speculating. Although some traders specialize in one activity versus another, it is frequently the case that a combination of approaches is used depending on the opportunity of the moment. It may be impossible for an outside observer to detect the strategy that any particular trade fits in, but it is still illustrative to describe the different approaches since each affects the market in its own way. Scalping, day trading, and position trading are the three major categories of speculating, differentiated only by the time horizon of the trader.

Scalping. Futures trading has no shortage of interesting jargon, and *scalper* is one of the most colorful, if not entirely descriptive, terms in the industry. A scalper is a floor trader who is willing to either buy or sell but at a differential known as the bid/ask spread. These traders work hard to gauge the flow of orders in the pit and later their bids and offers to maintain as close as possible a neutral, or flat, position.

If 162.00 (U.S. cents per British pound) was the last trade in the British pound pit and there was a perceived balance in buy and sell orders coming to the market, a scalper might bid 161.98 and offer at 162.02, being indifferent as to which side of the transaction was executed.

Suppose that a market buy order comes in and is filled at the offer. At that point the scalper would hope to encounter quickly a market sell order to take the 161.98 bid. If both trades occurred, the profit would be 0.04 per contract or $25.00.[19] The time horizon for this trader is very short, being measured in seconds in very active markets like T-bonds, Eurodollars, and the S&P 500 and no more than minutes in other markets.

The risk to the scalper is that after selling at 162.02, a wave of new buying enters that drives the price higher. The scalper must then compete with the other bidders to offset the existing short position and limit the loss. To be successful, the scalper has to act quickly to minimize the impact of losing trades and will hope that he or she can make many modestly profitable trades in order to maintain a livelihood. A successful scalper may be likened to Pete Rose or Ty Cobb in baseball—not many home runs but a steady stream of productive hits, and very rarely do you see a strikeout with runners in scoring position.

Because of the presence of scalpers and the liquidity they provide, other participants with longer time horizons have confidence that their orders will be filled near the current price. For someone buying 62,500 British pounds, having to pay implicitly $25 to a scalper is a modest cost indeed compared to the total value of the contract and how that value might react if there was little liquidity in the market. Prompt order execution is very important to traders, and most recognize the bid/ask spread as a fee to achieve that goal.

Competition among scalpers in busy markets insures that the wedge between the prevailing bid and offer will be small. In less active markets there is a lower chance that an offsetting order will come into the market before the underlying price moves, so the scalper has a wider bid/ask spread to compensate for the larger risk. There is a circularity at work here. Outsiders looking at a narrow bid/ask are more likely to trade, and with an increased flow of customer orders, the supply of scalping services increases. It works similarly, though in reverse, for less active markets.

The ideal environment for a scalper is one of active trading in a limited price-range market. The scalper is a unique speculator in that sudden price moves are not desirable; it is much preferred to have stability around which the scalper continuously trades. In such a world, the profits per trade are modest, but so are the risks.

Day trading is considerably different in philosophy from scalping. The scalper wants to avoid an exposure to the market whereas the day trader seeks out small pockets of opportunity in which an exposure can be established. As the name implies, day trading means entering each day with no position and exiting in a similar way. Positions may be held for minutes, or even hours, but not overnight. The day trader establishes and liquidates positions based on the trading session's developments, comfortable in the knowledge that overnight events will produce neither windfall nor catastrophe.

Going with the "feel" of the market, the day trader rarely looks at news stories or research reports as a source of trading information. The trader relies on the likelihood that once an item, like an analyst's opinion on next quarter's GNP, makes the news services, it has already been discovered and traded on by commercials that have strong incentives to invest in such information. Order flow is key, and the day trader knows that although in the long run information and orders may enter randomly as the efficient market hypothesis suggests, in the short run buy and sell orders are like bananas—they come in bunches. The day trader tries to pick when the crop is ripe.

Position trading. Extending the time horizon slightly produces the broad category of position trading. Any speculator holding open contracts for a matter of days or weeks is taking a position based on the opinion that the market should eventually move in the favorable direction. These traders are not interested in the small profits available to scalpers, and they largely ignore the daily dips and bulges that are the staple of the day trader. Instead, they hold a view, formed either by technical or fundamental analysis, that the market should move, and they hold this position until their view is confirmed, or they find it too expensive to maintain a losing position, or their opinion changes. Position traders are attracted to the futures market by the idea that the leverage provided by margin gives them an excellent vehicle to translate information into wealth. The key to success is having superior information, and it is a very rare commodity.

There is a long running debate about the impact of speculators on markets, and it hinges on the question of whether speculators cause markets to be more volatile. A devil theory of speculation states that since noncommercials are not involved in the fundamentals, any trade by this group cannot be a reflection of supply or demand and must consequently disturb the market.

The liquidity theory of speculation takes the opposite view. It states that there are enough commercials in a market so that the price will almost certainly reflect the best guess about supply and demand. As speculators enter, their bids and offers cannot disturb this equilibrium too much without eliciting a response from some group of commercials. By their actions speculators increase the chance that a commercial's bid or offer will find a ready counterpart in the ring.

For scalpers, the liquidity theory is certainly a more accurate description, but in trying to decide between these two extreme views for position traders, and even day traders, one finds neither satisfactory. If speculators added nothing but noise, commercial participants would quickly abandon the market, since the futures prices would be poor indicators on which to base their decisions. Conversely, if the price was never out of equilibrium there would be minimum incentive for speculators to enter.

The evidence that has accumulated shows that futures trading in all likelihood reduces the volatility of the underlying market (see Gray, 1963; Banerjee and Weaver, 1987; and Edwards, 1987, as good examples of this literature), while speculators, on average, lose money on their trades (see Rockwell, 1967; and Draper, 1985). The conclusion one can draw from this is that if misinformed speculators enter the market and bid the price too high, or offer it too low, commercial firms enter on the other side to restore equilibrium. This leads to mild variations in price, damped by the commercials' expertise. Since on average overall volatility is reduced with futures trading, it must be the case that the liquidity-induced stabilizing force of speculators is greater than any disturbing influence they may inject. But for speculators who make money, and there are some, they must either have good information, or be lucky, and from them there are only benefits in added liquidity and more accurate prices.

NOTES

1. A popular exercise among futures market historians is to try to identify the first futures markets. The problem is that the evolution of the markets is so gradual that the exercise is akin to identifying the first "man" from prehistoric remains. That futures are old is well documented (see Bear, 1986, and Williams, 1986), and it is obvious that forward contracts are much older.

2. Settlement based on closing prices was perceived by some to contribute to stock market volatility as arbitrageurs unwound program trades at the closing moments of the stock market. In 1987 steps were taken to change to settlement based on opening prices to eliminate the last-minute pressure on the markets. It is precisely this type of contract definition that traders in the markets should be keenly aware of. Program trading is discussed in greater detail in chapter 4.

3. The Mexican peso contract failed more because of unpredictable policies on the part of the Mexican government that interfered with the free trade in pesos than because the contract size was too small.

4. More precisely, the only parties receiving funds at final settlement are those holding contracts profiting vis-à-vis the previous day's settlement price. This is due to daily marking to the market, which is discussed in Section 2.5. The cumulative effect of the daily pays and collects is the total profit or loss for the entire holding period.

5. Johnson (1985) provided a good overview of the history and key topics of federal regulation of futures. The discussion of the CFTC-SEC jurisdictional issues is particularly helpful in appreciating the broad impact that financial futures market innovation has meant.

6. These jurisdictional disputes were most severe when stock index products were developed. In 1982 the turf was divided between the SEC and the CFTC in an agreement

informally called the Johnson-Shad Accord. In general the SEC has responsibility for narrowly defined indexes that behave similarly to individual stocks, and the CFTC covers broad-based indexes, but there is little assurance that the current ground rules will be effective as the markets continue to evolve. The regulation of futures is explored in detail in chapter 7.

7. Members are always in the name of individuals, although corporations frequently supply the financial guarantees to maintain the ongoing membership requirements. If a firm revokes its guarantee the individual member is suspended.

8. Appendix A of Kaufman (1984) gives a chronology of the CBOT seat prices from 1898 through 1982. November 1942 is remembered by few but should be kept in mind by all. At the worst point of World War II, four seats, which had traded as high as $62,000 in the busy days of 1929, were traded for $25 each.

9. Floor brokers have personal liability for execution errors so there is a great incentive to be accurate and to confirm trades with the opposite brokers. A mistake in a volatile market can easily erase a week's worth of commissions in a matter of minutes.

10. The CME has a rule that prohibits brokers trading their own account from occupying the outer tier of the S&P 500 pit. This ''top step'' rule has nothing to do with potential trading abuses. The physical congestion in the pit is so great that the exchange wants to insure accessibility of outside customer orders by reserving that section of the pit for brokers doing customer business.

11. Since regular memberships are held by individuals, clearing members are frequently required to hold more than one seat. This practice insures that the clearing member can continue processing trades in the event of the death or disability of one of its members.

12. Each 0.01 on a CME Eurodollar contract is $25, representing the effect on the value of a $1 million three-month obligation of a 0.01 percentage point change in the interest rate.

13. Since there must be a seller for every buyer, the sum of all long open positions must equal the sum of the shorts, and it is the typical practice at the market level to ignore any long or short designations.

14. Minimum original margins are set by the exchanges and clearing associations, and they can change frequently as market conditions demand. Examples in this book are not meant to convey specific information that must be confirmed by contacting a broker or the exchange.

15. Each full index point of the CME S&P 500 contract is worth $500. The minimum fluctuation is 0.05 points, or $25 per contract.

16. The hedging definition plays an important role in many regulatory matters, which are discussed in chapter 7.

17. Williams (1986) described in close detail the inventory hedge in the grain market. For the financial markets, virtually all of the Williams results are fungible.

18. Interestingly, when soybeans moved from just over $4 per bushel at the start of 1973 to over $12 by midyear, there was no complaint of excess speculation by the farm community. There was, however, some grumbling later when the fall crop came in around $6.

19. A CME British pound contract calls for delivery of 62,500 pounds. A change of 0.04 cents per pound equates to $25.

CHAPTER *3*

Basics of Options
on Futures

Options in many ways are similar to futures in that they provide a means to manage the allocation of resources over time. Unlike futures, however, the risk profile of an option is asymmetric. The buyer of an option can lose no more than the premium, and the potential gains are not bounded. Conversely, the seller has a maximum profit of the premium received but risks unlimited losses. This chapter explains the structure of options, the factors that influence their price, and basic trading strategies. In each of the subsequent chapters, total trading programs employing futures and options are developed.

3.1 BACKGROUND

Options on futures are a genuine infant industry, having been legally traded in the United States since Friday, October 1, 1982. On that day options on sugar futures began trading at the Coffee, Sugar & Cocoa Exchange (CSCE) in New York, and options on T-bonds commenced at the CBOT. The following Monday, COMEX began trading in gold futures options, and the CFTC pilot program allowing options on futures was off and running.

Immediately before that time options on commodities had been explicitly prohibited unless they were between commercial firms executed as part of their normal business. Prohibitions date from as early as 1874 when the state of Illinois outlawed trading in "privileges" (Carasik, 1981), and since that time there has been an on-again, off-again history of commodity option trading.

The highly leveraged aspects of options have long drawn suspicion from some parties that the instruments lacked a legitimate function. Furthermore, there have been some spectacular instances of fraud linked with commodity options that placed a cloud over these instruments. In virtually all of these cases, investors lost money not because they were trading in options per se but because they were dealing with dishonest firms.

Congress, as part of the 1974 Commodity Exchange Act, formally designated the CFTC to have regulatory authority over all commodity options. At the same time the law prohibited trade in options on all domestic agricultural futures and would allow trading in other areas (metals, currencies, financial instruments, and tropical commodities) only after the CFTC could document its ability to regulate those instruments. It took from 1975 until 1982 to develop the first pilot program for commodity options, and it was not until January 1984 that the second major program for domestic agricultural options was in place.

Once out of the blocks in 1982, the growth and evolution was swift. The original three contracts were quickly joined by options on foreign currencies and stock indices. In just four years activity had grown until there were 33 different options on futures trading (with varying degrees of success) on ten designated exchanges. By early 1987 the two pilot programs regulating options had been made permanent.

The importance of options cannot be overstated. Commentators who view futures or options in isolation are ignoring the synergy that molds the nature of both markets. Although many traders participate only in futures and others only in options, the links between the markets are so strong that anyone trying to understand either must look at the package or miss a major dimension.

3.2   WHAT IS AN OPTION CONTRACT?

An *option* is a contract that gives the owner the right, but not the obligation, to perform on the terms of the contract within the life of the option. For this privilege the owner pays a premium to the seller (also known as the writer or granter) who agrees to perform if called upon. Option clauses have been part of commercial contracts for ages, but it was not until the introduction of exchange-traded options, with the advantages of standardized terms, liquidity, and security, that option trading gained wide acceptance.

The year 1973 marked the beginning of the modern option era with the opening of the Chicago Board Options Exchange. The success of this enterprise under the regulatory domain of the SEC put additional pressure on the CFTC to meet congressional concerns about commodity options.

Options come in two types: *puts,* conveying the right to sell, and *calls,* which give the right to buy. The other standard features of option contracts include:

Definition of the underlying instrument

Term of the option (expiration date)

Exercise price

Form of settlement for exercised options

Just as in futures contracts, once the standard elements are defined, all that is left to negotiate is the price, or premium, to be paid for the option.

3.2.1   Definition of the Underlying Instrument

Options on futures usually provide for the buyer of a call, upon exercise, to receive a long futures contract, and similarly, the buyer of the put receives a short futures position. The definition of the underlying instrument is transferred implicitly to the definition of the futures contract, and it is important for traders to understand those specifications since they will affect the value of the option.

Other financial options either call for delivery of the actual instrument (Philadelphia Stock Exchange currency options) or are based on the cash value of an index or price (e.g., CBOE S&P 100 options; CME Eurodollar options). Here the definitions come into play directly and must be monitored to maintain accurate pricing.

3.2.2   Term of the Option

The term of the option gives the period during which the option may be exercised.[1] Options on futures typically are matched to the maturities of the underlying future. An important element for such instruments that call for physical deliveries on the futures is that the options expire *before* the underlying future. This allows holders of options to exercise and still have time to trade out of the futures position before having to participate in the delivery.

Exchange-traded options in the United States all have fixed expiration dates set on regular cycles, unlike many privately negotiated options that may have fixed maturities (e.g., 90 days) from the date of origin. The advantage of scheduled expiration dates is that they enhance transferability. Attention is focused on just a few maturities, and liquidity is concentrated. If you buy a September S&P 100 call option today and want to dispose of it next week, there will be a ready market. Options on financial futures and indices typically have most of their interest concentrated in one or two expirations extending only a few months, whereas agricultural options have had some success with maturities spanning more than one crop year.

3.2.3   Exercise Price

Also known as the "strike" or "striking" price, the *exercise price* is the level at which the owner of the option may effect the transaction. Standardization of exercise price is another attractive feature of exchange-traded options. Intervals between the strike prices are set so that there will be a wide enough range of options to fit most trading strategies without diffusing attention across too many options at the expense of liquidity.

London options and many dealer options have irregular strike prices, sometimes set equal to the current value of the underlying instrument. The major drawback to this approach is that as the underlying market changes, existing options are no longer "at-the-money." Their exercise prices are either "in-the-money" if the market has moved in the owner's favor, or they are "out-of-the-money" if it has moved adversely. Owners of the existing options can have difficulty selling them to third parties and frequently must go back to the original writers to discover what their current bid is. An alternative is for the optionholder to become a writer of a similar option to achieve an imperfect form of offset. Standardized strike prices avoid all of these problems by allowing ready offset of a position.

3.2.4   Form of Exercise

There are three basic types of options in terms of the effect of exercise: (1) exercise produces a futures position, (2) exercise creates a cash market position, or (3) exercise triggers a final adjustment in the owner's account based on the relative values of the strike price and the underlying price or index. This last alternative is cash settlement, and where effective, it provides a convenient way of trading on the value of a financial instrument without having to deal directly with it. All of the distinctions between physical deliveries and cash settlement discussed in the preceding chapter apply to the options as well, and exercising into a futures position is merely an intermediate step. However, each type of option produces a slightly different result and consequently must be evaluated accordingly.

3.2.5   Premium

Once the strike price, maturity, underlying commodity, or index and whether it is a put or a call have been decided, all that is left to negotiate is the price of the option. Called the premium, the option's price is affected by many factors in predictable ways. Each of these influences is explored in some detail below, but importantly, the key determinant of the premium is the supply and demand for the option at the moment of sale.

3.3   STRUCTURE OF THE EXCHANGES

Ten designated futures exchanges were trading options on futures at the start of 1987, less than five years after the inception of the first pilot program. The organization and governance of those exchanges was described in the previous chapter, and virtually everything stated there applies to options as well. One commercial group active in option exchanges and not discussed previously is the option professionals. This is a group of individuals who are experts in the fundamentals of option trading but may have no particular expertise in the underlying commodity. They perform many of the same services as floor traders in the futures ring, trading in a very risk controlled fashion and in doing so providing liquidity to the market. In the exchange organization they will sit on the option committee, which advises the exchange on matters concerning the form and trading rules of options.

The major difference between futures and options is in the system of margin. There is still a clearing association with the same mechanics of receipts and payments, but the margin rules for options are much more complex reflecting the wide range of risk profiles that option combinations can have.

Both long and short futures positions have risk, and it is immediately quantifiable. If one buys an S&P 500 contract at 300.00 and it later goes to 301.00, the buyer will have gained $500 and the seller will have lost an identical amount. Exchanges set their margins on the basis of expected volatility, and for an S&P 500 contract, a $500 move is well within the expected range. The buyer's account would be credited with the profit and the seller's debited. Only if the deduction dropped the seller's account below maintenance margin levels would additional money be called for.

Option margins work on the same general principle as futures. The aim is always to have sufficient funds to guarantee performance on the position but not to collect such a large amount as to discourage trading. However, there is a key difference because of the asymmetric risk profiles of option buyers and sellers.

A buyer of puts or calls can never lose more than the premium paid for the option. A general rule that has been maintained since the introduction of options on futures is that long options are paid for in their entirety at the time of purchase. This can be thought of as having 100 percent as the margin requirement for long option positions, with no subsequent obligations. The buyer in paying the premium has already provided for the maximum potential loss, so there is no reason to call for more funds to guarantee performance. If the option is profitable to exercise, it will be, and if it ends up out-of-the-money, it will expire worthless.

Writers of options have considerably more risk than the buyers, and this is reflected in the margin mechanism. Take a simple case of a single pound sterling call with a strike price of 180 and a premium of 5. The buyer has paid 5 U.S. cents per pound sterling for the right to buy at 180. As stated above, the most the buyer can lose is this premium, but such is not the case for the writer. If before expiration the value of sterling goes to 200 the option writer must be prepared to deliver the product at 180 (the strike price). This would produce a net loss of 15 cents per pound sterling equal to the difference between the option strike and the current market price (20 cents) tempered somewhat by the 5 cents per pound sterling premium collected. If the price had gone anywhere above 185 the writer of the option would be liable on a point-for-point basis to compensate the option owner. In writing options it is the potential gain that is limited, but the potential loss is unbounded.

Margins for short options are typically comprised of two parts reflecting the premium and the potential risk. The premium collected is held in the clearing system to guarantee the availability of the total current value of all options. We will see later that this is roughly akin to wearing suspenders with a belt. The risk portion of the margin is another cushion to cover the potential change in the value of the options and, like futures margin, is geared toward the volatility of the underlying market. As the market moves, the writer's margin account will be called for more funds if the position moves adversely and will be credited for profitable moves.

As option portfolios increase in complexity by combining long and short positions in calls and puts with different strikes and maturities, the margining problems can become more detailed, but the basic principles remain the same. In the early days of stock options, margin rules developed that were strategy based. If a particular combination of options had less risk than the options considered individually, the risk margin would be appropriately lowered. This approach works fine as long as the combinations are relatively simple, but as soon as the portfolios become more complex in terms of size and number of different combinations, inadequacies appear.

A solution that has been developed by the futures industry incorporates the risk of the entire portfolio as determined from option pricing models that are discussed in a later section. Tremendous strides have been made in the early years of options on futures to develop systems of risk analysis that help traders manage their strategies and allow the clearing organizations to collect adequate funds to protect the markets. The user of the options market need not be intimately familiar with the margin system's details. All that is essential is an understanding that the two components capturing the potential risk and the actual premium are evaluated on a daily mark-to-market basis in order to protect all participants.

Efforts have been made to allow buyers of options to operate under a less than 100 percent margin system. For example, if an option cost $1,000 per contract, the buyer would be required to post a margin chosen to reflect the risk of the position. Depending on the volatility, this number could be high, but it should always be a fraction of the total premium. As the option value changes, the position would be marked to market daily with appropriate account adjustments made.

There are two distinct advantages of futures-style margins. First, there is no unnecessary capital held in the system. Margin is collected from both long and shorts and reflects the risk of the position. Asking an option buyer always to pay full premium is akin to asking a long futures trader to pay the full value of a contract to insure performance. Financial security can be attained with much less capital committed than is currently done.

The second advantage concerns the flows of capital within the system. Currently, the long pays the option premium in full, and it flows to the account of the short who must maintain its marked-to-market value in the account. If the long option increases in value, the short places more money in the system, but these profits are not accessible to the long. To realize the gain, the position must be liquidated. With futures margins, positions are marked to market daily with winning accounts credited with gains and losing accounts debited. As long as there are sufficient funds in the account to cover the margins, profits may be withdrawn and put to other uses. There is no reason why options could not similarly be margined, but at present profits and losses do not flow.

By allowing funds to flow, a much more efficient use of the capital within the system is achieved. Someone who spreads long options against a futures position cannot currently take profits in the options to offset losses in futures. If options and futures were similarly margined, such gains and losses would be automatically offset.

The CFTC has resisted the idea of futures-style margins for options despite the fact that it provides for a much more efficient use of capital dedicated to premiums. There are vague fears of leverage on top of leverage leading to undesirable volatility, and there are further concerns that public customers buying options may be induced into committing more capital than is prudent, only to find that they are called on for more funds as the position moves against them.

The tide may eventually turn on this subject. After the 1987 stock market crash regulators from the Treasury Department, SEC, CFTC, and Federal Reserve dissected the major problems surrounding October 19 and concluded, among other things, that the asymmetric flow of funds between options and futures was a serious impediment to the smooth flow of capital. Some of the uncertainty about the adequacy of capital within the system might have been avoided if futures-style margins had applied to options. This was the first public mention of the advantages of such a system and could lead ultimately to the regulatory changes necessary for a full integration of options and futures margins.

3.4 OPTION PRICING THEORY

The original stock options traders traded intuitively. Market opinion interacted with notions of option basics to guide the over-the-counter (OTC) dealers in setting their bids and offers. To today's observer trained in mathematics and versed in the competing formal models of option prices, the old ways look primitive. But in fact the early OTC markets were very efficient because the traders had a good grasp of the fundamental elements: time, volatility, the cost of money, and striking price relative to the underlying value. This section describes the dominant models in use today, but the emphasis is on providing the kind of basic principles that guided the earliest option traders.

In 1973 the academic world saw the appearance of the now classic paper by Fischer Black and Myron Scholes that drew together a rapidly growing literature on option pricing. Their main contribution was to recognize that by modeling the arbitrage conditions that governed trading between the stock and option markets, explicit values for a theoretically perfect European call or put could be derived. In that same year in his "Theory of Rational Option Pricing" Robert Merton expanded on the Black-Scholes approach to offer a unified theory of all options valuation. It was a fortuitous moment to have the academicians present workable theories, since 1973 also marked the birth of the Chicago Board Options Exchange, the nation's first institution to offer organized markets in stock options.

Starting with some basic, and some would say self-evident, assumptions, guidelines can be developed to focus on the relative impact of key variables on an option. Before looking at explicit values, the relative impact of the key factors may be described.

3.4.1   Strike Price; Underlying Price

The most direct influence on an option's value is its strike price. Consider two call options on the S&P 500 futures contract with strikes of 250 and 260. From the buyer's perspective the 250 call should always be preferable because it gives the right to buy at the relatively lower price. The seller has a different view. The 250 option has a greater probability of having value at expiration than the 260 call, and if they are both valuable at expiration, the lower strike call will be worth more. This translates into higher risk for the writer of the low strike price call. These two views combine to produce a higher price, or premium, for the 250 call since the buyer is willing to pay more for the preferred option and the writer will demand more to compensate for the higher risk.

The value of low strike calls relative to higher strike instruments holds for all pairs, so the 270 call will have a lower premium than the 260, with the 280 cheaper yet, and so forth. For puts, which convey the right to sell at the strike price, the incentives and risks are reversed. High strike price puts will be more expensive than lower strike prices.

Although the basic ordering is important, it goes only a little way toward establishing an option's value. By looking at the price of the underlying instrument relative to the strike price, more insight may be gained. If the S&P futures contract is trading at 255, the 250 and 260 calls are fundamentally very different. If the options were to expire immediately the 250 call would be worth 5 points since it could be exercised and the futures immediately sold. The 260 call would hold no value since anyone could buy the futures in the market at a price lower than the strike value. The 250 call is said to be "in-the-money" while the 260 call is "out-of-the-money." (Note that for the same pair of puts, it is the 260 option that has value.) The 250 call is said to have 5 points of "intrinsic value," whereas the 260 call has none.

As the underlying futures price increases, the 250 call gains in intrinsic value, and if the futures touches 260, the 260 call is said to be "at-the-money." Further increases in the underlying instrument will produce commensurate gains for both options. This results in increasingly valuable calls as the futures price gains is reversed for puts, since they will lose intrinsic value with higher underlying prices.

If option prices were dependent only on intrinsic value, there would be no reason for the instruments to exist. In fact, if before expiration the futures is at 255, the 250 call will trade at a price higher than its 5-point intrinsic value, and the 260 call will have a positive price. It is this "premium over intrinsic value" that is of most interest to options traders, and this leads directly to the subject of time.

3.4.2 Time

Time is the essence of an option. For two options identical in every way except for the time remaining to expiration, the price of the longer term option will always be greater than the one with less time. As the time remaining goes to zero, the option's premium will approach its expected terminal value, which will be the amount the option is in-the-money or zero if the option is out-of-the-money. The excess premium above intrinsic value that exists for options before expiration is sometimes conveniently referred to as ''time value.'' Even an option that is currently out-of-the-money will have a positive price, all time value, reflecting the probability that at expiration the price of the underlying instrument will have increased above the strike price.

The effect of time on an option's price is not linear. As expiration approaches, ''time decay,'' which is the rate the premium over intrinsic value goes to zero, accelerates. Such decay is depicted in Figure 3.1. Under the simplest of assump-

Figure 3.1
Time Decay of an Option

time value

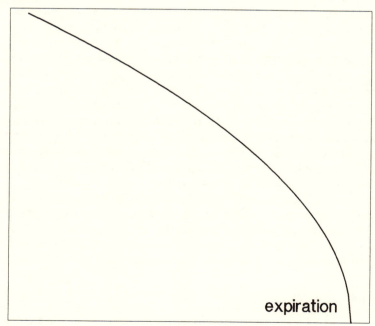

time

tions it can be shown that time value is approximately proportional to the square root of the time remaining to expiration. That is, an option with two weeks remaining does not have twice the time value of a one-week option; its value is 1.414 (the square root of two) times as great. It is the option with four weeks remaining that has twice the time value of a one-week option.

What happens as the length of an option extends indefinitely? Following the simple model above would produce an extremely large premium over intrinsic value, but this would be counterintuitive. We should never see an option to buy something, at any strike price, ever cost more than the item itself. If it did there would be an immediate risk free arbitrage opportunity from buying the instrument, selling the call, and pocketing the difference. No matter what happened to the price of the underlying instrument, the person doing this arbitrage could never lose on the transaction. Consequently, there is an upper bound on the time value.

3.4.3   Interest Rates

For options on individual stocks, the effect of interest on an option's value is reasonably direct. The analysis isolates the effect of interest on the option's price and ignores the fact that changing interest rates may impact the value of the stock, which would be analyzed separately. A person deciding between buying the stock directly and buying a call on it has a money-management decision to make. By purchasing the call, the outlay of funds for the full value of the stock is avoided temporarily, and this sum, less the cost of the call, can be invested to earn interest. As interest rates go up, it becomes relatively more attractive *not* to buy the stock, so the price of calls should go up.

For puts, the decision is between selling a stock now or buying the right to sell it later. If the stock is sold, the funds can immediately begin to earn interest, where the money is tied up if the put option is bought. In this case, with rising interest rates, puts lose attractiveness, and so their value should decline.

Options on futures pose a more complicated problem since, typically, a buyer of a futures contract does not tie up funds equal to the value of the contract and forego interest. On the contrary, by paying for the option premium in cash, a small amount of interest is missed by taking the option route, but this is typically a very small fraction of the total value of the futures contract.

In the applications chapters that follow it will be seen how interest expense is of vital importance in a wide range of futures and options strategies. However, for a basic options on futures pricing model, the pure impact of interest is much less important than it is in the stock options models, and it is a minor variable relative to strike price, underlying futures price, time, and volatility.

3.4.4   Volatility

Volatility drives options prices directly. Options on futures that historically exhibit wide price changes are priced higher than options on less volatile instruments to reflect the greater probability that any given price will be reached during the life of the option. As important as this variable is, it gives the practitioner the most problems, since, unlike the previously discussed variables, it is unobservable at the time the option is priced. The only relevant volatility is future volatility, and it is the perpetual riddle of options as to how best to estimate this factor.

Suppose that the major central banks announce a plan of fixed exchange rates, eliminating, at least temporarily, any volatility. The market for foreign currency options would have had its future variability removed. In-the-money options would converge to their intrinsic values, and out-of-the-money options would all go to zero. Unless there were signs that the agreement was faltering, this situation would persist, with there being no incentive to trade.

This extreme example may be unlikely, but it points out the one unique feature of options. Without volatility, options are redundant. There is no additional information contained in options prices that is not already being captured in the underlying futures. When there is any volatility, the option price gives the market opinion of it. The more volatility that is expected, the higher the price of both puts and calls. Whereas the futures market can be thought of as the reflection of the best informed opinion on future price levels, options are magnets that draw opinions together about volatility. As option prices change, one can identify the individual impacts of strike and futures price, time, and interest rates. Anything that is not explained can be viewed as the market's changing opinion about volatility.

3.4.5   Supply and Demand

After all of the analysis of the impact of time, volatility and so on, one has only a model of *ideal* behavior of a market instrument. The option models described below are very good, having been found descriptive of a wide range of markets and conditions. However, like all such models, they have limits, and supply and demand, as determined by all of the market participants, are the ultimate judges in determining an option's price. The only lesson from this comment is that there is no solace from thinking you have the ''right'' model and that the market is wrong. The ultimate judge of a model's usefulness is the profit/loss statement of your account. It is sometimes a cruel evaluator, but it is always consistent.

3.5   BASIC STRATEGIES

Option strategies range from elementary to complex, but the important element to keep in mind is that even the most complicated portfolios can be broken down into very simple components. An important exercise is to start with the risk characteristics of the simple pieces and combine them like building blocks into the risk profile of the portfolio. In each of the examples below, the impact of changes in the underlying instrument's price and time are shown in the charts.

Changing volatility is less easily depicted in the charts but is described since it is vital to understand that although the position may make you "long" or "short" the instrument, you will also be long or short volatility. The strategies are usually described generically to emphasize their wide applicability, although specific clarifying examples are provided.

A common mistake made by the purchasers of options is thinking about them only on the day they are bought and the day they expire. The fallacy here comes from ignoring the dynamic nature of the instrument. The holder of an option should continuously monitor the worth of the position and evaluate its value against current expectations. There is no reason to accept the full loss of premium as if the option was an all or nothing bet. Options can be traded like gambling devices, but they need not be, and the systematic interaction of the key option variables allows for a much more precise management of risk.

3.5.1   Long Call/Short Call

Buying a call is the easiest way to take a bullish position on an instrument and have limited risk. At expiration, if the instrument has moved up beyond the strike price plus the initial premium paid, the profit will be the point-for-point equivalent of the increase. The risk characteristics of a long call are shown in Figure 3.2. In all of these risk graphs, the solid line shows the option's value at expiration, and the dotted line is the expected value a month before expiration. *E* is the strike.

A long call is a "wasting asset." The passage of time reduces the value of the option toward its expiration value. The holder of the long call is, however, long volatility. A rapid increase in price that enhances the market's view of variance will have a doubly beneficial impact. In rare instances, the increase in volatility from an unexpectedly large drop in price can more than offset the effect of the price decline itself.

Speculative buying of calls should be the strategy of the risk averse bull. The more bullish the opinion, the higher should be the strike price purchased. With call options deep out-of-the-money, the premium is often a tiny fraction of the underlying instrument's price, and the trading strategy begins to take on the characteristics of a lottery ticket. The probability of success is small, but the initial layout is similarly minuscule. This can be a particularly effective strategy for someone expecting a sudden outbreak in volatility from a quiet period.

Long calls can be used with effectiveness by hedgers as well. Here the principle is one of insurance. For a firm that needs protection against an upward move in prices, a call insures against all moves above the strike price. Since the cost of the call falls with higher strike prices, the choice of option is analogous to choosing a different deductible. As the strike price increases, the owner is self-insured against a larger move, so consequently the cost of the policy should be lower. Buying deep out-of-the-money options is akin to buying disaster insur-

Figure 3.2
Long Call

profit/loss

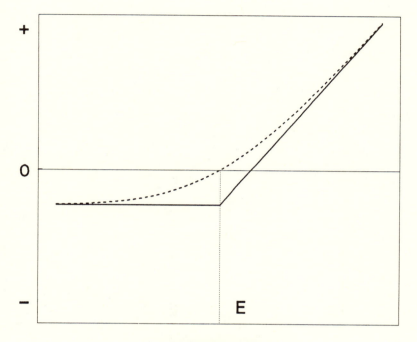

underlying price

ance. The premiums are not large, but protection is provided only against the most extreme moves.

Selling a call has the reverse risk characteristics (Figure 3.3). The most the writer can ever earn is the full amount of the premium, and this occurs only when the underlying instrument settles at or below the strike price at expiration. If prices rise above the strike price, the position will show a profit only to the point equal to the strike price plus the premium, and beyond that there is a point-for-point loss.

The passage of time helps the writer of calls since the value of any option shrinks toward the expiration value. In all cases this lowers the premium, reflecting the lower risk remaining. At a very practical level, this shrinkage also lowers the premium part of the margin requirement, freeing up capital to be employed in other uses. The call writer is short volatility. Any sudden increase in the size of price moves will mean more risk to the writer, and premium decay will be retarded.

Figure 3.3
Short Call

profit/loss

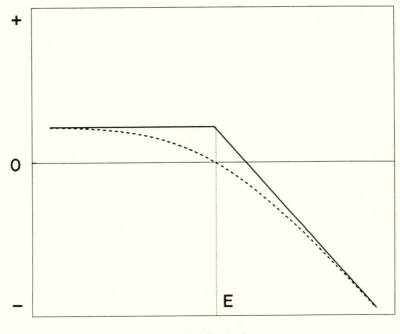

underlying price

Writing calls can be an effective hedging strategy for a firm that is moderately bearish and would be hurt by a price decline. By collecting the premium, some cushion is achieved against falling prices. If the price decline is expected to be severe, call writing is inappropriate because of this limitation. If prices rise, the call will be exercised against the writer. The owner of the call will be assigned a long position at the strike price, and the writer will be symmetrically assigned a short position. If a potential hedger is not comfortable with the possibility of such an assignment, call writing is not an appropriate hedging tool.

3.5.2   Long Put/Short Put

Buying a put is very similar to buying a call, except the purchaser's price outlook is bearish (Figure 3.4). The possible loss is limited to the premium, while gain is practically unlimited.[2] Just like the long call, time decay is an

Figure 3.4
Long Put

profit/loss

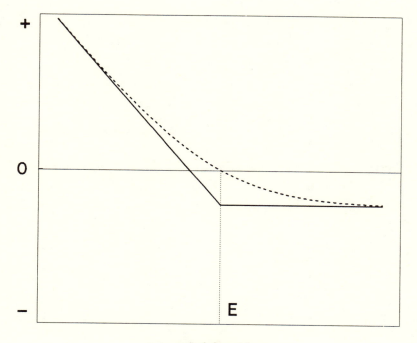

underlying price

enemy and volatility a friend to the owner of a put. It is the best leveraged strategy for the risk averse bearish speculator.

Buying puts can be an extremely useful strategy for commercial firms holding cash inventory of the underlying instrument. By going long puts, insurance is bought that protects the inventory against declines in price but does not eliminate potential gains if prices rise. By buying puts that are further out-of-the-money, premium is saved, but the inventory is subject to more risk. It is the same deductible insurance principle discussed for long calls.

Short puts have a risk profile very similar to that of short calls, except the risk is from falling prices (Figure 3.5). If the price stays constant or increases, the full premium will be received at expiration. Time decay helps, but there is always the risk that the markets will become more volatile, hurting the put writer.

Short put hedges are used by someone who has moderate expectations of increasing prices, which would lead to some financial damage. The premium

Figure 3.5
Short Put

profit/loss

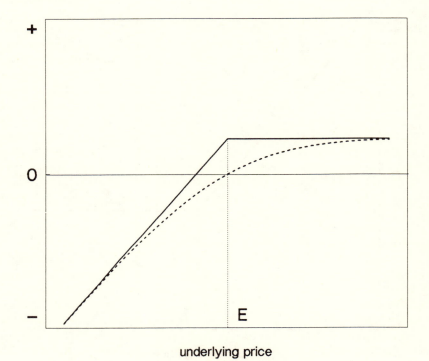

underlying price

collected offers a measure of protection against these price increases. The strategy runs the risk that in a rapidly declining market, the writer will be assigned a long position at the granted strike price. To someone holding a short cash position, this means that the profits from declining prices will be cut short at the point the put is exercised.

3.5.3   Synthetic/Arbitrage Relationships

Once the four basic option building blocks are understood, they may be combined with long and short futures to demonstrate some of the key arbitrage relationships that should be clearly understood by anyone trading in these markets. It is not expected that arbitrage will be a primary activity of the reader, but with this knowledge there is an immediate, easy way to assess whether the price of an individual call or put is fair relative to the underlying instrument and the other options.

Start with an example of someone who is long an at-the-money call because of a bullish opinion. If this view strengthens to the point where the owner is not seriously concerned about the possibility of a price decline, it may be worthwhile to sell the call and buy a futures. After all, with this opinion, there is no need for the limited risk characteristics of the call.

An alternative to this two-step adjustment is to take the single action of selling the same strike price put. If both of the options are at-the-money, their premiums should be the same, so the new premium collected should offset the price paid for the call. Figure 3.6 shows the effect of adding the two options. Any increase in price will result in a point-for-point profit from the long call with the short put expiring worthless. Any price decline, however, will mean that the short put will cost the writer on a point-for-point basis, with the long call adding no benefit.

From the final part of the diagram, it can be seen that the sum of a long at-the-money call and similar short put produces the identical risk profile of a long futures position. In fact, it is the *synthetic* equivalent to such a long futures.

Professional arbitrageurs watch synthetic positions closely for opportunities to profit. If the call price is too high relative to the put, the arbitrageur will sell the call, buy the put (establishing a synthetic short position), and then buy the future. The profit on this trade, known as a conversion, depends on the magnitude of the mispricing. An example will demonstrate the process.

Let the S&P 500 futures be priced at 250, and suppose that the 250 call is currently 2.10 bid and the 250 put is offered at 1.90.[3] By selling the call and buying the put, a synthetic short position is established at 250, but in this case a net premium of 0.2 is collected making the effective sale price 250.2. By immediately buying the futures directly at 250, a profit of 0.2 is insured at expiration.

Such conversions can be established at any strike price level. With the futures again at 250, let the 260 call be trading at 0.70 and the 260 put at 10.30. When the call is sold, and the put purchased, a synthetic short position is established at 250.4, which is determined by reducing the 260 strike price by the 9.6 net premium *paid*. By buying the futures contract at 250, a profit of 0.4 is insured.

Conversions are not the only arbitrage positions available. By buying a call and selling a put, a synthetic long position can be built and compared to a direct short position in futures. If this three-way trade is established, it is known as a reverse conversion. Although it is convenient to think of a pair of options compared to a futures position, it is important to realize that paired combinations of calls, puts, or futures can create the synthetic analog of the missing instrument. Table 3.1 gives a listing of the direct synthetic equivalents. The benefit in understanding these relationships comes from the ability to measure the relative worth of individual options. A strategy that requires going long calls can be executed directly or indirectly by buying a future and a put. Both alternatives should be evaluated before executing the trade. The reader should verify these synthetic relationships by combining the simple profit at expiration diagrams.

When all three components of any line from Table 3.1 are traded, the resultant profit at expiration line is flat at the level of the guaranteed profit. There is one

Figure 3.6
Long Call + Short Put = Synthetic Long Futures

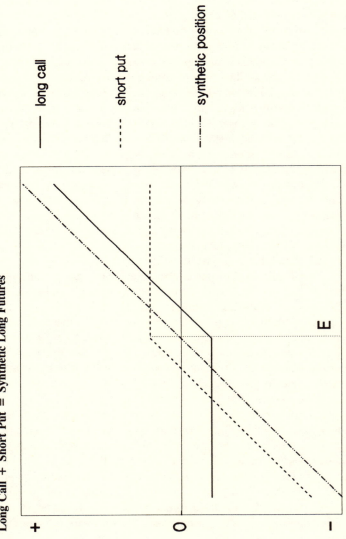

long call

short put

synthetic position

underlying price

+

O

–

E

Table 3.1
Synthetic Equivalents

Direct trades		Synthetic equivalent
long call	+ short put	long future
long call	+ short future	long put
short call	+ long put	short future
short call	+ long future	short put
long put	+ long future	long call
short put	+ short future	short call

other combination position that produces a flat profit line, and that is called a "box." A *box* is simply a combination of a long call and short put at one strike price with a short call and long put at another. From Table 3.1 it can be seen that this is effectively a simultaneous long and short future, which nets to no position at all. Boxes will be traded whenever the net premium received for written options exceeds the premium paid for the long options. A box is yet another tool of the arbitrageur that is effective in keeping option prices properly aligned.

3.5.4 Bull Spreads

For the trader that is less enthusiastic in his bullish opinion, a bull spread is an effective strategy. In its simplest form the spread is accomplished by buying a call at one strike price and selling another higher strike call (Figure 3.7). The sale accomplishes two things. First, it reduces the net cost of the bullish strategy by implicitly subsidizing the initial call's purchase, but it also restricts the potential profitability if prices rally more than originally anticipated. Unlike a single long call where profits are potentially unlimited, the maximum gain on a bull spread is the difference in the strike prices less the premium paid. For anyone who is only modestly bullish, that amount may be attractive relative to the risk.

Bull spreads are not restricted to calls. Any option spread that is successful with a moderate increase in prices falls into this category. Selling a put at one strike price and buying a put at a lower strike has similar risk characteristics. In this case there is a net premium received that will be kept in its entirety if prices rise. If prices fall, the net premium offers a measure of protection against the risk posed by the short put. If prices continue to decline, the long put at the lower strike will eventually be in-the-money, offsetting point for point the losses on the

Figure 3.7
Bull Spread

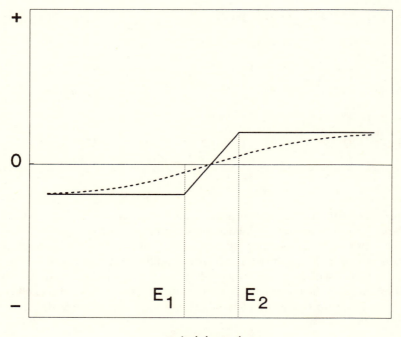

profit/loss

underlying price

higher strike short put. Just as in the case of the call bull spread, both the maximum gain and maximum loss are defined at the time the position is established.

The effects of both volatility and time are dependent upon the strike prices and the current underlying price. In the long call example, if the underlying price is near the upper strike price, time decay moves the position toward its maximum profit point faster. If, however, the futures price is close to the lower strike, time is an enemy of the position. Volatility effects are similarly dependent upon the current circumstances. If the futures price is well above the upper strike in a bull call spread, volatility hurts only because it increases the chance that the position will decline below the maximum potential profit. At the other extreme, an increase in volatility may be one way to salvage a position that appears headed for its maximum loss.

3.5.5   Bear Spreads

The opposite analogy to the bull spreads are the call and put bear spreads. The risk/profit profiles are very similar to the bull spreads except that the profit occurs when prices decline. Figure 3.8 shows how by selling a low strike price call and buying a higher strike call, a net premium is received and forms the maximum profit whenever the options expire with the underlying future lower than the short call's strike. A similar position can be established by being long one put and short another with a lower strike price.

The impact of time and volatility on bear spreads is mixed, just as in the case of bull spreads. It is important to remember that a mixed effect is *not* a neutral effect. Call and put spreads of all kinds should be constantly monitored so that the impact of any change in volatility will be anticipated and planned for.

If a trader is mildly bullish or bearish the advantage of option spreads comes from the additional leverage relative to a single outright position. An example

Figure 3.8
Bear Spread

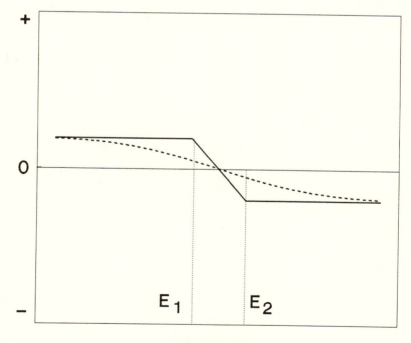

profit/loss

underlying price

will demonstrate this advantage. Suppose that the pound sterling is trading at 180 (¢/£), but an investor expects it to drop to 165, with a maximum exposure to 160. Suppose also that there is a fear that the market could move up in the short run before making the anticipated decline. Buying a put rather than selling the futures addresses this fear of a brief rally. Let the 180 put be trading at 5 cents. If the decline to 165 occurred there would be a total return at expiration of 15 cents, or a gain of 200 percent. Now suppose that the investor simultaneously sold a 160 put for 2 cents, making the net expense 3 cents. When prices fell to 165, the total return would still be 15 cents, but it would represent a 400 percent gain on the original outlay. This is the leverage benefit of option spreading. If the entire market believed that the potential decline in sterling was limited, the 160 put would have no value and such a strategy would have no advantage over the direct purchase of a put. Since market opinions do vary, this divergence of opinion can be used to custom fit a strategy to an opinion. Futures and cash markets offer this versatility, which suggests why the growth of options has been so rapid.

Figure 3.9
Long Straddle

profit/loss

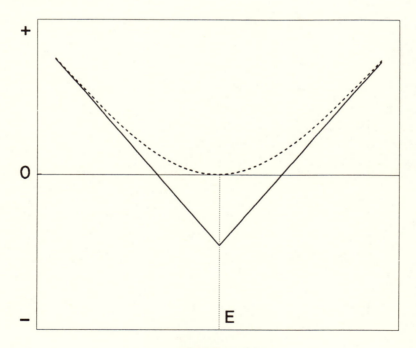

underlying price

3.5.6   Long Straddle

The strategy known as a long straddle consists of the simultaneous purchase of a call and a put at the same strike price (Figure 3.9). Typically, they are both at-the-money. The sentiment here is a pure expression of volatility. To profit, the move up or down must exceed the sum of the two premiums paid. The investor is not sure which way the market is about to move, but the belief is that it will move dramatically and soon. The owner of this position is long volatility, pure and simple. Note that if volatility does not increase, the position should not profit because the market has fully incorporated the expected price changes into the cost of the premiums. Only a sudden, significant move will produce a likelihood of profit in this position.

Time is the enemy of the holder of a long straddle. As expiration approaches, the effect is severe since both the put and the call are on the steepest portion of the time decay line. The appeal of this strategy is most evident around release

Figure 3.10
Short Straddle

profit/loss

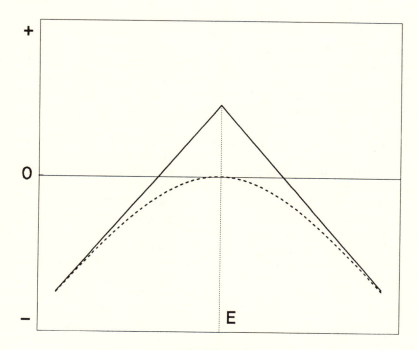

underlying price

dates for key market information. A long straddle in currency options around the trade figure release date is an expression that the number will appear at strong variance to expectations, producing an exaggerated movement in prices up or down. The writers of straddles know, however, that such dates are likely to be accompanied by a higher chance of a big move, and the options are usually priced accordingly.

3.5.7   Short Straddle

Writing a straddle is an attempt to sell time. By selling both a put and a call at the same strike price, the writer hopes that by the expiration date the underlying price will not have moved past the strike price plus or minus the sum of the premiums (Figure 3.10). The maximum gain is bounded by this sum, and it occurs only whenever the futures price exactly equals the strike at expiration. Time decay helps only the writer of straddles, and volatility increases are potentially lethal. A good time to consider this strategy is *after* a sudden price shock, like the October 1987 stock market crash. The volatility components of all puts and calls are at extremely high levels then, and there *may* be a return to more normal price changes. If this happens the profits to the short straddle trader can be great, but the risks of such an approach should not be minimized.

3.5.8   Strangles

The futures and options industry has no shortage of colorful terms, and the strategy known as a strangle is as descriptive as they come. The strangle is a slight variation on the straddle where the put has a lower strike price than the call. Typically, both are out-of-the-money when the position is established. Figure 3.11 shows a short strangle, and an example will suggest why it is so aptly named.

Consider pound sterling to be trading at 180 and let the 170 put and the 190 call both trade at 1.00 point. For simplicity, let these options be for physical currency with no intervening futures contract. By writing a strangle the investor collects 2.00 points, which is the maximum profit possible that occurs any time the futures settles between 170 and 190. To see why this is so, take any final value in this range. The put will not be exercised because it is more profitable to sell at the current price. Similarly, the call will expire worthless, and the writer will collect both premiums. At prices below 170 or above 190 one of the options will be exercised, and the profit will be diminished. The break-even points are 168 and 192, beyond which the loss potential is unlimited.

Now suppose that the market enters a particularly active stage with prices moving back and forth. It is possible with American options that may be exercised any time that prices could advance well above 190, at which point the owner of the call exercises his option, requiring the writer to buy sterling in the cash market at a price above 190 to deliver at 190 in fulfillment of the exercised

Figure 3.11
Short Strangle

profit/loss

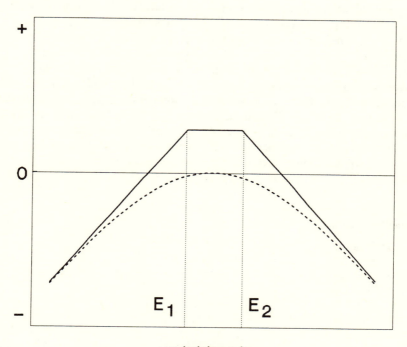

underlying price

call. After this occurs, prices could fall to below 170 at which point the put can be exercised requiring the writer to sell below 170 the sterling that had been put to him at 170. Although such an example is not typical, it happened frequently enough to give many the feeling of being strangled from both sides, leaving its name on the strategy.

Short strangles are typically entered into with a short time remaining until expiration. Since the total premium collected is smaller than that for a short straddle, the risk/reward ratio favors acting when the favorable impact of time decay is at its greatest. This strategy is an extremely risky one from the speculative short side since any shock to the market can prove devastating with very little collected premium to act as a cushion.

By contrast, from a hedger's perspective it can be an important inventory-management tool. If the hedger believes the market will remain in a trading range for the period of the option, he can sell a put at the low end of the range and a call with a strike near the high end. If prices drop, the product will be put to him at the low strike price. If they rise he will have inventory called from him at the higher strike. Prices in the middle will result in income from the premiums. If the hedger's expectation about the trading range market is correct, a short strangle guarantees that inventories will be built up at the low end of the range and will be drawn down at the high end. For intermediate prices, income will be generated that will subsidize the cost of holding the inventory.

A long strangle is merely the opposite position of the short strangle, with a long put at one strike combined with a long call at a higher price (Figure 3.12). Again, both are typically out-of-the-money to keep the expense minimized. The buyer of a long strangle is hoping for a big shock to the market and is indifferent as to the direction. This is as strong an expression of increased volatility expectations as you can create. Time decay, however, is the bane of the long strangle holder. If the price remains between the strike prices as the position matures, it may be advisable to liquidate with a few weeks remaining. This insures a small loss but avoids the most severe effects as time decay accelerates.

Figure 3.12
Long Strangle

profit/loss

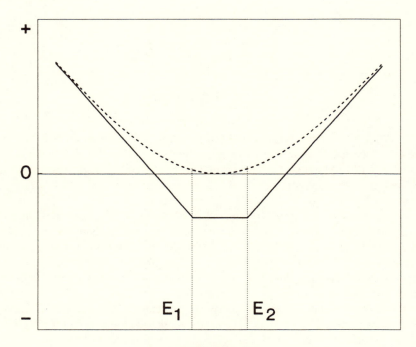

underlying price

3.5.9   An Options Menagerie

Butterflies and condors are strategies that suggest the presence of wings, and indeed the expiration profit/loss profile may appear that way to the more imaginative. Figure 3.13 shows a long butterfly, which is constructed by combining a bull spread between strike prices A and B and a bear spread between B and C. The width of the strike price intervals A-B and B-C are the same. Anyone putting on this position has the same expectations as the straddle writer but is being conservative. The hope is that prices will remain in a relatively narrow range, but if they do not, the maximum loss is limited by the wings.

Recalling that bull and bear spreads can be formed with pairs of either puts or calls, it should come as no surprise that butterflies may be constructed with all calls (long one call at strike price E_1, short two calls at E_2, and long one call at E_3) or all puts (long one put at E_1, short two puts at E_2, and long one put at E_3) or a combination consisting of one pair each of puts and calls. The logic behind the

Figure 3.13
Long Butterfly

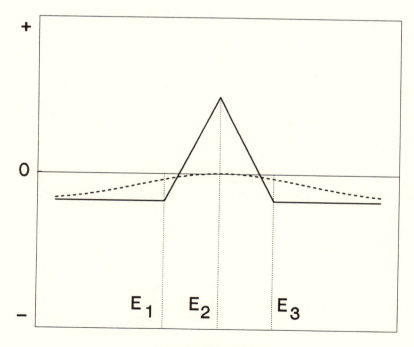

underlying price

profit/loss diagram can be seen by looking at an example of an all-call butterfly. Let the S&P 500 futures be trading at 250, with an expectation that it will stay in that neighborhood but a fear that it might not. Assume also the following call prices: 240 strike at 12.00 (10.00 intrinsic plus 2.00 premium above intrinsic), 250 strike at 5.50, and the 260 strike at 2.00. By buying the 240 (12.00 point debit), selling two 250s (13.00 point credit), and buying the 260 (2.00 point debit), a net expense of 1.00 point is incurred. Now consider the payoffs at expiration:

1. At any price below 240, all of the calls expire worthless; net result is 1.00 point loss.

2. Between 240 and 250, the long 240 call is exercised, but the others expire worthless; net result is the difference between the final price and 240 less the 1.00 point net premium. The break-even point is 241, and the maximum gain occurs at 250 with a total profit of 9.00 points.

3. Between 250 and 260, three options will be exercised: the 240 long call and both 250 short calls *against* the owner of the position. For every point above 250, there is a 2.00 point loss accruing from the short 250 calls to be offset only partially by the continued 1.00 point gains of the 240 call. The net effect is a one-for-one loss from any prices above 250, with the position dipping back into the red at 259 (you should be able to show this).

4. At prices above 260, all four options are exercised, with the profits from the long 240 and 260 calls fully offsetting the losses from the short 250 calls. The net result is the maximum loss of the 1.00 point in net premium paid.

Similar examples can be constructed with all put or mixed butterflies, but they add no unique insights to the strategy. One wrinkle that does show an important property of relative call prices comes from making a minor adjustment in the beginning premium of the 250 call. Suppose that the price of that option alone was bid up from 6.50 to 7.50. What implications would that have for the strategy? In this case the butterfly becomes very attractive since by trading all of the parts as prescribed, there is a net premium *received* of 1.00 point. In no case can the holder do worse than a 1.00 point profit, and if the settlement occurs at 250, there will be a maximum gain of 11.00 points. It should be apparent that arbitrageurs would quickly sell the 250 calls and buy the 240 and 260 calls until the prices again would produce a net premium paid, and a genuine risk/reward trade-off. What can be seen from this is that for equally spaced call strike price intervals, the differences in premiums should decline as the strike price pairs increase. Originally the 240–250 difference was 5.50 and the 250–260 difference was 4.50. When the 250 strike premium was set at 7.50, these values were reversed. For puts, the differences will get smaller with declining strike prices. Unless these conditions hold, risk free profits will be available.

Just as in bull and bear spreads, the respective impacts of time and volatility are mixed. If the underlying futures price is near the middle strike, time decay helps and volatility hurts. The opposite situation holds if the price is outside the profit range.

It is possible to imagine a short butterfly as simply the flip of the long butterfly, but it is difficult to imagine why anyone would deliberately take on this position. To profit, however modestly, requires a radical up or down move, and for most outcomes around the middle strike, a considerably larger loss is expected. For those expecting a significant increase in volatility, a long straddle would seem preferred, but it is possible that if the in- and out-of-the-money options are sufficiently expensive, it may pay to sell the wings in an attempt to minimize the net outlay of the straddle.

A condor has a different profile than a butterfly when it is flying toward you, and this has prompted options strategists to dub a combination of a bull spread at one pair of strikes with a bear spread at a higher pair, a condor (Figure 3.14). The only restriction is that the strike price intervals defining the condor be equidistant. Like a butterfly, a condor can be comprised of all calls, all puts or an appropriate combination.

Returning to the S&P 500 example, a condor could be constructed by going long a 240 put and a 270 put and selling both a 250 and 260 put. Like the

Figure 3.14
Long Condor

profit/loss

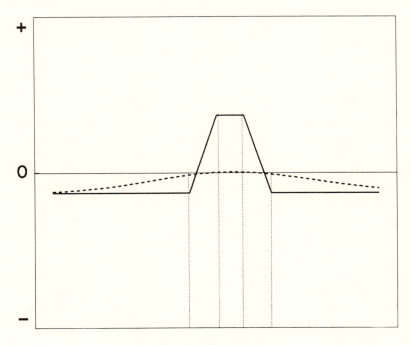

underlying price

butterfly, the premiums paid will be expected to exceed the premiums received. If not, risk free profits are available. The logic of the profit/loss profile shown in Figure 3.14 can be derived in a similar fashion to the butterfly. If the futures price ends up below 240, all of the puts will be exercised; above 270, none of them will be. In either case the loss is at its maximum value. Between 250 and 260 profit is maximized at a value of the strike price interval less the net premium. The break-even points are at 240 plus the net premium and 270 less the net premium.[4]

Time and volatility play the same roles with condors as they do with butterflies. Also similar is the lack of apparent speculative motivation to do the trade from the short side unless the values of the ''wing'' options are high relative to the body.

3.5.10   Summary on Strategies

This section has presented several simple and complex option strategies that can meet the needs of a wide range of traders. It has by no means exhausted the possibilities of how options can be, or in fact are, combined. Professional option advisors have catalogued scores of strategies and present them almost cookbook style—a recipe for every occasion. But the main point here is that any combination may be analyzed by adding very simple profit/loss diagrams. It is a skill every option trader, whether speculative or commercial, should possess. Only with this knowledge can the trader appreciate how the strategy fits with his or her opinions and, most importantly, what risks are posed from the passage of time or a change in volatility.

3.6   FORMAL MODELS OF OPTIONS PRICING

The most important breakthrough in the theory of option pricing occurred with the publication of Fischer Black and Myron Scholes's seminal 1973 paper. This study started a growth industry extending well beyond the original topic. Black-Scholes's key contribution was the recognition of arbitrage relationships that tie together the prices of options, interest rates, and the value of the underlying security. Importantly, there is no need to guess about the direction of the stock price or interest rates to determine a ''fair'' option value. The Black-Scholes model, and the multitude of variations that have followed, all take current conditions as given and then derive option values that preclude arbitrage opportunities.

The Black-Scholes model was derived using stochastic differential equations, and consequently, much of the intuition of the model is hidden behind some formidable mathematics. A simpler approach, called the *binomial* model, was presented by John Cox, Stephen Ross, and Mark Rubinstein (1979). This model starts out with an extremely simple set of assumptions but can be made increasingly realistic to achieve the degree of computational precision (and complication) desired. The beauty of the binomial model lies in its ability to demonstrate the key arbitrage relationships that ultimately govern the characteristics of option trading.

In the more than 15 years since the introduction of Black-Scholes, there have been scores of computer programs for both mainframes and PCs to perform the key option calculations. Knowing the intricacies of the particular model behind the program is not essential to its successful use, but an understanding of the basics is required if appropriate strategies are to be developed.[5] This section begins with the simplest one-period binomial model and then presents the Black (1976) continuous-time commodity option pricing model used most widely today in evaluating options on futures.

3.6.1   The Binomial Model

The single-period binomial model demonstrates the key elements of option pricing starting from very simple assumptions. An example from the deutsche mark futures market will provide a test case. Suppose that the next deutsche mark futures is currently priced at 60 (cents per deutsche mark) and that in the next period we know it will change to either 66 or 57 (up 10 percent or down 5 percent). Suppose also that the interest rate over the period is 5 percent. What is the value of a one-period call that has a strike price of 0.60? In other words, what will it cost to guarantee that I can buy deutsche marks a period from now at today's price?

The first response most people have to this model is that it is so preposterous in its assumptions that it cannot be useful for anything. Prices obviously move in many unpredictable ways, and planning horizons are never for "a single period." But what is demonstrated here are the basics, and this simple model holds everything needed to accomplish that end. In the example, specific numbers are used, but later a general form is presented.

The binomial model is presented in the "tree" below, one for the futures and one for the option. In the one-period model, the tree has only two branches (Model 1).

The option tree states that the call, which has an unknown value of C today, will be worth 6 if the futures price moves up to 66 (6 is its intrinsic value), or it will expire worthless if the futures declines to 57.

There are boundaries that can be immediately placed on the value of C. First, $C > 0$, because there is a chance that the futures will increase in value; the call must have some value. Second, $C < 6$. If C were greater than the maximum intrinsic value, it would never pay to buy the call. It would be cheaper to buy the futures at the highest possible price than pay the premium and acquire the futures at the strike price.

These boundaries provide a starting point but little else. To move on, assume that the price of the call initially was 5. Also assume that a portfolio was constructed of three short calls and two long futures. This ratio was not chosen at

Model 1

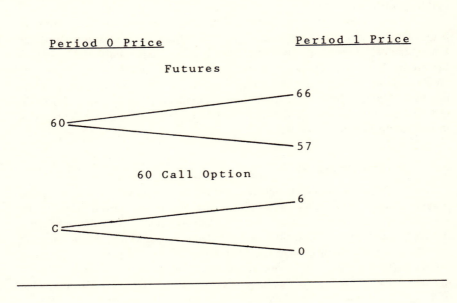

Period 0 Price   Period 1 Price

Futures

60 → 66

60 → 57

60 Call Option

C → 6

C → 0

random but reflects the *hedge ratio,* which is derived below. The portfolio also has an outcome tree (Model 2).

There are three components to the returns in period 1. First is the profit or loss on the two long futures contracts. Second are the three option premiums that have been invested at 5 percent interest. Finally, there is the terminal value of the options, which is the liability from writing the options. The fact that there is a profit of 9.75 cents per deutsche mark in either case derives from the choice of the hedge ratio. Different proportions of options and futures would give varying returns.

What is remarkable is that a strategy could be developed that would produce a guaranteed return no matter which futures outcome occurred. Arbitrage is possible in this world since writers of the options can receive gains with no chance of loss. This is the first indication that $C = 5$ is too high for an equilibrium. As more competition comes from arbitrageurs to perform this trade, the price of the option should be lowered.

Suppose that instead of a price of 5 the option's initial value was 1. In this world construct a portfolio of three *long* calls and two *short* futures. The payoff tree for this trade has the same components as the prior example with the signs reversed (Model 3).

Here the return comes from the futures profit plus the terminal value of the long option, reduced by the opportunity cost of the money invested initially in

Model 2

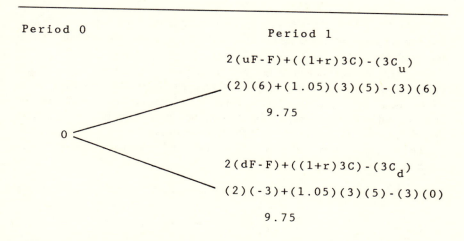

Period 0   Period 1

$$2(uF-F)+((1+r)3C)-(3C_u)$$

$$(2)(6)+(1.05)(3)(5)-(3)(6)$$

9.75

0

$$2(dF-F)+((1+r)3C)-(3C_d)$$

$$(2)(-3)+(1.05)(3)(5)-(3)(0)$$

9.75

where,

F	=	futures price at time 0
u	=	"up"; rate of price increase
d	=	"down"; rate of price decline
r	=	interest rate for period
C	=	call value at time 0
C_u	=	call value at time 1 after up futures move
C_d	=	call value at time 1 after down futures move

Model 3

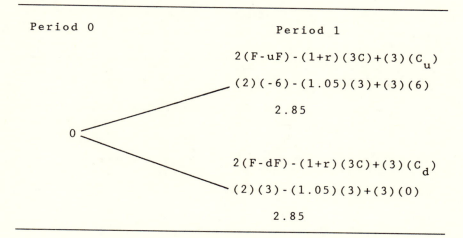

Period 0   Period 1

$$2(F-uF)-(1+r)(3C)+(3)(C_u)$$

$$(2)(-6)-(1.05)(3)+(3)(6)$$

2.85

0

$$2(F-dF)-(1+r)(3C)+(3)(C_d)$$

$$(2)(3)-(1.05)(3)+(3)(0)$$

2.85

the calls. Once again there is a guaranteed return from either outcome, suggesting that arbitrageurs will enter and bid up the price of the calls until this gain is not available.

If $C = 5$ induces traders to sell options and $C = 1$ produces certain profits from long positions in options, the equilibrium value of the calls must be between these values. A crude iteration process of testing trading strategies for riskless profits would eventually hone in on the equilibrium, but with a general binomial model the call price can be calculated directly.

Start with the general value of the call at the end of period 1, where E is the exercise price:

$$C_u = \text{Max } [0, uF - E] \qquad (3.1)$$

$$C_d = \text{Max } [0, dF - E] \qquad (3.2)$$

Recalling that the option's strike price is assumed to be the initial futures value, these equations state that the call will be worth the larger of the futures price change or zero. This is the equivalent of intrinsic value for options that expire in-the-money and zero for those out-of-the-money.

Let h stand for the hedge ratio, or the number of futures per call written. (See Model 4.) The hedge ratio is the optimal proportion of futures to options, that is, the ratio that produces the identical return under either outcome. It is found by setting the "up" outcome equal to the "down" outcome and solving for h.

$$h = (C_u - C_d)/((u - d)F) \qquad (3.3)$$

In this example $C_u = 6$, $C_d = 0$, $u = 1.10$, $d = 0.95$, and $F = 60$. Placing these in the above equation gives $h = \frac{6}{9}$ or $\frac{2}{3}$. There should be two long futures for every three short calls.

Since either outcome is certain, if the call's initial premium is too high, it will pay to write calls against the futures. If the premium is too low, the reverse

Model 4

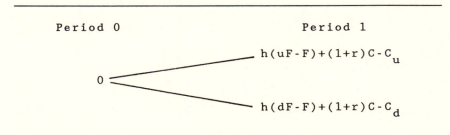

arbitrage will guarantee profits. At only one value of C will there be no incentive to arbitrage because either trade will produce zero returns in both outcomes. *This is the equilibrium value of C.*

By setting either of the period 1 outcomes equal to zero, one can solve for C using the hedge ratio above. In equilibrium,

$$C = (pC_u + (1 - p)C_d)/(1 + r) \tag{3.4}$$

where,

$$p = (1 - d)/(u - d), \text{ and} \tag{3.5}$$

$$(1 - p) = (u - 1)/(u - d) \tag{3.6}$$

The equilibrium value of C is a discounted weighted average of the possible terminal values of the call, where the weights are a function of the size of the up and down moves. Solving for C in the example gives,

$$C = ((.05/.15)6 + (.10/.15)0)/1.05 \tag{3.7}$$

$$= 2/1.05 = 1.905$$

Placing this value back into either of the terminal return values produces no profit opportunities.

It may not seem evident at first, but the general solution contains all but one of the elements that were considered important contributing factors to a call's value: strike price relative to the underlying price, volatility, and interest rates. The missing element of time will be added later.

To see how each of these factors is important, start with the original assumptions and change them one by one. Suppose that instead of a strike price of 60, the value of a 63 call was desired. C_u would now be 3, and C_d would still reflect an out-of-the-money call expiring worthless. Plugging this new value into the equation gives $C = 1/1.05 = 0.952$. As expected, higher strike price calls cost less, and you should demonstrate that all calls with strikes at or above 66 are worthless.

The impact of a varying interest rate is direct since it appears only in the denominator of the equation. Higher rates increase the opportunity cost of buying options and increase the return to writing them. Both factors combine to unambiguously lower premiums.

Volatility increases should increase an option's value. To show this, change the payoff tree as shown in Model 5. This example is more volatile than the original case, but if the probabilities of moving up and down are the same as the first example, the means of the two distributions are identical. In this example, u and d have changed to 1.15 and 0.90, respectively, reflecting the greater range of

Model 5

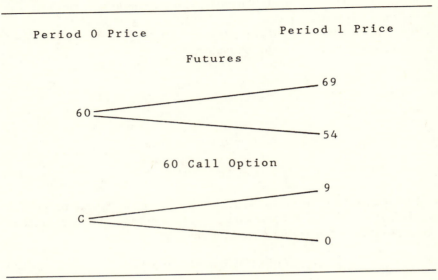

Period 0 Price   Period 1 Price

Futures

69

60

54

60 Call Option

9

C

0

---

values. Solving for C here gives a value of $3.6/1.05 = 3.429$, almost twice as great to capture the greater volatility.

Demonstrating the impact of time involves expanding the binomial model beyond the single-period case. Applying the same ''up'' and ''down'' factors to a beginning value F produces a slightly more diverse tree in the two-period case. There is also a corresponding tree for calls (Model 6).

Note that in the multiplicative model the order of the steps makes no difference to the ultimate outcome. One step up followed by a step down produces a price identical to a down-up sequence. The other important feature is that each one-period step may be viewed as the single-period valuation problem already explored. For example, stepping back one step from the final outcome and applying Equation 3.4 gives,

$$C_u = (pC_{uu} + (1 - p)C_{ud})/(1 + r) \qquad (3.8)$$

$$C_d = (pC_{ud} + (1 - p)C_{dd})/(1 + r) \qquad (3.9)$$

No matter how many steps make up the total process, the problem can be broken into one-period bites and solved recursively. For the two-period case the solution for C becomes,

$$C = (p^2C_{uu} + 2p(1 - p)C_{ud} + (1 - p)^2C_{dd})/(1 + r)^2 \qquad (3.10)$$

Model 6

Period 0 Price   Period 1 Price   Period 2 Price

Futures

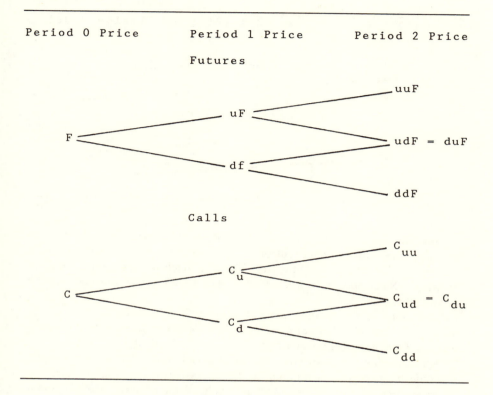

Calls

---

and, in general, the solution for n periods progresses by binomial expansion to become,

$$C = \frac{1}{(1 + r)^n} \sum_{k=0}^{n} \frac{n!}{k!(n - k)!} p^k(1 - p)^{n-k} \text{Max}[0, u^k d^{n-k}F - E] \qquad (3.11)$$

The first terms in the summation are the coefficients of the binomial equation in p and $1 - p$. Each coefficient is multiplied by the intrinsic value of the option calculated after the futures contract has taken k up steps out of a total of n.

To see the impact of additional time, the original example can be expanded, as shown in Model 7.

Placing these values into the binomial formula gives:

$$C = ((1/3)^2 12.6 + (4/9)2.7 + (2/3)^2 0)/(1.05)^2 \qquad (3.12)$$

$$= 2.6/(1.05)^2 = 2.358$$

which is greater than the one-period value of 1.905.

Model 7

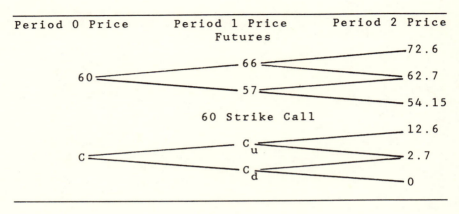

Period 0 Price   Period 1 Price   Period 2 Price
                            Futures
60   66   72.6
                                       62.7
                           57   54.15

60 Strike Call
                           C_u 12.6
C   2.7
                           C_d 0

Time adds to the value of an option because as more steps are allowed, there are more potentially profitable outcomes. After having F move to uF, there is the chance of additional appreciation to u^2F and a much higher intrinsic value at expiration. Since options cannot fall below zero in value, steps down do not pose a symmetric risk.

Continuous solving of this option equation as it grows would show an ever increasing value of C but *not* at a linear rate. Doubling of the time frame will increase C by less than a factor of two.

Before moving on to expand the binomial model to the continuous-time case, it should be noted that at no point in the discussion were *probabilities* of the different steps discussed. It is tempting to believe that once the size of u and d have been determined, the two events are equally likely. This is not necessary for the binomial model to work. By developing hedge ratios that generate equivalent payouts for all outcomes, it makes no difference whether the chance of an up move is 50-50 or 1 in 20. The arbitrageur will secure a profit from mispriced options no matter what the frequency of outcomes. This demonstrates the broad abilities of the binomial model to work under very basic assumptions that are not dependent on market opinion.

As flexible as the binomial model is, several of its assumptions strain the imagination. Prices do not move in simple up/down steps on a fixed schedule of periodicity, and the possible outcomes for a deutsche mark future are not limited to a discrete set of values. But the binomial model can be stretched to get closer to reality.

Suppose that the original one-period model spanned an eight-hour trading day. Modifying the sizes of u, d, and r to reflect the change, an eight-period hourly model could be developed. This would have nine possible price outcomes ranging from u^8F to d^8F, greatly expanding the range of possibilities. But there is no reason to stop with an hourly model. A minute-by-minute binomial model would have 480 steps, and if the market ticked every second, n would expand quickly to

28,800. As the length of the time interval shrinks, the number of steps and possible outcomes grows to approximate the continuous-time model.

3.6.2 Black–Scholes

Black–Scholes began with a continuous-time model for stocks, which can be shown to be the limit of the binomial model for that security as n goes to infinity. The equation for stocks is,

$$C = SN(d_1) - Ee^{-rT}N(d_2) \tag{3.13}$$

where $d_1 = (1n(S/E) + (r + .5\sigma^2)T)/\sigma\sqrt{T}$ and $d_2 = d_1 - \sigma\sqrt{T}$

Table 3.2 gives a list of all symbols used in these models.

Table 3.2
Symbols Used in Option Models

P	put price
C	call price
S	underlying stock price
F	underlying futures price
E	exercise price of the option
r	interest rate
T	time to maturity in years
u	"up" move factor in binomial model
d	"down" move factor in binomial model
ln x	the natural logarithm function
e^x	the exponentiation function
N(x)	the cumulative normal distribution
N'(x)	the normal probability density function
	$= (1/\sqrt{2\pi})e^{-.5x^2}$
	annualized standard deviation of the underlying distribution of returns

The world under examination here, however, covers options on futures. Recognizing that futures purchases and sales do not require the acquisition or sale of an asset, Black (1976) modified Equation 3.13 to cover options on futures.

$$C = [FN(d_1) - EN(d_2)]e^{-rT} \qquad (3.14)$$

$$d_1 = (1n(F/E) + .5\sigma^2 T)/\sigma\sqrt{T}$$

$$d_2 = d_1 - \sigma\sqrt{T}$$

Here F takes the place of S in the stock model, and there are other differences stemming from the impact of interest on the alternative arbitrage instruments. The similarities between the stock and futures models are evident, but it may not be clear what connection can be made between either model and the binomial models that lie behind them. The derivations are complex and do not add much toward understanding the interaction among the forces. It is necessary to know only that as n becomes large, the binomial equation converges to the normal, and that σ, the standard deviation of the underlying price changes, is related to the size of u and d.

Looking at an extreme case will point out an important feature of the equation. Assume that the futures price has no volatility, that is, $\sigma = 0$. In this case d_1 and d_2 both get very large implying the cumulative normal distribution approaches 1; the entire distribution is covered. In this case,

$$C = [F - E]e^{-rT} \qquad (3.15)$$

which is the discounted value of the intrinsic value of the option. Just as in the binomial case, the minimum value of any call is zero, so in this example out-of-the-money calls will never have value. This is to be expected in a world that never changes.

For nonzero volatilities the equation does not simplify as readily. To appreciate the various interactions, it is necessary to look at the derivatives of Equation 3.14 with respect to its key variables.

3.6.3   A Greek Alphabet Soup

The quickest way to feel lost among options traders is to listen to their conversation about strategy without benefit of a glossary of option jargon. From delta neutrality to being long gamma, the potential for confusion is vast. But like most jargons, option labels are not that difficult to understand once the shorthand is deciphered.

Delta. The delta of an option is the change in the theoretical value that comes from a change in the underlying futures price. It is the derivative of Equation 3.14 with respect to F.

$$dC/dF = e^{-rT}N(d_1) \tag{3.16}$$

Since $N(d_1)$ is limited to between zero and 1.0, delta is similarly bounded. For options that are deep out-of-the-money, delta will be close to zero. Options that are deep in-the-money will move in a closely parallel fashion to the futures contract and have a delta near 1.0. Not surprisingly, at-the-money options have a delta near 0.5.

One of the important elements of the binomial model is the hedge ratio, and in the Black model the hedge ratio is easily found by taking the inverse of delta. For example, if a call had a delta of 0.5, a "delta-neutral" position could be constructed by combining two short calls with a long future or two long calls with a short future. The concept implies that gains or losses in the underlying futures will be completely offset by opposite moves in the options. An option with a delta of 0.5 has the same risk as half a futures, whereas a delta of 0.1 implies an option equal to one-tenth of a futures. If the calls were not priced according to the Black model *and* the delta of the position did not change over the term of the option, it would be possible to earn arbitrage profits by trading calls against futures according to the hedge ratio.

Although the theory is complete at any given price, the delta of an option is not constant as prices change. Establishing a delta neutral portfolio today provides no guarantees that delta will not change, transforming the position into a net long or net short exposure.

If delta never changed, an option would behave just like a scaled-down future. Delta must change, however, because of the limited-risk character of an option. Begin with an at-the-money call with a delta of 0.5. If the option moves out-of-the-money, its lowest possible value is bounded by zero. As the price of the underlying instrument continues to fall, after some point there will be no further reduction in the option value. The delta will have fallen from 0.5 to zero as the futures price declined. Figure 3.15 shows the variation of delta of an at-the-money call as the underlying price changes. To keep a balanced portfolio would require continuous adjustment of the number of options according to the hedge ratio.

The rate at which delta changes is a critical factor in portfolio management and gives an indication of the risk in a delta-neutral portfolio. The underlying price can change quickly at any time, necessitating a rapid adjustment to maintain a flat book. If the price change occurs overnight or over a weekend when the markets are closed, the adjustment will not proceed instantaneously or at prices that can avoid losses. By the time neutrality is reestablished, the trades will have been placed defensively, often at losses.

Gamma. To gauge the exposure faced by a delta-neutral portfolio requires the measurement of how fast delta can change. This is given by gamma, the second derivative of the call price equation with respect to the underlying price.

$$d^2C/dF^2 = e^{-rT}N'(d_1)/F\sigma\sqrt{T} \tag{3.17}$$

Figure 3.15
Call Delta

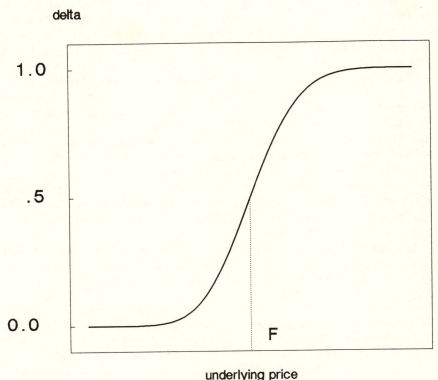

underlying price

Gamma is a function of the strike price relative to the futures, the volatility, and the time to expiration. Starting with an at-the-money call, Figure 3.16 shows the gamma is not terribly important as the underlying price shifts to make the option either deep in-the-money or deep out-of-the-money. Another important element in this equation is time. As an option nears expiration and is near the money, delta can change radically. One day before expiration a call with a strike that is one standard deviation away from the current price may have a delta of 0.2, suggesting a strategy of writing five calls for each long futures. This is not an enterprise for the faint of heart. With a one standard deviation move up, which can be expected to occur approximately once every six days, this "neutral" position would become a net exposure of four lots short. The gamma, and hence risk, of this position is extremely high.

At the opposite extreme is an option with a great deal of time remaining. In the equation, as T gets large gamma declines for all underlying prices and strikes. This means that delta-neutral positions with considerable time to expiration are

Figure 3.16
Gamma

gamma

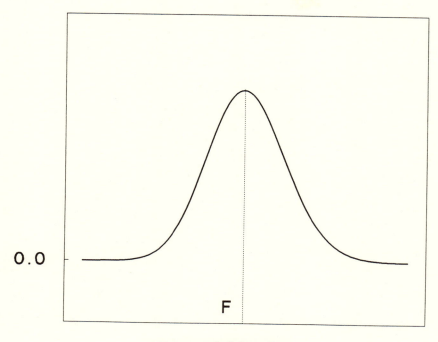

0.0

F

underlying price

relatively safe. There are firms that offer over-the-counter multiyear options. The ability to offer these products is made possible by the low gamma. Delta-neutral portfolios are created that may be reasonably maintained because there is very little chance that a surprise event will occur to alter radically an option's value and generate a market exposure.

Vega. In the section dealing with strategies, emphasis was placed on the need for an awareness of the impact of volatility on the value of an option's position. In terms of the option pricing model, this is formally the derivative of the call price with respect to σ. This derivative, vega, is,

$$dC/d\sigma = e^{-rT}FN'(d_1)\sqrt{T} \tag{3.18}$$

The key values here are the strike price and the underlying futures. At-the-money options ($E = F$) are much more sensitive to changes in volatility than either in- or out-of-the money options. This is shown in Figure 3.17. The impact

Figure 3.17
Vega

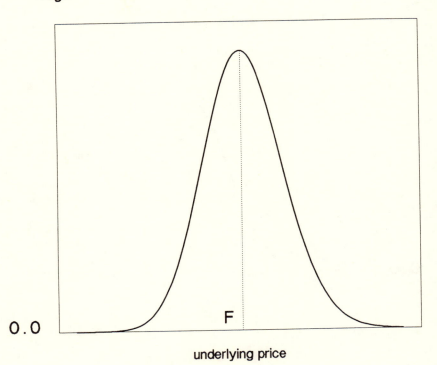

underlying price

of volatility on deep in-the-money options is minor because they are always priced near their intrinsic values. For deep out options it takes not only a major change in volatility but also the underlying price level to have much of an influence. Vega, which only sounds like it should be a Greek letter, but in fact is not, is sometimes called by other names. Different writers have called the impact of volatility on option prices kappa, omega, zeta, or sigma. The lack of uniformity is a suggestion as to how new some of this theory is. The labels may be confusing, but it is important to remember that by any name, volatility changes will have a major impact on an option's price.

Rho. As mentioned previously, the influence of changing interest rates on a futures option is complex because they impact not only the option decision but also the carry structure of the futures. Let S be the spot value of the underlying security. Then,

$$F = e^{hT}S \qquad\qquad (3.19)$$

where h is defined to be the holding cost for the commodity. In a carry market h is positive, implying futures are more expensive than spot. Inversions imply a negative h.

Rho is the influence of interest rates on an option's value.

$$dC/dr = -TC + e^{-rT}FN(d_1)[T(dh/dr) + (dS/dr)/S] \qquad (3.20)$$

This is complex, relying not only on the relative values of h and r but also on dh/dr and dS/dr.

In some financial markets the total holding cost is the interest rate, implying that $h = r$ and $dh/dr = 1$. If we can also assume that the spot price is independent of interest rates ($dS/dr = 0$), this simplifies Equation 3.20 considerably.

$$dC/dr = Te^{-rT}EN(d_2) \qquad (3.21)$$

The key factor here is time. Higher interest rates will always lead to greater premiums, and the more time left in the option, the greater the impact.

Theta. Time decay was previously discussed in Section 3.4.2, and Figure 3.1 showed how the effect of time is most dramatic as an option approaches expiration. Theta is the measurement of this effect and, by convention, is defined as the *negative* of the derivative of an option's price with respect to time. A large negative theta implies rapid time decay, while a theta near zero suggests that whatever value the option has will not be greatly affected by the passage of time.

$$dC/dT = -rC + Fe^{-rT}N'(d_1)\sigma/(2\sqrt{T}) \qquad (3.22)$$

Very similar to the effects of gamma and vega, theta is most potent for options with strike prices near the current futures price. Neither deep in-the-money nor deep out-of-the-money options have significant time values to decay, and hence theta is small. While theta is an important indicator, an option trader ought to be keenly aware of the time exposure of his or her portfolio without having to examine this value.

3.6.4   Put Pricing

The value of a put could be derived in the same way as a call by exploiting the arbitrage relationships across futures, interest bearing instruments, and the put, but this will not be necessary. Using the characteristics of a conversion discussed in Section 3.5.3 brings about a much quicker solution. Recall that someone buying a put and selling a call (with the same strike price) has created the equivalent of a short futures position at the strike price less the net premium paid. Knowing the futures price and the call value is enough to determine the put. Let F_1 be the value of the futures at expiration.

$$(F - F_1) = Ce^{rT} - \text{Max}[0, F_1 - E]$$
$$- Pe^{rT} + \text{Max}[0, E - F_1] \qquad (3.23)$$

The terms on the right-hand side correspond to: (1) the total value of the invested call premium collected; (2) the terminal value of the short call (a liability); (3) the cost of financing the purchased put premium; and (4) the terminal value of the long put (an asset). Since E, the strike price, is identical for both the put and call, at most one option can expire with an intrinsic value. If it is the call, solving Equation 3.23 becomes,

$$P = C + e^{-rT}(E - F) \qquad (3.24)$$

and it is easily shown that the same value is obtained when it is the put that ends up in-the-money.

The intuition behind this formula is compelling. For at-the-money options ($E = F$), the put premium equals that of the call, a result first discussed in Section 3.5.3 on conversions. For the in-the-money puts ($E > F$) the call will be out-of-the-money, implying that its entire premium will be time value. This means that the put will equal the call's time value plus the discounted intrinsic value. It is discounted because the buyer of the put will lose the use of the funds for the life of the contract. For out-of-the-money puts, the reverse logic from the previous case applies.

The various derivatives of the put price equation are similar to that of the call. They are presented here without their derivations.

$$\text{Delta: } dP/dF = e^{-rT}(N(d_1) - 1) \qquad (3.25)$$

$$\text{Gamma: } d_2P/dF_2 = e^{-rT}N'(d_1)/F\sigma\sqrt{T} \qquad (3.26)$$

$$\text{Vega: } dP/d\sigma = e^{-rT}FN'(d_1)\sqrt{T} \qquad (3.27)$$

$$\text{Rho: } dP/dr = dC/dr + e^{-rT}[TF(1 - dh/dr)$$
$$- TE - e^{hT}(dS/dr)] \qquad (3.28)$$

$$\text{Theta: } dP/dT = -rP + Fe^{-rT}N'(d_1)\sigma/(2\sqrt{T}) \qquad (3.29)$$

Simplifying 3.28 along the lines to arrive at rho for calls (Equation 3.21) gives,

$$dP/dr = e^{-rT}TE(N(d_2) - 1) \qquad (3.30)$$

A comparison with the corresponding call equations will reveal that gamma and vega are the same for puts and calls with the same strike price. This is in keeping with the arbitrage relationships. An increase in volatility ought to increase both the put and call by the same amount or else arbitrage opportunities would be created. A similar argument can be made for gamma, the rate of change of delta.

The key equation is 3.25, the calculation of delta. For the put, delta is always negative (since $N(d_1) - 1$ is always less than zero), implying that as a futures price increases the value of a put declines. Similar to the case of a call, the put delta is bounded by zero and -1, implying that the *absolute* movement of a put will always be expected to be less than that of the futures. Starting with an at-the-money put, the theoretical delta is given in Figure 3.18.

Puts that are deep in-the-money have deltas close to -1, that is, they behave much like a *short* futures. Out-of-the-money puts have deltas closer to zero.

Figures 3.15 and 3.18 appear to be mirror images of one another, suggesting that by adding a long call's delta and a short put's delta you would get a value of 1. From the Table 3.1 synthetic positions, you would also expect such a result. This is usually very nearly true, but is literally true only for at-the-money op-

Figure 3.18
Put Delta

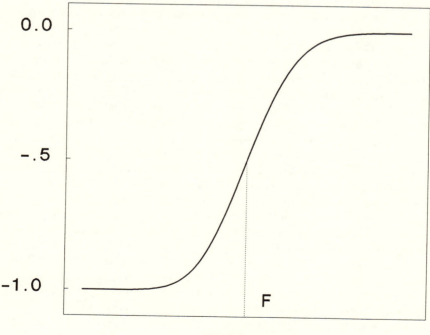

delta

underlying price

tions. In all other cases the culprits are time and the cost of money, which react to drive a wedge between the actual position and the synthetic equivalent. To see this effect add the delta of a long call to that of a short put.

$$\text{Sum} = e^{-rT}N(d_1) - e^{-rT}(N(d_1) - 1) \tag{3.31}$$

$$= e^{-rT}$$

If either r or T equals zero, the sum equals 1. As time or interest costs expand a minor deviation begins to appear. What this means to the options trader is that there is a bit of sand thrown into the gears, keeping the synthetic position from moving as quickly as the underlying futures. There is nothing wrong with this, but it must be kept in mind when building effective outright option and arbitrage positions.

3.6.5 Pricing of American Options

In all of the previous discussions, the models have presumed that there was no chance of early exercise, that is, the options were European. American options allow for exercise any time prior to expiration and are consequently more valuable. This is particularly important for dividend-paying stocks where there may be an incentive to exercise prior to the ex-dividend date, but it is still a factor on options on futures where there are no dividends. One might think that failure to capture this feature in the pricing model is a serious defect, but this is not true.

Robert Geske (1979) and Robert Whaley (1986) discussed the analytical aspects of pricing American options, and Geske and Richard Roll (1984) discussed some of the empirical research that has explored biases in Black–Scholes and how an American model can address them. The analytical approaches are cumbersome, even by option pricing standards, and the empirical work suggests that the bias from using the wrong model is usually small. This has not prevented researchers from pursuing even more analytically complete approaches.

We will not go into any detail on the subject here. For options on futures it is important to note that in only extreme cases does the owner of an option have an incentive to exercise early. Out-of-the-money options will not be exercised because it makes no sense to acquire something with negative intrinsic value when the positive time value could be sold back to the market. In-the-money options will be exercised only when it becomes too expensive to hold them and the market does not value them as options.

This occurs with positions that move deep into the money. Being profitable is not the problem, but the option equity may not be used for other investment purposes. Deep in-the-money options have the same risk as futures but tie up more funds than a futures margin. If risk like a futures is desired, it makes sense to hold it in the lowest cost fashion.

The owner of such an option may wish to sell it and buy a future, but who would be willing to buy? Any long in the market would have to pay the premium in full and consequently tie up funds. The bottom line is that the option will always be priced at *parity,* equal to its intrinsic value. The solution is to exercise the option early to free up these funds and let them earn interest.

If this is the major difference in behavior between American and European options, one can see why the pricing issues are subtle. American options will never be priced below parity, because if they were, they could be purchased, immediately exercised, and a riskless profit acquired. This suggests that European options may fall below parity, which is true before expiration. The bottom line, however, is that for the broad group of options on futures that hedgers and speculators are concerned with, there are many more important pricing questions, like estimated volatility, than any distinction between American and European formats.

3.6.6 Option Pricing with Futures-Style Margins

It was previously mentioned that attempts were being made to bring about futures-style margining for options. If that ever came about, the futures option pricing model could be greatly simplified. No longer would there be any need to consider borrowing to pay for a premium or investing premiums from short options. With this simplification, interest rates drop out of the equations altogether. The Black equations become:

$$\text{Call Price: } C = FN(d_1) - EN(d_2) \tag{3.32}$$

$$\text{Put Price: } P = C + E - F \tag{3.33}$$

$$\text{Call Delta: } dC/dF = N(d_1) \tag{3.34}$$

$$\text{Put Delta: } dP/dF = N(d_1) - 1 \tag{3.35}$$

$$\text{Put and Call Gamma: } d^2C/dF^2 = d^2P/dF^2 = N'(d_1)/F\sigma\sqrt{T} \tag{3.36}$$

$$\text{Put and Call Vega: } dC/d\sigma = dP/d\sigma = FN'(d_1)\sqrt{T} \tag{3.37}$$

$$\text{Put and Call Theta: } dC/dT = dP/dT = FN'(d_1)\sigma/2\sqrt{T} \tag{3.38}$$

These equations are considerably easier than their earlier counterparts and there is no rho to consider.

Both call and put prices are higher since the writer no longer gets to earn interest on the premium, but the counterpoint is that the long no longer has to give up this interest. It should also be noted that now the sum of the put and call deltas always equals 1, meaning a synthetic futures position should behave exactly like its direct counterpart. A final virtue is that since funds are never tied up in the form of inaccessible premium, there is never an incentive to exercise a futures-style option early. This means that the equations derived for European-style options apply equally well to American options, eliminating considerably more complications.

The economic benefits of futures-style margining were explained in Section 3.3. A final argument for their adoption would come from the theoreticians who would like to simplify their lives.

3.6.7 Option Pricing Summary

This section began with a simple one-period binomial model and quickly grew to a continuous-time environment capable of accommodating numerous assumptions. Few practitioners will have great need for the detail presented, but the equations represent key relationships about which any option trader, speculator, or hedger should have an intuitive grasp. When considering software for trading options, all of the key variables should be presented, and the user should appreciate the differences in the basic assumptions used (binomial versus Black, American versus European, and so on). Only in that way will the trader be in control of the model rather than the other way around.

Academic reputations have been made by considering the impact of subtle changes in assumptions on option pricing. There have been many underlying price distributions examined. Some have been in the same family as, but less restrictive than, the lognormal distribution of Black. Others have eliminated continuous-price movements by allowing for "jumps" on occasion. For options professionals, these have been important investigations because competition across arbitrageurs is keen and any advantage important. But for the hedger using options, there have been rapidly diminishing returns in this area.

It is important to have a good grasp of value before placing a trade, but how much difference does it make to a hedging strategy if the underlying distribution is "fat tailed" or lognormally distributed? The option hedger can rely on the market to have a degree of efficiency in incorporating the most effective model. With the difference across assumptions amounting to a few points at most, these distinctions should not form the basis of a decision whether or not to hedge. The model at hand should act only as a guide toward sound financial decisions.

If option modeling was a completely precise science, considerably more space would have been devoted to the nuances across models. In fact, there is a large problem that theoreticians would love to avoid. Volatility is possibly the key variable in any model, and yesterday's volatility is of absolutely no use in the equations. Tomorrow's volatility is what is needed to get an accurate option price, and no one is advertising a guarantee of what that value might be.

If the market thinks upcoming volatility will be 15 percent, any subtle variations between American and European option model pricing will be swept away if the volatility indeed turns out to be 20 percent for the period. The unpredictability of volatility makes vega a critical parameter to assess and makes clarity of decision making concerning volatility almost as important as one's opinion on price. Estimates of volatility take on great importance in this world, and the next section suggests several approaches to this problem.

3.7   ESTIMATING VOLATILITY

In all of the option pricing models described there were a handful of parameters that combined to produce the fair values. Time to maturity, strike versus underlying price, and the rate of interest are all observable and not subject to debate. Volatility, however, must be estimated since what is relevant is the variability of future price moves, and this is a big unknown. There are many valid approaches to volatility estimation, and each successful options trader believes his or her method is superior. This section will not prescribe one technique over another but will point out some benefits and shortfalls of each.

There are only two types of volatility, implied and historical. *Implied volatility* is simply that which is produced when the market price is substituted into the option pricing model. Basically, the logic is: "If the option trades in the market at *C,* and it is right, what is the volatility expected to generate that price?" Implied volatility is a critical concept, but if one always accepts it as the best estimate possible, no speculative trades should be entered into because the market's opinion will be your own.

Implied volatility should be compared to your own view of volatility. Recall that in many option strategies the trader is not only bullish or bearish in terms of underlying price but also long or short volatility. A bull may want to buy a call, but the strategy is considerably less attractive if the implied volatility is high relative to the trader's opinion, because the expectation is for volatility changes to work against the price move. At the opposite end of the scale, if implied volatility is low relative to expectations, these long option strategies have added appeal.

Historical volatility is, as its name implies, the volatility of the past. Traders use it because it is available and the past is an important component in forming impressions of what the future might hold. But probabilities can be deceiving. An event that objectively has a probability of 1 in 100,000 may not have occurred in 20 or 50 years of trials. But one should not assume from history that the probability is zero. It is precisely this kind of situation that caught many options traders in the October 1987 stock market crash.

On Friday, October 16, the market fell by 108 points as measured by the Dow Jones, 15 points by the S&P 500. That move by itself increased the world's estimation of the stock market's volatility. Call and put prices both immediately reflected this, as implied volatilities skyrocketed. To any trader who thought this was a quirk, there was a strong temptation to sell volatility. That would be done by putting on a price-neutral, but short-volatility, options and futures position.

The ensuing events of the following week showed the fallacy of relying on historical odds. Just because an event had never happened before did not preclude it happening. The irony here is that once such an event happens, it is also a mistake to overestimate the probability of its reoccurrence.

Figure 3.19 shows the implied volatility of the at-the-money S&P 500 call from October 1, 1987, through year end. What is clear from the pattern in hindsight is that the volatilities of the week of October 19 could not persist. However, for anyone participating in the market that week, such a conclusion was by no means evident. Stating that "the market can't get more volatile" is like stating that a rallying price has topped out. The logic behind such a statement may be compelling, but if it is wrong, it can be roughly akin to trying to stop a freight train by standing in front of it.

With all of these potential difficulties, how does the market come to a consensus on volatility? Just as prices are subject to close statistical scrutiny, volatilities are similarly examined in an attempt to gain insight into their behavior.

The simplest method of estimating historical volatility is to pick a time span

Figure 3.19
S&P Implied Volatility

annual volatility

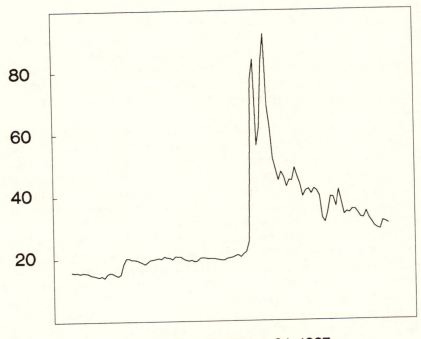

July 15 -- December 31, 1987

and examine the standard deviation of the daily price changes for that period. A modest refinement that puts the value into an intuitive framework looks at the standard deviation of the daily changes in the logarithms of the prices, which is a measure of the daily percentage change in price. Once this is found it is multiplied by the square root of 252 (the typical number of business days in a year) to get at an annual volatility expressed in percentage terms. Like the practice for rates, expressing volatility in an annualized form is a widely accepted convention.

There are a number of simplifying assumptions in this model. First, changes from Friday to Monday are treated the same as any change from Monday to Tuesday or Wednesday to Thursday. Such weekend changes are probably larger on average, but this is addressed in the annualization process of using 252 as the number of business days in a year. If there was continuous trading, true daily observations could be made, and the daily standard deviation would be annualized by multiplying by the square root of 365. The second major assumption is that volatility expands with the square root of time. Moving from one day to a year, the assumption has strong empirical support, but in general this view should be tested rather than assumed.

What is the relevant historical sample? Here is where the art of estimating volatility emerges. Recall that the objective is to forecast future volatility, and to that end only relevant data should be included. Is last year's exchange rate volatility that surrounded trade talks relevant? How important is the week of the 1987 stock market crash when pricing options in 1990 or 2000?

Typically, the target is short term (less than a six-month option) and the history examined even shorter. The thinking is that the market quickly reflects relevant information, and to form an accurate view of the near future, one does not want to include too much of a stale past. This is a view that serves its users well in periods without large shocks, but it is precisely those shocks that can be so costly to option writers.

By picking too short a period the volatility estimates are unduly influenced by the most immediate past. Volatility calculated on a single week's prices is probably naive and would likely find its user bouncing from one strategy to the next as the estimated volatilities alternated above and below the implied market volatilities.

A starting point that strikes a middle ground between too short and choppy volatilities and too long estimates that contain irrelevant data is 60 business days (59 price changes), which is roughly three months. The simple standard deviation of the daily logarithms of the price change is given by:

$$V_{60} = \sqrt{(\Sigma(x_i - \bar{x})^2/58)} \qquad (3.39)$$

where $x_i = \ln P_{T+1-i} - \ln P_{T-i}$

$\bar{x} = \Sigma x_i/59$

Similar expressions may be formed for 20- or 40-day or even longer samples for comparison. Any time there is a significant difference across the samples, it is a warning sign for closer scrutiny.

One problem with the simple standard deviation calculations is that the importance of an event yesterday is identical to that of a price change two or three months ago. To combat this problem the volatility may be calculated as a *weighted* standard deviation of the log price changes.

$$V = \sqrt{(\Sigma w_i (x_i - \bar{x})^2 / (n - 1))} \qquad (3.40)$$

where w_i are the weights that decline as the price changes fade into the past. With sixty observations you might want the most recent change to have a weight ten times the most distant. This would produce a very gradual erosion of the influence until the most distant contribution is barely noticeable. Such weighting schemes are popular because of this ability to maintain smoothness as old observations fall out of the sample, but it is still essential for the user to be comfortable with the number of observations and the pattern of weights.

Another technique for measuring volatility works from minimal assumptions. Suppose that the trader is interested in writing one-month options and has no prior expectation that the next 30 days should be extraordinarily volatile or quiet. A direct measure of volatility would be to look at the distribution of 30-day price changes going back through time. Ten years of history would give 120 observations, and doubling the span would double the observations making up the sample.

One might argue that it is irrelevant to include events from political and economic regimes that no longer exist. Currencies before Breton Woods were controlled; grains in the 1960s were dominated by government farm programs and not the marketplace. Including these events would intuitively lower estimated volatilities, calculated from recent market-oriented times.

But the question remains of how the political probabilities should be accounted for. If a major political figure announced two years ago that the dollar was too high, setting off a precipitous short-term decline, is it not appropriate to include that event to allow for the chance of a similar occurrence? Fortunately, truly outrageous comments are rare, or at least the market is sufficiently numbed to their frequency so that a large market impact is rare. But extremes do occur, and this vast sampling from history is one of the few ways to capture them and simultaneously keep them in perspective.

The choice of volatility estimators is wide, and as previously stated, there are no simple answers. Most option traders rely on historical volatility calculated over the most recent few months, tempered by a healthy dose of subjective opinion. There appears to be a tendency for market volatility to be mean reverting. Markets that are quiet will eventually heat up, and active markets will someday cool, but such shifts are neither regular nor predictable. No matter which approach is used, the savvy option trader will know the current implied volatility of the market, its position relative to historical volatility, and, most importantly, the exposure of any position to unexpected changes.

3.8   SUMMARY

This chapter began with the basic risk characteristics of puts and calls and moved through simple and complex strategies, ultimately reaching option pricing. Each step is important to the trader seeking to find the appropriate set of tools to manage risk or express a speculative opinion. In the subsequent chapters, specific hedging programs are developed, demonstrating how the generic strategies have actually been adapted to a variety of situations. In each of the examples, the risk objective is described and the positions to accomplish that objective critiqued.

There are examples of successful strategies as well as some that had been viewed as holding considerable promise before their defects became known. Fortunately, lessons can be learned from both the successes and the failures of previous traders. There is no need to reinvent the wheel, but it is important to understand enough of the basic characteristics to know when a wheel will prove useful or when a simple lever is the more appropriate tool. By understanding options the reader will gain an ability to take the tools at his or her disposal and create programs to address particular risk management needs.

NOTES

1. Most options discussed here are "American" options that provide for the right to exercise any time before expiration. "European" options are more restrictive, allowing exercise only at expiration. Examples are constructed with American options unless specifically stated otherwise.

2. The potential gain is limited to the full value of the strike price since prices cannot fall below zero, but for most instances, when comparing the gain to the original premium, this is "practically unlimited."

3. It is important in examining the profitability of such arbitrage opportunities to look at the bids and offers and not last sale prices. What may appear to be a profitable trade may not be executable in practice.

4. Starting with the first set of prices in the butterfly example, the reader should be able to show that if the 270 call is priced at 0.50, an all-call condor has a maximum loss potential of 4.00 points, a maximum gain of 6.00, and break-even points at 244 and 266.

5. A reader wishing to explore these models in detail is referred to Richard Bookstaber (1981) or John Cox and Mark Rubinstein (1985).

CHAPTER 4

Equities Market Strategies

Equities trading had been evolving rapidly through the 1960s and early 1970s when the first organized market for stock based "derivative products" was started in 1973. The Chicago Board Options Exchange was an important departure from the over-the-counter option market that it largely replaced. For the first time market makers on the floor of an organized exchange were available continuously to quote call options for a variety of well-capitalized issues. Throughout the 1970s the market continued to evolve, adding puts and expanding the number of stocks covered. As more exchanges began offering options on individual stocks, it became clearer that the total demand for option services was not being met, because increasingly, the institutional investor thought in terms of portfolios and not individual stocks.

By the late 1970s several exchanges were working toward the goal of futures on stock indices. The Kansas City Board of Trade developed a proposal to trade a contract based on the broad-based Value Line Index, but the product faced considerable regulatory opposition because of its innovative features. One of the thorniest problems at the time was how delivery would be accomplished. Delivery of a basket consisting of each of the index stocks was impractical, and even if it could be made cost effective, it probably would lead to a product regulated by the SEC, a fate most CFTC-regulated commodities exchanges did not relish. Cash settlement, where on expiration day there would simply be a variation margin payment based on the final settlement price, was an untried concept, suspected by many. Physical deliveries had always been used by futures markets to insure convergence of spot and futures price at expiration. Many needed to be convinced that the mechanism of cash settlement could produce a liquidation that was accurate and not subject to manipulation.

The cash settlement question was finally tested not in the area of equities indexes, but in Eurodollars (see chapter 5). The advantages of cash settlement were identified for markets where physical delivery was undesirable or impractical, and there was an actively quoted cash market against which to base the settlement. Fortunately for stock index futures, one of the key hurdles had been crossed in a market subject to considerably less publicity.

In 1982, at the urging of many forward-thinking participants in the securities industry, the KCBT Value Line contract was approved, and shortly thereafter the CME S&P 500 contract began trading. The latter contract very quickly established itself as the industry standard. In the months that followed, several exchanges tried to make a mark with both broad- and narrow-based index futures of their own, but none has come close to achieving the depth of liquidity of the CME product.

While stock index futures were blossoming, a closely related set of developments was occurring in options. At the CBOE, a cash-settled option based on the S&P 100 was launched along with a wide array of cash and futures based index options at other exchanges. Like the S&P 500 future, this option, widely known by its ticker symbol OEX, quickly became the dominant product in its area.

These developments did not occur without complaint. There were those stock market traditionalists who looked only at the leverage of the new instruments and warned that the grain gamblers had invaded their back yard. Others viewed the ability to trade entire indexes with alarm, stating that true investors were interested in building their portfolios stock by stock after examining the fundamentals. This view was maintained despite years of mounting evidence that it was extremely difficult for any significant portfolio to outperform the averages in the long run, and many active managers did appreciably worse after accounting for commissions.

4.1   THE ROLE OF STOCK INDEX FUTURES

Stock index futures in general, and the S&P 500 contract in particular, proved to be an instrument rapidly embraced by the institutional equities trader. This does not mean that the product is universally used by all participants. On the contrary, because of regulatory constraints some firms like insurance companies are restricted from hedging completely with futures, and for some dealers who have historically maintained a relatively "flat" book with little exposure from up or down moves, there is little benefit from the product. But enough professionals have seen the inherent advantages to make stock index futures and options the most significant financial development of the 1980s.

To see what these advantages are, start with a portfolio manager who for strategic reasons is 80 percent invested in stocks and 20 percent in cash earning short-term interest. Furthermore, assume that the manager's view of the market has recently dimmed so that the desired mix is 60–40 invested in favor of stocks. What are the options available to the manager? One course would be to sell immediately 20 percent of all stocks to make sure that the target was reached before the expected move. Unfortunately, even in today's liquid markets it might be very costly to do that. There is a strong likelihood that prices would move adversely because of the large, rapid sales. A second alternative would be to minimize the impact of such sales by spreading them out over time at a pace the market could tolerate. The risk here is that in the interim, the entire market could have the adverse move that the manager was trying to avoid.

By using futures, both objectives can be achieved simultaneously. The first step is to sell a quantity of stock index futures roughly equivalent to 20 percent of the portfolio's value. This insulates that fraction of the portfolio from any general market move. In fact, as will be demonstrated below, it produces the synthetic equivalent of Treasury bills. With the hedge in place, the fund manager can go about the disposal of the *right* 20 percent of the portfolio with minimum negative impact from the sales. As the actual stocks are sold, the short index futures would be bought back in equivalent amounts to maintain the match of the hedge. Ultimately, all of the target stocks would be disposed of, and there would be no futures position remaining. This is the classic portfolio hedge, and it allows for the rapid adjustment of stock positions because the liquidity in the stock index futures market is fundamentally greater than that of the vast majority of individual stocks.

Another advantage of this approach comes from the ability to adjust strategies in a low-cost environment. Suppose that the fund manager got the portfolio to 70–30 and decided the outlook was less risky than originally perceived. If 70–30 was a good stopping point, the balance of the futures would simply be bought back, and no further adjustment would be required. The savings here would be from the stock commissions that were not spent either from the sales of stocks down to 60–40 or the purchases back to 70–30. Additionally, there is the fact that the bid/ask spread of the S&P 500 futures was faced once establishing the position and once getting out. This is a considerable advantage over the sum of the individual bid/asks of the stocks.

There are then three areas in which the advantages of stock index futures are strong: commissions, the number of bid/ask spreads faced, and the extent of market impact from the trade. Estimating the magnitude of these effects presents a strong case as to why stock index futures were embraced as quickly as they were.

Start with the S&P 500 index at 250 and a simple portfolio of $10 million (evaluated at the midpoint of the S&P bid/ask spread). Using a rule of thumb that the average price of a share equals the S&P 500 divided by 5, there are 200,000 $50 shares in the portfolio. At the institutional level commissions in stocks can be around 7 cents per share and for futures a reasonable number is $25 per round turn contract. The bid/ask spread in stocks is rarely less than an eighth (12.5 cents) on a $50 stock, and in futures the bid/ask is typically 0.10 index point or less. To compute the comparisons for these factors the remaining needed piece of information is that an S&P 500 futures contract is valued at $500 times the index.

To sell the stocks directly would require the sale of 200,000 shares for a commission charge of $14,000 and a bid/ask impact of $12,500.[1] By comparison selling the portfolio synthetically would entail 80 contracts ($10 million divided by $125,000 contract value). Total commissions, which include unwinding the position, are $2,000 (= 80 × $25), and the bid/ask spread effect will also be $2,000 (again half the spread amount applied to the entire transaction). The comparisons of direct costs are dramatic but ignore the liquidity effects. If placing a $10 million lot sell order moves the entire S&P 500 futures down 0.10, and it usually does not, there is an additional $4,000 expense. In stocks, there may be an additional eighth or more liquidity effect from a quick sale implying another $12,500 impact. As the magnitude of the purchases or sales grows, so does the relative importance of the greater liquidity in the S&P 500 futures.

Although the advantages of these futures are large, they in no way imply that futures can or should substitute for the actual stocks in all situations. The key advantages are in the short run, as temporary replacements for the actual equities. Since futures expire on a quarterly cycle, any positions established for a long-term strategy would have to be "rolled over" periodically, reducing the savings in all areas.[2] Just as grain futures complement the cash markets they serve, stock index futures offer another tool to the equity professional's arsenal, adding liquidity to the implementation of most equities strategies.

What are the risks from this kind of hedging? Like all hedges the biggest risk comes from variation in the basis. If the portfolio manager's stocks do not move in parallel with the index, the net result could be better or worse than the complete neutrality of the ideal hedge. It is the manager's responsibility to gauge this basis risk and plan accordingly. The reverse side of the coin is the possibility of the manager's stocks outperforming the index. Suppose that the market as a whole fell 10 percent but that because of superior stock selection, the actual portfolio fell only 6 percent. A fully hedged position would have protected against the full market decline. Combining this hedge with the actual decline will produce a 4 percent gain, exactly the margin by which the stocks outperformed the broad average. This relative gain will still be realized as the hedge is unwound.

4.2   A MODEL OF STOCK INDEX FUTURES PRICING

To identify the theoretically fair value of a stock index futures contract it is possible to build a simple arbitrage relationship. This is the same type of analysis done in chapter 3 on options to derive equilibrium values and is most useful in identifying the important parameters in the problem. Looking at a simple one-period model, start by buying a portfolio at the beginning of the period under review that has a price $P(0)$. Just before the end of the period you will receive some dividend D, and you will sell the portfolio that may have gone up or down to some price $P(1)$.

Now consider an alternative investment involving a stock index futures contract that will expire at the end of the period. Let it currently be priced at $F(0)$. Note that buying a futures contract involves no current expense, only the posting of margin, which can earn interest. The second half of this investment involves calculating the discounted present value of the futures plus the expected dividend and placing that amount in some secure instrument like Treasury bills that mature at the end of the period (the margin on the future can come from this amount). Putting these two payment-receipt streams in a chart gives:

Investment	Cash Flow at 0	Cash Flow at 1
1.	$-P(0)$	$P(1) + D$
2.	$-(F(0) + D)/(1 + r)$	$[F(1) - F(0)] + [F(0) + D]$
		$= F(1) + D$
		$= P(1) + D$

where r is the rate of interest earned and also the discount rate. The minus signs at period 0 signify cash outflows.

In the second investment the cash flow at the end of the investment consists of two parts. There is the profit on the futures of $[F(1) - F(0)]$, which is positive only if stocks increased over the period, plus $[F(0) + D]$, which represents the end value of the funds invested. Note that the impact of the original futures price cancels out, leaving the final return equal to $F(1) + D$. Since futures converge to cash at expiration by definition, $F(1) = P(1)$, and we have constructed two investments that *must* have identical payoffs at the end of the period. Since this is true, if an investor was offered the choice of the two initial opportunities, he would choose the cheaper of the two, so in equilibrium they must be equal. That is,

$$P(0) = (F(0) + D)/(1 + r) \qquad (4.1)$$

or after rearranging terms to solve for the futures price,

$$F(0) = P(0)(1 + r) - D \qquad (4.2)$$

This expression is the theoretical fair value of a stock index futures contract. It states that the futures price should be the current value of the index as it would grow at current interest, less any dividend paid to the owner of stock. As interest rates increase, so does the futures price relative to the spot price. This is simply a compensation for the larger discount rate. Larger dividends reduce the futures price, which is to be expected since the holder of a long futures does not participate in the disbursement of dividends, but they should not affect the value of the cash index. Let d be the expected *dividend rate* so $D = dP(0)$. Rewriting Equation 4.2,

$$F(0) = P(0)(1 + r) - dP(0) \qquad (4.3)$$

$$= P(0)(1 + r - d)$$

This equation states that as long as the expected dividend rate is less than the rate of interest, the futures price should exceed the spot index. The one-period model can easily be extended to a multiperiod model, with the arbitrage involving futures with different maturities. In general, by comparing the relevant interest and dividend rates, the entire structure of futures prices may be determined. Care must be taken to apply the proper interest rate for each different length strategy, with the shape of the term structure being very important in practice.

As previously mentioned, the deferred months in stock index futures have limited activity. This is because it is very easy and cheap to trade futures market spreads, and it takes only a limited amount of trading to keep these markets in line with the carrying costs suggested in Equation 4.3. There is indeed very little independent price discovery going on in the back months since the term structure is determined in the interest rate markets and dividends are relatively predictable. The net result is that because most of the hedging is short term, only the near contract attracts liquidity and consequently has a lower bid/ask spread. As new outright traders come to the market who have a longer hedging horizon, they can choose between an accurately priced but illiquid deferred month that matches their horizon or a very liquid near month that can be rolled over as needed. The history to date suggests that the near-term liquidity is dominant in the decision analysis since the vast majority of all open interest and volume is in the spot month.

4.3 BASIC OPTION HEDGES

There are two basic option strategies that have direct applications for stocks. They both were developed using options on individual stocks but can be easily applied to index options to cover an entire portfolio. The first strategy calls for buying puts as insurance against a market decline. Figure 4.1 shows how the risk/profit profile of a portfolio changes by adding the put. The upside potential of the portfolio is reduced by the cost of the put, but any downside below the strike price is eliminated. The degree of insurance desired will affect the cost of the program. The greater the decline that is tolerable, the lower is the cost of the insurance and consequently the drag on any upside move. This is the purest form of "portfolio insurance," a subject that will be examined in greater detail in a later section.

The profit/loss picture in Figure 4.1 shows how the ultimate price gets translated into gains and losses, but it does little to explain how the distribution of outcomes is altered by the strategy. Figure 4.2 starts with the assumption that future prices are distributed normally around today's price, *P*. If an out-of-the-

Figure 4.1
Basic Portfolio Hedge

profit/loss

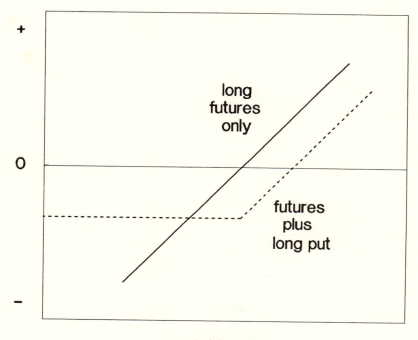

underlying price

money put is purchased, two things occur. For any outcome below the strike price *E*, the actual return is *E* less the premium paid, which can be called *E'*. All of the probability in the distribution to the left of *E'* is stacked up on that point. If the ultimate price is above *E*, the return will equal the final price less the premium paid for the put. This results in a parallel shift left of the return distribution by the amount of the premium paid.

If the option was priced to reflect the actual distribution, that is, it was at its actuarial fair value, the mean of the altered return function would be lowered by the time value of the purchased option.[3] The benefit from this shift is that the second and third moments of the distribution would have been radically altered. The variance of the returns would decline as the extreme downside values would be completely eliminated, and the skew would move from symmetry to a favorable asymmetry where there is still upside potential but limited downside risk. These trade-offs are at the heart of risk management decisions.

There is a debate about who should use this type of strategy. Any investor with

Figure 4.2
Protected Portfolio Outcomes

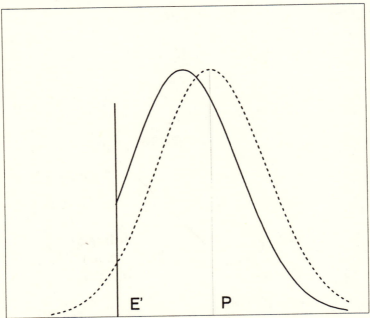

underlying return

a long equity exposure could routinely buy puts, just as a homeowner would carry fire insurance (even if the mortgage bank did not require it). If this was the approach taken, the same portfolio could be created by combining T-bills and stock index calls. Note that the hedged position in Figure 4.1 looks exactly like a long call. The costs of this approach would no doubt be lower since the expenses of individual stock purchases could be avoided.

Another school states that long-term investors like pension funds should not pay for insurance they do not need. The theory goes that this strategy protects against short-run volatility that should even out in the long run. If a retirement fund has a charter to invest in stocks, it should do that and recognize that it will get the long-run return for that product. By allocating funds between stocks and other assets, the individual saving for retirement can decide on the makeup of risk and return. Any attempt to improve returns by market-timing strategies in a fund dedicated to long-run stock investment is bound to fail.

This latter view may have a few radical adherents, but it basically is an abrogation of the role of any stock fund manager who has not established pure indexing as the fund's objective. There is a great deal of room between the extremes of always insure and never insure, and what is necessary is a careful examination of the perceived risks and a decision about how to best manage them. Buying puts is an effective approach whenever the decision maker is fundamentally bullish but has significant concerns about downside risk.

Another popular stock option strategy involves covered call writing. The proponents of this strategy argue that the market is basically efficient so that the current price is an accurate reflection of information available today. As such, there should not be a tendency for the market, on average, to move up or down. By writing out-of-the-money calls, the premiums collected will augment dividend income since there is an expectation that the calls will expire worthless. If prices do blip up, the calls will be exercised, but this results in the sale of stock at a higher than current price, and there is the benefit of the sale of time. This option strategy, like most, exploits the differences in opinions across traders. If everyone believed that no sustained increase in stock prices was likely, there would be no value to the call and no possibility of income to the covered call writer. Before executing this strategy the risk characteristics should be appreciated. Figure 4.3 shows the combination.

Figure 4.3
Covered Call Writing

profit/loss

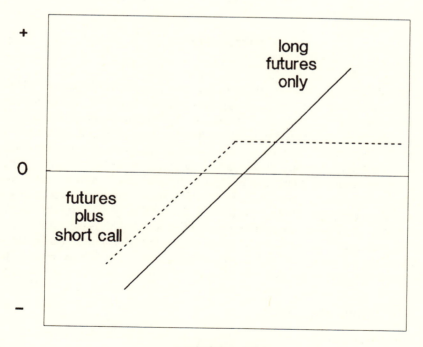

underlying price

Figure 4.4
Covered Call Outcomes

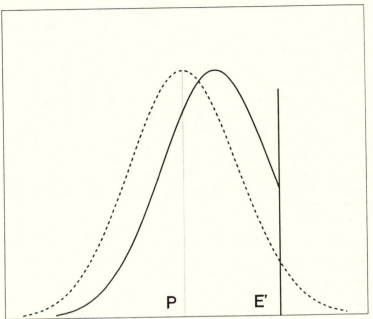

underlying return

By writing calls against the portfolio, the risk characteristics are converted into the equivalent of a short put, a strategy that was described as being appropriate whenever the decision maker was mildly bullish. This fits squarely with the view of the proponents of the strategy. The market should not be going down if it is fairly priced currently, and one can test the degree of conviction that the market is not going up by seeing which strikes the covered call writers are selling. Writing at-the-money calls maximizes the premium over intrinsic value and would be the purest expression of a belief in market neutrality. Higher strikes would indicate a more bullish inclination. The effect of this strategy on the probability distribution of returns is given in Figure 4.4. This is the mirror image of the purchased put case. Here the top part of the probability distribution is lopped off and stacked at the exercise price plus the premium received. The trade-off here is a higher mean versus less attractive skewness.

4.4   INDEX ARBITRAGE

The pricing model in section 4.2 gave the theoretically fair futures price given the underlying value of the index and the cost of funds. The logic behind this model is no more complicated than the idea that the price of gold in New York should be equal to that in London, assuming it entailed no costs to buy in one market, transport the material, and sell in the other market, which is not the case. In the gold example one would expect the prices in two locations to be closely, but not perfectly, corresponding. Any price move in one market that kept the prices within the cost of transport would be permissable because no profit opportunities would be present. The limits of independent price moves are sometimes referred to in the economics literature as the ''gold points,'' and they are represented in Figure 4.5. A similar principle dictates index arbitrage between stocks and index futures. Any price difference within the gold points cannot be arbitraged profitably.

Stock index arbitrage is commonly known as program trading, but this label has been applied loosely to any combination of stock and futures trading in which decisions are triggered by a computer model rather than an independent thought process. This is a curious distinction made by many that ignores the fact that the computers did not program themselves. In this discussion, whenever program

Figure 4.5
''Gold Points''

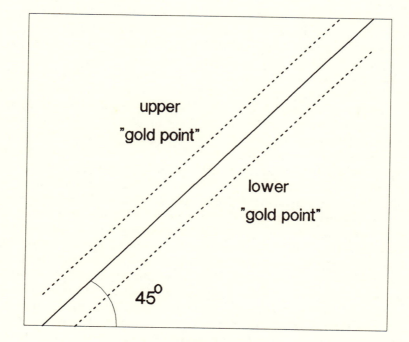

London price

upper
''gold point''

lower
''gold point''

45°

NY price

trading is mentioned it will refer narrowly to stock index arbitrage. There are several computer-assisted strategies and each should be evaluated on its own merits rather than lumped into a generic category.

Identifying the determinants of the gold points for stock index arbitrage is more than an exercise for any firm contemplating this arbitrage directly. Anyone considering stock futures hedging in general should understand these elements if they want to assure themselves that they are buying and selling at appropriate times. Start with an easy case of the stock index futures trading at a premium over its theoretical fair value. The optimal strategy is to sell the futures and buy the basket of stocks making up the index. The costs incurred in this strategy are the commissions on the round turn futures (you typically pay this even if you hold the position to expiration and cash settlement), the impact of the bid/ask spread in futures when selling the position (assumes you hold the position to expiration; if not, double this), and the commissions and bid/ask spread effect for buying and selling each stock. The magnitude of these effects has been discussed previously, but the important additional ingredient is the cost of funds necessary to buy the stock and finance any variation margin payments over the life of the position. These are the quantifiable costs, and at interest rates and liquidity levels that characterized much of the 1980s, "gold points" typically ranged from 100 to 150 basis points, or 1.0 to 1.5 full index points, of the S&P 500 index.

If the situation were reversed, with futures trading beneath cash, a complication would enter. To sell stocks short one must meet the conditions of the "up-tick" rule. This rule states that before stocks can be sold short, the price must have moved up at least one tick. For the program trader this means that evaluating the profitability of the arbitrage is complicated by the fact that the stocks could tick down several times before the short sale is executed. Anyone who routinely maintains a diversified portfolio of stocks in inventory is not affected by the rule since outright sales are not similarly restricted. Consequently, the short-sale rule skews the benefits of program trading toward those firms that maintain inventories of stocks.

If this was the complete picture we should never expect a divergence between the index and the futures prices to exceed the "gold points." For the vast majority of traders this should be a great comfort since the accuracy of the futures price is of great importance in determining the efficiency of a hedge.[4] Unfortunately, because of market dynamics, there can be many more risks involved. First, the market bid/ask spread may have widened by the time the trades are executed, or either market may have moved adversely, reducing the profit potential of the trade. In a variant on Murphy's Law these forces rarely seem to come into play to expand the profit of the trade. Market-timing risk is difficult to quantify, but it is very real and must be considered when planning for the trades.

Another risk comes from the confusion of appearance and reality. The S&P 500 cash index, like all cash indices, is comprised of the last traded prices of all of the stocks. At the opening of the market the first few minutes can be particularly deceiving on days when the market is moving dramatically up or down. Until all of the stocks are open the cash index is comprised of some opening prices and some prices from the previous day's close. At these moments huge wedges can apparently develop between futures and spot because the futures markets are not bound to simple arithmetic constructions. Pit traders quickly and accurately extrapolate to form the basis of their early trading. If an index arbitrageur tried to act on the apparent wedge, the profitability would be gone by the time all parts of the trade were implemented.

This effect happens regularly at the opening whenever there is a significant move from the previous night's close, but it is in no way restricted to that time. Frequently, in active markets the tape of stock prices will be delayed because of the sheer volume of information that has to be transmitted. In these cases illusory wedges can develop between cash and futures that signify nothing more than a time lag. Sometimes it is erroneously stated that futures "led" stocks down, when in fact the moves were contemporaneous, but with reporting time differences.

Once an index arbitrage position is established it must be unwound. Such positions rely on the fact that futures and the cash index converge by definition at expiration. However, if the two markets come into line before expiration, both sides of the position are unwound. This has the advantage of realizing the expected profit sooner (which in a world of continuous discounting translates into more profit), and it frees up the capital to be employed in other, possibly nonarbitrage, activities.

If the arbitrage cannot be unwound profitably early, cash settlement insures a profitable liquidation at expiration. However, the mechanics of the expiration process led to concern over "triple witching hours" and ultimately brought about a modification of how major stock index futures settled. *Triple witching hours* refers to those moments four times a year when stock index futures, options, and options on stocks simultaneously expired. They were called witching hours because of the strange things that sometimes occurred at the point of expiration. If during the life of a futures contract there had been good opportunities to establish, but not liquidate, index arbitrage programs, there would be considerable stock sales or purchases to unwind when the futures expired.

Since the futures were cash settled, the holder of a long or short position would have to do nothing active to liquidate that portion of the position, but "market on close" orders (MOC) would be entered for all of the stocks in the portfolio. If the initial arbitrage was to buy futures and sell stocks, there would be MOC buy orders to unwind the position. The MOC sell orders would accompany the reverse arbitrage position. Note that the arbitrageur is completely indifferent about the ultimate settlement price because, by definition, the market prices received for the stocks will be used to determine the final settlement of the futures contract, and the cash and futures positions are completely offsetting.

The MOC orders should pose no problem if the amount of purchases and sales from this activity balance out or are small relative to the total order flow on the close. Unfortunately, this was not always the case. Arbitrage activity can bunch up on one side of the market or another, and if there have been no reversal opportunities before the expiration, there can be sizable orders awaiting the final bell. Such situations arose in 1986 and 1987 causing violent swings, up and down, as the specialist system of the NYSE was pressed into handling large orders at a most vulnerable time, 3 p.m., right before a weekend, the Friday expiration time of the futures. Specialists with limited capital were not eager to alter their position radically before the weekend. The price moves were sometimes dramatic, but they were clearly temporary blips caused by the sudden rush of orders at the close. Anyone trying to cash in on these high or low prices was usually frustrated to discover they were too late. The market had already closed. By Monday morning the stocks had generally retraced their steps.

The closing volatility stemmed from inadequate information before the close. If it had been possible to let the world know about the pending orders, capital could have been marshaled to take advantage of the opportunity and ultimately cushion the shock. From this premise the solution was discovered. Beginning in the summer of 1987, the rules of the CME S&P 500 contract were changed to move the last trading day up to the third Thursday of the expiration month with settlement based on the following morning's *opening* value. The NYSE simultaneously instituted special expiration Friday opening rules for many key stocks. One-half hour before the opening, order imbalances would be announced by specialists. Fifteen minutes later the expected opening prices would be given to the public. With these modifications, broad segments of the investing public could be aware of the impact of arbitrage liquidations. If large sales were expected, buyers could assemble to take advantage of the anticipated lower prices. By moving this process to the opening, the specialists were given more latitude to handle order imbalances since any shift in inventory from the opening could be adjusted over the course of the day. This flexibility had not been available with settlements based on the close.

The asymmetry of cash settlement had a great deal to do with the initial problems of the expiration Fridays. If the futures contract had called for delivery, the arbitrage would have been symmetric. A seller of futures and buyer of stocks arbitrageur would have delivered the stocks to fulfil the obligation of the futures. In that case the demand is known and comes from the longs remaining in futures. With cash settlement the longs at the expiration of the futures may have many motivations, not necessarily including the ultimate ownership of stocks. At settlement they may simply walk away with their final variation margin payment, leaving the arbitrageur to transact with whomever is available in the equities market. Because there was no delivery process there was a chance that the futures and "true" spot could diverge, even though definitially convergence did occur. What was important were the careful steps that were taken by both exchanges to modify their rules to improve the access to these market orders. With the change in the final settlement price process, the futures became a more accurate indicator of the market, and the market itself became less prone to temporary shocks. This is a classic example of how careful modification of rules can serve to improve both markets while retaining the benefits of an important stabilizing activity.

Program trading can be succinctly described as a process that brings capital to bear on situations of mispricing. There are no sure things, only situations where the probabilities of a profitable trade are such that the risks are worth taking.[5] To the extent that arbitrage capital is available, both stock and futures markets are more liquid and accurate environments. Because of program trading, stock market hedgers can be assured that the price they see in the index futures market is a fair reflection of the underlying cash market.

4.5   DYNAMIC RISK MANAGEMENT STRATEGIES

The term *portfolio insurance* has been used previously in describing the purchase of puts to protect against the erosion of value in a portfolio. Although the basic principal is straightforward, in practice there have been several difficulties. First, the term of the most liquid exchange-traded options is fairly short, frequently under six months and sometimes as short as three. Such an issue makes it difficult to secure longer term coverage without incurring fairly large costs. Recalling that time's affect on premium is not linear, but geometric, buying a string of four three-month options should be twice as expensive as buying a year-long option, if such an instrument were available. For these reasons, alternative risk strategies have been developed.

Dynamic asset allocation is a plan of combining a portfolio with a dynamic futures strategy to replicate the behavior of a portfolio protected by puts. A simplistic example will demonstrate the idea. Suppose that a fund is fully invested when the S&P 500 is at 300. The manager is concerned about a significant decline during the next year (anything more than 10 percent) but does not want to miss out on additional appreciation. To protect the portfolio, stop loss orders can be placed to sell the portfolio's equivalent amount of S&P 500 futures *if the market declines to 270.* If this event occurs, the portfolio is liquidated synthetically. Any further decline in the portfolio will produce offsetting gains and losses in futures and cash. If the market rallies, the futures would be bought back to restore the upside potential. Although actual strategies are much more sophisticated, having several decision points rather than just one, this example captures the spirit of the approach.

A variation on the theme is to adjust the strategy according to the level of the index. If the market advanced from 300 to 330, the stop loss order could be lifted from 270 to 297, reestablishing 10 percent as the maximum permitted loss. In the five-year bull market that ran from 1982 to 1987, such a practice was gaining popularity as fund managers sought protection without giving up the potential for further appreciation.

This strategy is identical to owning an out-of-the-money put, except that there is no direct payment of a premium. Is this the proverbial free lunch? Those who acted as if it was were sorely disappointed when the truth of the situation became clear. First, there were management fees to develop the plan, but they were known and small relative to the cost of a put. Second, there is the unknown cost of selling futures at 270, buying them back if the market rebounds, and doing this any number of times if the market bounces around the trigger point. In a perfectly functioning market, you would expect to be able to sell and buy precisely at 270 every time. In practice however, you would likely sell lower than where the contracts are bought back. Each time this happens, a loss plus commissions occurs. It is useful to think of an option's premium as being a prepayment alternative to the expected losses from the futures strategy, which also are an increasing function of volatility.

If these were all of the costs to dynamic asset allocation, there would be little question of its superiority to a direct options strategy. However, there is an important missing element. Futures and cash markets can move very quickly, sometimes "gapping" past a price at which desired transactions were resting. To see how this happens it is necessary to examine how a stop loss order works.

A stop loss order rests in a broker's desk, not to be activated unless the price is touched. Sell stops are placed below the current price, buy stops above. If a market declines to the point that a sell stop is touched, it becomes a market order to be executed at the next available price. However, if a broker is holding unfilled market sell orders when a sell stop is activated, it goes to the back of the queue, so to speak. It will be executed in turn, and in quickly moving markets, the fill may occur at a price well away from the trigger point. This can occur even more dramatically in the case of market openings occurring at prices well away from the previous close. "Gapping," as it is called, can result in a market jumping right over the stop loss order, triggering it at an automatically disadvantaged position.

This is the major risk of dynamic asset allocation. Each time the market stays up, and the strategy produces an apparent free lunch, there is the risk that a stop protecting against a 10 percent decline will not get filled until the market declines 15 percent, producing a very expensive option replication. A direct option can never have this problem because the strike price is predetermined. The maximum loss is always the full value of the premium, and this is known in advance.

In the early days of portfolio insurance, there was limited understanding of how great the ultimate costs of dynamic asset allocation could be. It was frequently assumed that the liquidity of the futures market would be so great that the stop loss orders would be executable in tight ranges around the trigger points. The events of October 1987 proved the fallacy of this view.

Even before the crash, researchers had begun to explore the use of short-term options to replicate the risk characteristics provided by long-term options. The principle here uses the fact that a portfolio of options, each having its own delta and gamma, will itself have an aggregate delta and gamma. By simulating the behavior of each option over a wide range of prices, researchers have been able to construct synthetic long-term puts, from a combination of shorter term options. These synthetics can have very stable characteristics over a broad range of prices, and they are cheaper than a simple string of short-term options. Given these factors, and the considerable advantage of avoiding much of the uncertainty from the stop loss futures strategies, it appears that the concept of dynamic asset allocation will increasingly be associated with dynamic options rather than futures strategies.

There is an opposite approach to dynamic asset allocation called tactical asset allocation (TAA). This is an updated dynamic counterpart to the old adage "buy on dips, sell on bulges." Although not necessarily involving futures or options, it is a strategy worth discussing simply as an alternative to dynamic asset allocation. The advocates of TAA stress that it is not a short-term trading system but instead strives to make appropriate allocative decisions between stocks and cash, or stocks, bonds, and cash, by assessing which category is relatively overpriced for the intermediate planning horizon.

The approach uses whatever valuation model the fund manager is comfortable with. Some look at business cycles, or dividend yields, in a historical context. Once the criteria are established, if stocks move from being underpriced to being overpriced relative to Treasury bills, the fund reduces its exposure to stocks and increases its share of cash equivalents. Obviously for TAA to work, the valuation model used must be accurate, but there are many fund managers who believe that the trends in stock prices are "mean reverting," that is they cannot go up forever at too high a pace or stay lower than average for long. The TAA followers were net sellers throughout the 700 point increase in the Dow during the first nine months of 1987. Although they may have been doubting their approach in August, by October they received considerable reinforcement of their views.

4.6 OCTOBER 1987 AND ITS AFTERMATH

The third week in October 1987 produced market conditions that many had previously believed were impossible. After steadily accumulating a 35 percent gain through the first nine months of the year, the market retreated broadly and quickly, eventually stabilizing just below the year's starting value. Before the smoke had cleared, the studies began. The crash of 1987 has been, and will continue to be, one of the most thoroughly analyzed events of the century. Most of the work done has been careful and thorough, but unfortunately, much of the widely publicized commentary has been emotional and highly partisan. Sorting fact from myth is a difficult process and importantly involves identifying the role of futures and options.

A chronology of the events is worth a quick review. The market had rallied throughout the summer reaching record highs in late August. September began with a correction, but the severity was no worse than several that had preceded it during the previous months of 1987. As October began, the Dow stood at 2639, nearly 40.0 percent above where it began the year. But storm clouds had begun to gather. Interest rates had been creeping steadily upward, and concern was building over the trade deficit and the strength of the dollar. On Monday, October 12, the Dow Jones Industrial Average stood at 2471, a 9.2 percent decline from the summer's high close of 2722 on August 25. By week's end the Dow stood at 2246, a further 9.1 percent drop, with the biggest decline occurring on Friday the 16th.

Monday the 19th began for U.S. traders long before the opening bell. Many were called and warned of the impending decline that could be anticipated by the activities in some Asian and most European markets that morning. The Dow dropped 508 points on the day to 1738, a 22.6 percent drop over the previous close. Volume topped 600 million shares, and the tape of transaction prices ran at times up to two hours late.

As calamitous as the 19th was, the 20th proved more daunting in many respects. The day began with a rally above 1900, but fear held sway and by midmorning the declining market was gathering momentum. Rumors circulated wildly about firms collapsing. Banks were calling in lines of credit instead of affirming them, and liquidity was evaporating in virtually all equities-related markets. Many stocks stopped trading, sometimes with a formal suspension, often not. Around 11:15 A.M. eastern time, the major stock index futures and options markets suspended trading because the underlying cash market was so thin that there was little accurate information to trade on.

The history of the events on the 20th that ultimately stemmed the tide has yet to be fully chronicled, but it seems clear that the Federal Reserve was active all morning in assuring banks that adequate funds would be made available to maintain credit liquidity. Simultaneously, and perhaps not coincidentally, some major industrial concerns entered the market to buy their own shares at what appeared to be bargain-basement prices. The market reversed, many more stocks began trading actively, and the futures and options reopened around noon. By the end of the day the Dow had advanced to 1841, its largest single day gain ever, but not before the system was stretched to its limits. The balance of the week was spent searching for some ground on which to reestablish a base of normalcy. Trading for many sessions after the 20th was marked by hesitancy and fear.

In the immediate wake of the crash there were accusatory fingers pointing in many directions. The traditional stock traders blamed all derivative products as the source of the "meltdown." Futures hedgers acknowledged that there had been massive selling of index futures, but there had also been equally important wholesale dumping of stocks in the cash market. Before the pieces had been completely sorted, three popular themes emerged. The problem was much too large to have a single cause, so three bogeymen appeared. First, "program trading," which was broadly applied to include index arbitrage and portfolio insurance, sparked the crash because of massive selling triggered by computer decisions. Second, regulatory lapses allowed this to occur. With the SEC watching only stocks and equity options and the CFTC looking at index futures and their related options, no one was minding the whole store. Finally, because of low futures margins, well below the 50 percent mandated for stocks, speculation was encouraged that eventually produced an unstable bubble bound to produce a crash.

These themes are provocative, and they certainly made good press. They made many people feel better by allowing them to externalize the blame. Unfortunately, the careful studies that have been generated since the crash lend no support to any of these themes. The cause of the crash may never be precisely determined, but efforts to improve the markets in the long run have not been aided by emotionalism.

There have been reports filed by regulators, independent commissions, and exchanges. Of all of the studies produced in the year immediately following the event, four have gained a measure of prominence, but not all were executed with equal care. The first major public study was done by Nicholas Katzenbach (1987) working under a commission from the New York Stock Exchange. Katzenbach made no use of trading data but instead examined the issue impressionistically. The heart of this study may be summarized quickly. The stock market is for long-term investment, whereas futures and options are for short-run speculation. Program trading acts as a pipeline transporting the effects of speculation to the cash market. If futures cannot be banned outright because they may serve some hedging function, any activity like program trading that would link the markets should be made prohibitively expensive. Katzenbach concluded that if baskets of stock were to be traded, that activity would best be placed on the floor of the NYSE where it could be properly monitored.

The Katzenbach effort fanned the flames of the debate between prostock and antistock index traders. It had considerable intuitive appeal to many who were uneasy with the new instruments and strategies. However, when the data behind the events were examined closely, the Katzenbach conclusions could not be supported.

Within six months of the crash three government-funded studies were produced that dissected the events surrounding October 19. The CFTC, the Brady Task Force, and a working group comprised of representatives of the Treasury Department, the SEC, the CFTC, and the Federal Reserve, all made extensive and careful examinations. Any given study of a major event can suffer from blind spots, but great care was taken to avoid this here. There were no stones left unturned.

A preliminary CFTC study was published in late 1987, with two follow-ups appearing early in 1988 (Commodities Futures Trading Commissions, 1987a, 1988a, 1988b). Knowing that the Brady Task Force would be looking at the broader themes, the CFTC staff took it upon themselves to study the microdata of the event.[6] Their findings confirmed early estimates that index-arbitrage-related selling of stocks was a minor proportion of the total selling activity during the decline and that selling of futures and stocks by institutions practicing portfolio insurance strategies was similarly dwarfed by other institutional sales.[7] Particularly telling was the finding that one mutual fund group accounted for 17.5 million shares (34 percent of the total) of selling in the first half hour of trading on the 19th.

The Brady Task Force was created to be a forum where seasoned practitioners could examine the data collected by impartial government agents. The most important finding of the Task Force was that equities, options, and futures markets are intimately linked and that it would be impossible and ultimately counterproductive to try to insulate activity in one arena from the rest. The Task Force carefully reviewed the trading data, noting the institutional nature of the vast majority of the selling, and pointed out that neither index arbitrage nor portfolio insurance could be blamed as causes of the crash.

The study ended without identifying a definitive cause and instead argued that macroeconomic events had combined to trigger a decline in a possibly over-valued market. The major recommendations included coordination of trading limits and halts across all related markets and a call for a more comprehensive regulatory fabric. While recognizing that speculation could not be blamed for the crash, the Task Force still recommended that "margins should be made con-sistent to control speculation and financial leverage" (Brady, 1988). These rec-ommendations were most general, with the difficult task of working out the details being left to others.

The Working Group on Financial Markets (1988) took the longest to evaluate the situation and, to the more activist inclined members of Congress, came up with the least. The group's specific charge was to make specific recommenda-tions to address the problems identified by the crash. This study is possibly the most comprehensive document produced during the immediate aftermath. Largely because it was comprised of professionals from the SEC, the CFTC, the Treasury, and the Fed, the group could avoid some of the compromises of exposition that came from industry members of the Brady Task Force represent-ing competing factions. Statements sometimes popped into the Brady report that could not be derived from the data, but such was not the case with the Working Group.

The major conclusions were solidly stated and firmly supported by the events. Speculators were not the cause of the decline. Neither were program traders. Margins had been adequate to protect the financial integrity of the system.[8] The main problems had stemmed from investor fear generated by uncertainty and inefficiencies in the flow of capital across stocks, options, and futures.

The recommendations of the Working Group were positive and built upon the themes begun in the Brady Task Force report. Recognizing that exchanges may have maintained differences stemming from their individual histories, they rec-ommended a coordinated set of "circuit breakers" so that trading halts would occur simultaneously in all related markets at times of crisis. This was a major difficulty on October 20 when there was widespread confusion about which markets were open for business. The second recommendation was for better coordination across clearing houses, possibly leading to cross-margining of futures and options and futures-style margins for options.

There also were no apparent regulatory blind spots that needed repairing. The exchanges regulated by the CFTC maintained a close dialogue with the SEC throughout the crisis despite having no legal obligation to do so. There was great cooperation across regulators and the exchanges. Quite telling is the fact that there is not a single suggestion in the major studies of what a "superregulator" would have done differently to prevent or lessen any of the events of October 1987. But the Working Group noted that, despite the cooperation during the event, there was need for better planning before the next crisis.

Throughout the summer of 1988 the major exchanges worked toward a functional coordinated plan to recognize this goal. The program that emerged recognizes that despite the differences in the underlying instruments, rough correspondence is achievable. For example, each full point change in the S&P 500 is roughly equivalent to an 8 point move in the Dow. By placing trading limits and halts in each market at equivalent prices, coordination could be attained.

The core of the program was a two-step plan of "circuit breakers," or temporary trading halts, that would occur in all equities-related markets whenever the Dow declined significantly. There would be a one-hour halt after a 250 point decline, and if, upon reopening, the market continued to fall a total of 400 points, the markets would halt for an additional two hours. Since the futures markets tend to be more timely in their pricing than the cash markets, the S&P 500 futures would have intermediate price limits of 30 and 50 S&P points, which correspond approximately to the Dow trigger points.

A typical scenario to be protected against would start with the market beginning a rapid decline. The cash market tape would likely be delayed because of the heavy trading, but the futures would price the current, if unreported, situation. Once the S&P 500 futures fell 30 points, there would be a temporary futures price limit in effect. The pit would remain open but would only be allowed to trade higher. If the Dow ultimately fell 250 points, trading would be suspended in all markets for one hour, after which the individual stocks would follow their opening procedures to resume trading, and the futures would begin trading once 50 percent of the capitalization of the S&P 500 index had resumed. The 30 point price limit would have expired after the halt. A further decline to 50 S&P points down would be met with another futures price limit, followed by a marketwide two-hour trading halt if the Dow fell a total of 400 points.

The spirit of these circuit breakers is to provide an opportunity to pause during a frenetic market and reassess the situation. Some critics have claimed that the threat of a trading halt would stampede traders into selling faster and exacerbate the decline. These comments stem from an ignorance of how similar approaches have worked for years in other markets in other countries. Commodity markets in England have price limits that when touched lead to trading pauses. In a declining market this gives traders the opportunity to call potential buyers to assess and possibly encourage demand, without having to worry about the second-to-second variation in the futures market. It is difficult enough to monitor cash or futures in an active market, but when trading reaches a certain pace, it can have a paralyzing effect, driving traders and the liquidity they provide out of the market. Trading pauses allow for regrouping and a clearer evaluation of the situation.

Many users of the market looked at the proposed 250 and 400 point trading halts as falling short of the mark. They reasoned that on only one day in history had the Dow declined that much, and laying down plans on how to respond to the next October 19 was going to do little to restore the confidence of the investing public. They noted that whenever the Dow moves down by around 100 points, market liquidity begins to be severely impeded, and they asked for some form of action well before the circuit breakers would come into play.

To respond to that concern the NYSE and the CME developed what has been dubbed "shock absorbers." The CME has an opening price limit of 5 points to cushion against a sudden change in market prices at the opening bell. Extending at most for 10 minutes, this is the first pause possible. If the S&P 500 futures declines by 12 points during the day, a limit is touched that stays in effect for 30 minutes. At the moment the futures are limit offered, the NYSE is notified, and it begins a rerouting of all basket orders in its automated order transmission system. These "program trades," no matter what their strategic origin, are routed to an accumulation file for several minutes, after which time order imbalances are announced. If the imbalances are large, the stocks may suspend trading and reopen once an equilibrium can be determined. If the imbalances are minor, they are filled by the specialist and trading continues.

This plan was designed to meet the concern over institutional "cascade" selling, which during the normal course of trading can swamp a specialist in any given stock. In addition to the NYSE providing for a rerouting and special management of these program orders, individual investors are given higher priority within the order system to insure fair execution of their orders. The shock-absorber plan replaces the NYSE program of eliminating program trades from the automatic routing system whenever the Dow moved 50 points in either direction. This program, commonly known as the "50 point DOT collar," was implemented unilaterally by the NYSE after the crash as an attempt to purge the system of program trading's perceived harmful effects. After several months it was widely viewed as being ineffective because the major institutions could route orders manually on the floor of the exchange. Additionally, in the year following the crash, the perspective on program trading had shifted. No longer was it widely believed that such trading caused the crash. Instead, the view became more practical, with the concern being that massive orders might clog the system leading to operational inefficiencies.

The recommendation for coordination across markets in terms of limits and halts was not also extended to the area of margins. The Working Group recognized the fundamental difference between futures margins, which are good-faith deposits established by both the buyer and the seller, and stock margins. They carefully noted that the level of coverage provided by futures margins during the crash was adequate to cover the risk of even this extreme event. There was no evidence to suggest that highly leveraged speculators caused or exacerbated the decline, so the cries for higher futures margins should not be heeded.

In a study that received remarkably little publicity (United States House of Representatives, 1988), the House Committee on Banking, Finance and Urban Affairs examined the entire situation and concluded that the case for harmonizing margins across markets was "surprisingly weak." It went on to state that "'excessive speculation' is a phantom." Any attempts to fight this phantom by raising futures margins would only succeed in driving important liquidity away from the markets and in all likelihood into the arms of foreign competition. One may long debate the impact of low stock margins among the public before the 1929 crash, but laying the blame in 1987 on leveraged futures speculators is at complete variance with the facts.

The problem of margins is complex. That futures have approximately 15 percent of the total value up in margins versus stocks' 50 percent is irrelevant because of the fundamental differences in the basic settlement mechanisms. Futures generally have next-day settlement, and each account is marked to market daily. Stocks settle in five days, and there are no variation payments made. When margined equities go on the same strict settlement basis as futures, it will be meaningful to speak of equal percentage rates as constituting a level playing field. In the interim, the Working Group suggested cross-margining as a mechanism to avoid bottlenecks in the capital system.

Cross-margining involves either placing all related stock, options, and futures under the same clearing umbrella so that funds may pass from one type of investment to another or establishing links across the different clearing organizations to facilitate these capital flows. Complete cash pass-through would require not only linkages but also futures-style margining of options, which, as discussed in chapter 3, is much more efficient but to date has proved elusive to implement. In the year following the crash many strides toward improving the industry clearing mechanism have been taken. The Options Clearing Corporation (OCC), which is the primary clearing agency for equity index options as well as individual stock options, has begun working with the CME to bring about cross-margining for equity related products. Because of the complexity of the problem, coordination has been slower to evolve than circuit breakers and shock absorbers.

If all of the recommendations of the Working Group are implemented, it will mark an impressive degree of cooperation across groups that have frequently been in tough competition. But still unanswered is the question of the ultimate cause of the crash. Richard Roll (1988) produced one of the most innovative looks at the crash searching for a key to the puzzle. Unlike most Americans who fail to recognize any events outside our borders, Roll realized that the crash was a global event. October 1987 was in fact the only month in the years from 1981 through 1987 when all 23 national markets studied in Asia, Europe, and North

America moved in the same direction. In addition to recognizing that options, futures, and stocks form one integrated market in the United States, there was strong evidence to suggest an increasing global integration of markets.

Despite the uniform direction of the move, Roll noticed that the ultimate magnitude of the change varied across nations. He wondered whether institutional characteristics of the markets might explain the variation, and his results were suggestive. Unfortunately, Roll's findings are better at rejecting certain hypotheses than in pinpointing the ultimate cause, but they are most instructive nonetheless. He found only a weak correlation between the existence of ''program trading'' and the extent of a market's decline, and interestingly, it was in the ''wrong'' direction. The nations that had identifiable forms of computer-directed trading actually had smaller declines in October. Price limits and regularly scheduled trading breaks during the trading session seemed also to limit the extent of the decline. Ultimately, however, he found no evidence of any institutional causes or promoters of the crash, with all of the statistical tests very weak. In the end, Roll was left with changing ''fundamentals'' as the root cause of the crash.

After all of these studies have been completed, laying the blame at the foot of macroeconomic events is still less than satisfying. It was not a surprise that the U.S. budget and trade deficits were in disarray. Interest rates had advanced nearly 150 basis points over two months, not two trading sessions. Why should a market retreat by one-third with such decisive force? The question cries out for an answer, and it lies in speculative trading, although not the kind alluded to by the stock market traditionalists.

Instead of looking at what caused the crash, a more useful activity would have been to discover what caused a near 40 percent advance in equities during the first nine months of 1987. The data examined by the government agencies tell us that it was not the leveraged speculator who drove prices upward but institutions representing the ''long-term'' investor. There lies the source of the problem. Fund managers in this country and many others are rewarded for their relative performance over short-time horizons. They may be investing pension funds against which there are obligations that span decades, but all too often it is last year's or quarter's performance that spells the difference between having additional funds to manage or losing accounts.

When such traders become the dominant force in a market, perverse results can occur. Ask a fixed-income fund manager about performance in 1980. The answer might be that the fund earned 8 percent. When confronted with the facts that inflation in 1980 was in double digits and that the bond fund lost assets in real terms, the manager might reply, ''But I was in the top 20 percent of all comparable funds.'' The fact that the owners of the fund were severely damaged by an inability even to cover inflation should have been the key concern but typically was not. Equities managers are similarly oriented to relative performance, and the 1982–86 bull market put special pressures on these decision makers.

The markets were moving rapidly upward. Normal healthy returns were seen as paltry by comparison to what had recently been achieved. The prudent manager who moved toward cash as the stock market advanced was viewed as weak and short-sighted as to the ultimate potential of the market. That this potential always seemed to be 300 to 500 points above the current level bothered few. Those who deviated from the herd mentality chanced missing out on the next big move. If a correction occurred, everyone would be hurt, but the relative rankings might stay intact.

Ultimately, the market did reflect the fundamentals, and when the herd changed direction, it did not move at a trot. The seeds of the crash were planted the moment anyone believed a 35 percent increase in nine months was "normal" in the face of weak budget, trade, and dollar pictures. The trigger might have been any number of events: interest rates above 10 percent, no progress on trade deficits, Secretary Baker's comments that the dollar might be allowed to fall. It was likely the unfortunate confluence of many streams that caused the dam to break, but that it would break should not have been in question.

The role of futures in this episode is important but not in the way commonly portrayed. Portfolio insurers had believed they could use stock index futures to change quickly their stock/cash mix without having much impact on the market. They clearly overestimated the potential liquidity that would be present when the market made a major turn. More importantly, by their actions, they abetted the market advance. If the portfolio insurers had bought puts instead of placing stop loss orders, their bearish sentiment would have been expressed in the markets, and it is possible that the rally of 1987 would have been much more sedate.

If the portfolio insurers had been in the market buying puts, they would have had to bid prices attractive enough to induce writers to trade. Writers of these puts would have sold stocks or stock index futures to hedge their risk, and in turn the bearish feelings would be revealed to all. Instead, by relying on stop loss sell orders, which are not revealed to the market until declines have commenced, portfolio insurers kept the extent of their bearish sentiment to themselves. The market frequently needs clear signals to guide it along, and although published reports on the extent of portfolio insurance gave clues to the size of the potential selling, those signals could be ignored or discounted. Buying puts is a market signal that cannot be ignored since it is a pure expression of market sentiment.

It seems clear that many thought they could use futures to shift their positions quickly without market impact. Because of this sense of security these managers may have overinvested in stocks relative to cash before the crash. By being nearly fully invested there was the hope of having maximum participation in any continued rally without having to suffer the drag of option premiums paid out. For the individual portfolio insurer it seemed an ideal approach, but as the activity grew in the aggregate, the liquidity was not there to carry it out.

As previously mentioned, the data show that portfolio insurance programs were large before the crash, but they cannot be blamed for either the rise or the fall. Their share was still minor relative to the market as a whole. There were many other fund managers who were much more problematic because they had not concerned themselves with the tools available to manage stock market risk. They were blindly following a pack. The market crashed not because of margins, regulatory blunders, or computer-driven decisions. It fell as dramatically as it did because of the myopia and the short-term system of incentives that drove the U.S. stock market relentlessly beyond any level that was sustainable. Once this fact was realized the correction was inevitable.

The users of stock index futures and options should be forgiven if they have not learned everything there is to know about their products. These contracts have been trading only since 1982, whereas agricultural futures have been in existence for over 100 years. It takes experience in bull, bear, and flat markets to learn what can and cannot be accomplished. The answer to the stock market crash is not a Luddite solution of breaking all the machines and moving back to simpler, slower times. The real solution is to recognize the strengths of the individual markets and apply the variety of tools in situations in which they are most suitable. Only through knowledge and careful trading discipline involving all markets will long-term success be achieved. While the industry is still moving up the learning curve, one can only hope that the crash will serve as a reminder that long-term performance is not best measured by short-run relative results.

NOTES

1. Since it was assumed that the portfolio was evaluated at the midpoint of the bid/ask spread of 12.5 cents, any sale is assumed to occur at the bid, 6.25 cents away from the midpoint. Hence the total impact is $0.0625 \times 200,000 = \$12,500$.

2. One might inquire why someone with a long-term strategy would not trade the deferred futures and avoid these rollover costs. In fact, because of the ease of intertemporal arbitrage, which will be described below, there is very little need for back-month stock index futures, and liquidity has never developed beyond the first one or two contracts.

3. The proof of this requires the use of Riemann-Stieltjes integrals. A simple case for an at-the-money put is shown in the appendix to this chapter.

4. This does not imply that a hedger should be indifferent as long as the futures price is within the gold points limit of cash. Every effort should be made to buy futures when they are cheap relative to cash and conversely. The basics of basis hedging should never be forgotten.

5. See Kawaller (1987) for an enlightening description of these risks.

6. The CFTC staff was already in gear for these studies having produced extensive analysis of the one-hour, 115 point market decline in January 1987 (Commodity Futures Trading Commission, 1987b).

7. Index arbitrage accounted for 6 to 13 percent of selling activity on October 14, 16, and 19 and fell to near zero thereafter as the NYSE took institutional steps to curtail it. These steps may have relaxed the burden on some overtaxed NYSE computers, but persistent volatility, including some major declines, after the 19th suggested that index arbitrage was not the causal factor.

8. This point led to the only formal dissenting view. Despite agreeing that futures

margins had been adequate during the crash, SEC Chairman Ruder argued that they should be raised to control volatility. The other participants firmly rejected this view.

Appendix: The Expected Return from a Put-Protected Portfolio

Calculating the expected return of an investment requires a knowledge of the underlying distribution. The first moment of the distribution, the mean, is the expected value. Higher moments also contain important information. The second moment is the variance, and the third moment is the skewness of the distribution.

Any statistics text will provide the algebra required for calculating these moments from a discrete distribution, but typically, only more advanced texts provide solutions, involving calculus, to the continuous case. When options are added to a portfolio, the resulting return distribution is no longer continuous. As shown in the chapter, the part of the return distribution that corresponds to the option being in the money is stacked up on a point. This produces a return distribution that has both discrete and continuous portions, and regular integration over the entire space is no longer valid.

To address this problem requires the use of Riemann-Stieltjes integrals, which can break up the distribution into the appropriate discrete and continuous parts. These integrals are typically discussed in advanced calculus texts. To demonstrate the proposition that the mean of a put-protected portfolio is lower than that of the unprotected portfolio by the amount of the time value of the option, a simple example is provided. This example will avoid the need for much complicated integration by looking at a distribution symmetric around the current price and an at-the-money put. The basic procedure can be applied to more complicated examples as well but will require the explicit solution of the integrals.

Let the current price, P_o, be 100, and the put option being bought to protect the portfolio be at-the-money ($E = 100$). Suppose that the market price of the option is p, which is 10. This is all time value. The most important assumption is that the distribution is symmetric around the current price. The mean of the unprotected distribution is given by:

$$\mu = \int_{-\infty}^{+\infty} P f(P)\, dP = \int_{-\infty}^{100} P f(P)\, dP + \int_{100}^{+\infty} P f(p)\, dP \qquad (A.1)$$

$$= \quad 100 \quad = \quad 50 \quad + \quad 50$$

The symmetry condition insures that the mean equals 100, the current value, and that if the total integral is broken in two at the median of the distribution, each part will contribute half to the total.

The portfolio that is protected by the purchase of the at-the-money put has a different mean distribution. Recalling that the premium equals 10, the mean is:

$$\mu' = \int_{-\infty}^{100} (E - 10)\, f(P)\, dP + \int_{100}^{+\infty} (P - 10)\, f(P)\, dP \qquad (A.2)$$

$$= (E - 10) \int_{-\infty}^{100} f(P)\, dP + \int_{100}^{+\infty} (P - 10)\, f(P)\, dP$$

$$= (E - 10)\, \text{PROB}(P < 100) - 10\, \text{PROB}(P > 100) + \int_{100}^{+\infty} P\, f(P)\, dP$$

The last expression is derived by taking the constant term out of the integrals and recognizing that the integral of $f(P)dP$ over any region is simply the probability of the price being in that region. Because of the symmetry assumption, A.2 is easy to solve. The final integral term in A.2 equals 50, as shown in A.1. The probability that P will either be under or over 100 is 0.5. Placing the value of E into A.2 gives:

$$\mu' = (90)(.5) - (10)(.5) + 50 \qquad (A.3)$$

$$= 90$$

which is the value of the unprotected expected return less the time value of the option.

This example demonstrated the proposed effect for protective puts under fairly restrictive conditions. Similar approaches can be taken with any combination of options and futures, although as previously mentioned, the mathematics is more complicated. Calculating the moments of the distribution in this way requires explicit distributions that may not always be known with certainty, but the general guidance offered can still be useful.

It is also important to go beyond the mean of the distribution. In the example of the purchased put, variance falls and the third movement moves from symmetry to a favorable skew. An analysis of the effects on the various moments of the distribution was performed by Richard Bookstaber and Roger Clarke (1984). Using Monte Carlo simulation methods, they explored how purchased puts, covered writing of calls, and other option strategies influence the mean, variance, and skew of the return streams. Only by looking at all three moments can the strategy be properly evaluated in terms of how it fits into the portfolio. Traditional evaluation techniques that stress the mean and variance cannot capture the entire picture and can give potentially very misleading results.

CHAPTER 5

Interest Rate Market Strategies

It is convenient to think of the strategies for using interest rate markets as a group, but it is a heterogeneous one. Financing needs span both short and long periods, and the risks at either end of the spectrum can be different. The unifying theme comes from the yield curve and its behavior through time. As the curve shifts in a parallel fashion, one set of problems emerge. If the slope changes, there are completely different issues.

As futures and options on interest rate instruments have evolved since 1975, traders have learned which markets and strategies offer them the protection they need. Many instruments have been developed and have fallen by the wayside. A few have climbed to the very top of the industry, representing the pinnacle of success in terms of liquidity and breadth of coverage. This chapter first explores the rapid evolution of interest rate futures and options and then turns to the mechanics of yield curve risk. Finally, the instruments and strategies that form a smorgasbord of risk management opportunity are presented.

5.1   GROWTH OF THE MARKETS

The time was 1973–74. Inflation was running at a double-digit rate, and for the first time since World War II price controls were lifted. Interest rates were at postwar highs, with short rates higher than long. Banking regulations that dictated ceilings on interest rates caused a phenomenal draining of deposits from the system, as savers scrambled into investments providing some real return. Money-market mutual funds were invented as an instrument allowing the individual investor access to the interest rates faced by institutions. In 1973–74 the glue holding together the relatively quieter times of the 1950s and 1960s began to age and crack. New tools were needed to face the new challenges.

In 1975 the Chicago Board of Trade got the ball rolling with its Government National Mortgage Association (GNMA) contract. The Chicago Mercantile Exchange followed shortly thereafter with its 90-day Treasury bill futures. The world's two largest futures exchanges staked out opposite ends of the yield curve, and it has been a division in the United States that has persisted throughout the interest rate futures' brief history. In the beginning it was difficult to find bankers who had anything good to say about the new instruments. These innovations were at best characterized as unnecessary and at worst as a mechanism bringing chaos to a traditional group of cash market traders. But the environment called for a way to manage the record volatility, and interest rate futures would quickly prove their worth. Today it is difficult to find a major banker who does not count on these products as integral risk management and trading tools.

The chronology of interest rate products began with GNMAs and T-bills in 1975 and 1976, respectively, but quickly added T-bonds and commercial paper (1977), T-notes (1979), and domestic CDs and Eurodollars (1981). In addition to this list are many variations on the same theme. Competing exchanges scrambled to try different maturities and even identical products. The Darwinian theory of the survival of the fittest has proved to be a descriptive model in this area, with the majority of entrants failing to make much of an impact.

Even those contracts that were the standard-bearers of their day were not immune to the competition. The CBOT GNMA contract defined the turf, but after the introduction of the T-bond contract, various warts became apparent, and the contract fell into disfavor. The CBOT has on more than one occasion tried to repackage the GNMA contract on the theory that mortgage-rate risk has sufficiently unique properties to deserve its own contract. The market, however, has had a different view, and today the contract that started it all is not traded in any form.

On the short end of the yield curve the situation is similar, though less extreme. Within five years of its introduction, the CME T-bill contract was the focus of considerable academic and practical study. It was *the* short-term instrument, and the writers discussing its virtues could have hardly expected the extent of its ultimate decline. The T-bill fell victim to the success of the Eurodollar contract, which drew away traders who had used bill futures as a cross-hedge for short-term private instruments. As activity grew in Eurodollars, it proved itself to be a more flexible instrument in many ways than the original bill contract. After a decade of trading, the CME T-bill futures became a solid, dependable contract, regularly trading about a million lots annually, but far behind the industry standards it once set.

Differentiating across competing interest rate products is best done across two dimensions, time and credit risk. Position on the yield curve has already been discussed, but the other key determinant is credit quality. The U.S. Treasury instruments typically define the risk free rate of return.[1] Privately issued paper or agency paper that is not backed by the full faith and promise of the U.S. government carries greater default risk and hence lower prices. The commercial paper contract was the first to explore this aspect of pricing, but it ultimately gave way to the Eurodollar contract. Ten years after the start of trading there were surprisingly few contracts available. Of those trading, most clearly defined an area on the time-quality grid. Contracts that settled in too close to existing instruments either took over the neighborhood or died.

5.2   THE MAJOR CONTRACTS

Many publications devoting considerable space to careful contract descriptions have outlived the contracts they examined. The point of this section is to provide a general characterization of the contracts without too much institutional detail since the particulars of any contract can change quickly. Beginning at the short end of the yield curve and working to the longer maturities, the basic characteristics of the instruments are presented. Unlike stock index futures of the previous chapter, the various interest rate futures have important differences in form as well as in the definition of the underlying instrument. When considering delivery specifications in particular, the basic features become much more important to accurate pricing decisions. Fortunately, the options on these futures are fairly standard and will need no special treatment.

5.2.1   Treasury Bills

The CME 13-week Treasury bill contract calls for delivery of $1 million in U.S. Treasury bills that mature 90, 91, or 92 days from the first delivery date. To insure that there is adequate deliverable supply, it is possible to deliver bills for which the original maturities were 26 or 52 weeks but which now have 13 weeks remaining before maturity.

T-bills are discount securities, which means they pay no explicit interest. They are quoted in the cash market in terms of their annualized discount rate expressed as a percentage. For example, suppose that a million dollar 90-day bill was priced at $980,000. The discount for 90 days is 2 percent, and it is the custom of the cash trade to compute the annualized rate as a simple multiple of the time period. There is no compounding. Expressed in terms of its annualized price, this bill would be 92.00.

The pricing of the futures contract parallels the cash market closely. The contract calls for delivery of bills of appropriate maturity that have a face value of $1 million. Each 0.01 of the price equals $25. If a trader takes delivery on a T-bill futures contract, instruments will be delivered from the seller on the Fed wire.

During the latter half of the 1970s, T-bill futures dominated trading on the short end of the yield curve. Although T-bills represent the safest form of interest rate instruments, they are not the best trading tool available. First, the pool of 13-

week bills is small relative to the universe of short-term debt instruments. Second, many individuals, businesses, and money-market mutual funds that hold T-bills do so with little regard for the price risk. They hold T-bills as the safest interest bearing alternative to cash, and if rates should increase suddenly, most of these owners will take their lumps for the few remaining weeks and then roll into a higher yielding series. Such an attitude does not produce a great demand for hedging services.

Finally, for the vast majority of entities dealing with short-term debt, the creditworthiness of the U.S. government is irrelevant to their risk. This was most clearly seen after the October 1987 stock market crash when there was a "flight to quality." As investors scrambled to acquire T-bills, short-term rates on these instruments fell faster than those on private, more risky, short-term debt. Anyone who had hedged an inventory of private debt by going short T-bill futures faced a significant loss from the adverse movement of the basis. For all of these reasons, Eurodollar futures have become the instrument of choice for trading short-term rate risk.

5.2.2   Eurodollars

An early attempt to address the problem of private credit quality was the development of futures on domestic certificates of deposit (CDs). These contracts called for the delivery of three-month negotiable certificates of deposit from banks on the CME-approved list. The list was formulated to insure minimal credit risk. The contract was initially successful, but in time it became clear that only those CDs from the least creditworthy of the approved banks would be delivered. This was just an example of the "cheapest-to-deliver" principle described in chapter 2. Unfortunately, as the credit markets entered into a period of great volatility in the late 1970s and early 1980s, banks that had once been thought unshakable had problems spring up around them. The basis risk *within* the private credit market due to quality variation proved as troublesome as the basis risk between T-bill futures and private debt.

In 1981 an elegant solution to the problem was found in the development of Eurodollar futures. This contract is based on the London Interbank offer rate (LIBOR) for dollar-denominated time deposits of three months. These time deposits, unlike certificates of deposit, are nonnegotiable, making the concept of delivery problematic. For this reason, Eurodollars became the first cash-settled contract.

Closely paralleling the T-bill contract in terms of contract size and maturity dates, the price of the Eurodollar contract is equal to an index formed by subtracting the annualized *return* from 100. Unlike T-bills, which are priced according to the discount, Eurodollar cash market quotes are based on an add-on interest rate. Consequently, a T-bill future priced at 92.00 would imply a higher yield than an identically priced Eurodollar future.[2]

Cash settlement eliminates the need for an elaborate formula to calculate the invoice price of a delivered futures contract. The buyer and seller both know that each day their positions will be marked to market daily based on the settlement price. The last trading day is no different except that the final settlement price is not determined by the futures market participants in the pit. Instead, a large number of randomly selected prime London banks are polled as to what their offer rate is for 90-day dollar-denominated funds. Similar to diving scores, the two high and low quotes are discarded and the remaining quotes averaged. On the final settlement day this procedure is done twice, once at the close and once at a randomly selected time within a 90-minute window before the close. The procedure is purposely complicated to minimize the chance that any participant in the process can greatly influence the final settlement price by his or her actions. The point is to get a representative final value, and if there was an opportunity to distort that value by placing a poor quote in the sample, the hedgers who were counting on convergence of cash and futures at expiration would find the contract's utility greatly impaired.

The cash settlement procedure must be effective because the contract has been a huge success. By 1988 the open interest had grown to more than 500,000 contracts, representing $500 billion of exposure. Annual volume had reached 20 million lots making it one of the world's most actively traded futures contracts. The published examples of short-term interest rate hedging using domestic CDs can all be relegated to a historical footnote.

5.2.3 Treasury Notes

The part of the yield curve between the very short and the very long has always held great interest for scholars and exchanges. Unfortunately, traders have found it less intriguing. Treasury note futures of various durations have served specialized markets well, but none has ever moved beyond being a niche contract.

The only distinguishing feature between notes and bonds is the original maturities. Treasury notes are issued in maturities of 2, 3, 4, 5, 7, and 10 years at regular government auctions. Bonds at one time were issued with 15-, 20-, and 30-year maturities, but with the suspension of the auction of the 20s in 1986, only the 30-year bond is currently issued.

The pricing of these contracts is in terms of percentage of par in points, typically expressed in terms of $\frac{1}{32}$ of a point. Par value is 100 points. Occasionally, when cash market practice dictates, the price can be quoted in 64ths, 128ths, and sometimes 256ths of a point.

Several exchanges have made excursions into the T-note territory. The Chicago Board of Trade began in 1979 with a four- to six-year note contract. The IMM of the CME countered with a four-year instrument, and COMEX launched a two-year contract. None of these contracts caught on, perhaps because the interest rate volatility of the time was too great. With wide swings in both short and long rates, it was no time to experiment with new contracts when trades using the existing T-bill and T-bond contracts could be combined to cover the entire yield curve.

The first note contract to make an impact was the CBOT $6\frac{1}{2}$- to 10-year $100,000 instrument based on an 8 percent par coupon. By moving out toward the long end of the range, the contract's initial progress was helped immeasurably by the ability of CBOT locals to spread their risk to the very liquid bond contract. Since its inception in 1982, this contract has grown steadily, serving the community of government securities traders seeking hedging protection for their inventories.

The most recent entrants into this field have been five-year note contracts from the Finex division of the New York Cotton Exchange and the CBOT. The initial trading experience of these instruments has suggested that there may be a demand for this shorter maturity as well, but many other interest rate contracts launched over the years were initially more robust and have since waned.

5.2.4   Treasury Bonds

In August 1977 the CBOT launched its T-bond futures contract, opening a significant chapter in the management of risk. Ten years later, volume in this futures and the options on it placed these instruments one-two among all such futures and options globally. There have been years in the late 1980s when if these two instruments had seceded from the CBOT, they would have formed the largest futures and options exchange in the world, relegating all of the remaining CBOT contracts to third place behind the CME. T-bond futures and options together form a juggernaut of massive proportions.

The terms of the bond contract are hardly simple. The price is similar to that of the T-note, expressed as a percentage of par in points with a minimum fluctuation being $\frac{1}{32}$ of a point.[3] Par value is 100 points, and the size is $100,000. The acceptable delivery instruments are T-bonds with a minimum maturity of 15 years, and if they are callable, they cannot be eligible to be called for at least 15 years. This puts a huge array of deliverable instruments into the opportunity set. Actual delivery occurs with the short initiating a bank-book-entry wire transfer on the Federal Reserve System and the long paying in federal funds to that bank.

Over time, as new 30-year bonds are auctioned, different coupons appear. Deciding how to value a 17-year, $14\frac{1}{2}$ percent coupon instrument compared with a 28-year $9\frac{1}{2}$ percent coupon involves complicated algebra that is discussed in the next section. The basic principal however relies on a "conversion factor" for each instrument that converts all potential deliverable instruments to a common basis. This does not mean that they will all have the same price, and the participants in this market watch the conversions closely to identify which of the instruments is cheapest to deliver. For futures with several months to expiration, the cheapest-to-deliver bond is not known with certainty, and the price of the futures must track the general yield curve. Of particular importance is the most recently auctioned 30-year bond. As a futures contract nears maturity, the delivery picture becomes clearer, and the price of the future will closely parallel the bond expected to be cheapest to deliver.[4]

The success of the bond contract has crushed several potential competitors including the various incarnations of the CBOT's own GNMA contract. It cannot be suggested that this is always the perfect contract in terms of close matching of risk for a particular cash instrument. Instead, it is a classic example of a market that is so liquid that knowledgeable traders will accept a degree of basis risk as a reasonable trade-off. In the strategies section, the mortgage-backed securities examples will be constructed against T-bond futures and options, thus reflecting the reality of cash market practice rather than the theoretically more satisfying hedging models with GNMAs.

5.2.5   Other Interest Rate Instruments

In addition to contracts that span the range of the yield curve, there have been innovations that are noteworthy because of some unique feature. Cash settlement of Eurodollars marked a significant departure from the norm, and it opened the minds of many to opportunities that lay beyond the existing menu of contracts.

Eurodollars almost had to be cash settled to succeed. T-bonds, on the other hand, could be cash settled using an elaborate survey mechanism, but why bother? There is no problem with adequacy of deliverable supply, and traders generate considerable activity positioning themselves versus the cheapest-to-deliver instrument. Making a departure from the traditional delivery mechanism requires a strong reason.

One sector of interest rate trading that stands apart from the rest is municipal bonds. These instruments are affected not only by the general movement in interest rates but also by the creditworthiness of the issuers and the tax code. Holders of municipal bonds have often found significant basis risk between their portfolio and the instruments available for hedging.

The CBOT addressed this problem in 1985 with the introduction of its municipal bond index contract. In this case, cash settlement seemed preferable to delivery in order to avoid a cheapest-to-deliver problem that was potentially much worse than that experienced by the domestic CD contract. The CBOT created an index from a representative group of medium-maturity municipal bonds. At settlement, prices from the cash market would be sampled to determine the final value. Unlike Eurodollars where the sample is based on a homogeneous instrument, the municipal bond index covers a range of issues. If one of the issues falls in value because of a radical change in the creditworthiness of the issuer, the impact on the index as a whole is minimal. If the contract had been constructed as a delivery vehicle, it would be certain that any bond falling radically in value would form the deliverable supply.

The municipal bond contract has never posted exciting volume figures. Instead, it has built slowly, exploiting its basis risk advantage for a select group of specialized traders.

Indexes of bonds have had mixed success, but that has not deterred new entrants. The CME has received CFTC approval for, but has not yet begun to trade, a contract based on its "Treasury Index." Here the analogy is with the CME's successful S&P 500 futures contract.

Interest rate futures have always relied on identifying distinct pieces of the debt world and providing holders of those pieces a good hedging tool. What does a bond/note portfolio manager use for risk management? He or she pairs off parts of the portfolio with the relevant future or option and thereby achieves total coverage.

The CME's Treasury Index contract offers the opportunity for "one-stop" shopping. Just as a stock portfolio manager may hedge stock-by-stock using individual equity options, the bond fund manager can use today's interest rate futures and options. But a more efficient method is found for the stock manager using S&P 500 futures. The Treasury Index contract will provide the same kind of portfolio coverage for the bond fund.

It remains to be seen if either the municipal bond index or the Treasury Index will enjoy long-term success. But as sophistication grows among traders and holders of debt instruments, the likelihood increases that the contracts will survive. What is important is the identification of unique risk and the provision of a cost effective means of addressing it.

5.3   ESSENTIAL INTEREST RATE MATHEMATICS

Interest rate hedging depends on the ability to match the risk characteristics of the cash market instrument or portfolio to the behavior of the futures or option contract. This requires some basic mathematics combined with the conventions of the cash market. Readers completely familiar with discounting, yields, compounding, and the mathematics of the term structure of the interest rate may skip this section without loss of continuity. The following sections provide the algebraic formulations that are most frequently used in the analysis of interest rate hedges, as well as the futures market conventions for the main contracts.

5.3.1   T-Bill and Eurodollar Conventions

The simplest interest bearing instruments are discount securities like T-bills. Typically, such vehicles are quoted in terms of their discount versus a par value of 100. For example, a one-year, $1 million T-bill might be sold at original auction for a price of $930,000, a discount of $70,000 versus its ultimate maturity value. This bill has a price of 93.00 and in one year will return 7.53 percent to the owner. This return is calculated from Equation 5.1.

$$r = (P_T - P_O)/P_O \qquad (5.1)$$

where r = percentage return
           P_T = terminal value of the instrument
           P_O = today's value

This return captures the percentage markup only from the day of purchase to the point of maturity.

In the example of the one-year bill, the return is immediately recognizable in its raw form as an annualized value. If the maturity of the instrument is different from a year, however, the calculated return is less revealing. Suppose that a 90-day bill could be bought for $982,000, again having a value at maturity of $1 million. The simple return would be $r = (1,000,000 - 982,000)/982,000 = 1.83\%$.

When comparing this bill to the one-year alternative, the returns are not directly comparable since the time to maturity is not the same. An adjustment is called for, and it is the customary practice for T-bills and most instruments with one year or less to maturity to make a linear adjustment for time:

$$y = ar \qquad (5.2)$$

where y = quoted annual return
        a = annualization factor

For T-bills in the cash market, the accepted practice is for $a = 360/T$, where T is the number of days to maturity. This produces the following annual return equation for T-bills:

$$y = (P_T - P_O)/P_O * (360/T) \qquad (5.3)$$

In the example above the annualized return would be 7.33 percent.

The cash and futures markets for T-bills rely on these simple formulas for determining their prices. Starting with the cash quote for a T-bill:

$$P = 100 - D \qquad (5.4)$$

where P = cash price for a T-bill (per $100 face value)
       D = annualized discount in percent (e.g., 7.52%)

The annualized discount is conceptually near the annualized return:

$$D = (P_T - P_O)/P_T * (360/T) * 100 \qquad (5.5)$$

The difference between Equations 5.3 and 5.5 is the denominator in the first part of the expression. The discount is calculated in terms of the terminal value rather than the current price. There is also the trivial multiplication by 100 to put the discount in terms of a percent.

The actual invoice price of a T-bill, P_O, incorporates the face value of the instrument, and the number of days remaining, T:

$$P_O = \$1,000,000 * (1 - DT/36,000) \qquad (5.6)$$

The T-bill futures price is a formula similar to Equation 5.4:

$$F = 100 - D_F \qquad (5.7)$$

where F = futures price
          D_F = annualized discount in percent on the contract

If a trader takes delivery on a T-bill futures contract, instruments will be delivered from the seller on the Fed wire. The invoice price will be:

$$P_F = \$1,000,000 * [1 - (D_F T/36,000)] \qquad (5.8)$$

In this case, T refers to the number of days remaining on the bills delivered, and D_F is the annualized discount calculated from the final settlement price placed into Equation 5.7.

It is useful to draw out the differences between the T-bill conventions and the practice with Eurodollar time deposits. Superficially, the futures contracts appear similar in terms of maturity times and size. In fact, there are important distinctions. The cash market Eurodollar conventions emphasize the explicit interest paid on the deposits versus the emphasis on discounts for T-bills.

$$I = \$1,000,000 * (iT/36,000) \qquad (5.9)$$

where I = interest payment at end of the period on a $1 million deposit
          i = annual interest rate in percent
          T = length of deposit period in days

Since the emphasis in the cash market is on the interest rate, there is no cash market "price" formula. A very simple one was constructed for the Eurodollar futures so that as interest rates rose, prices would fall, just like the market for traded securities:

$$F = 100 - i \qquad (5.10)$$

Comparing Equations 5.7 and 5.10 it should be obvious that a T-bill future and a Eurodollar future with the same price represent very different instruments. Since the T-bill is quoted in terms of discount, its implied return will be higher than the comparably priced Eurodollar future.

Annualizing returns and interest rates is an area that has several rules that may not be completely grounded in logic, but their use is so widespread that there is virtually no chance that the old customs will be changed. You should have noted that for both T-bills and Eurodollars the time adjustment is linear, based on a 360-day year. This is a very widely used convention, but it is not universal. The trader should always be aware of the terms under which an interest rate is quoted. The second point is that even though the return is annualized, care still must be taken in comparing the returns of instruments of different maturities. The process of linear annualization ignores the fact that interest earned in the maturity period of the bill or time deposit can form new capital to be reinvested for the remainder of the year.

In the two examples above the one-year bill paid 7.52 percent and the 90-day vehicle had an annualized return of 7.33 percent. Superficially, if an investor were offered the choice of the one-year instrument or a string of four 90-day bills all returning 7.33 percent, guaranteed, it might appear an easy choice. But the question should be asked whether the interest in any given 90-day period can be *re*invested at the guaranteed rate. If the answer is yes, a little more work is required before the true yield is evident.

The *compound* annualized yield is found by assuming that the simple return could be earned repeatedly for a total period of a year. It is calculated by raising one plus the simple return to the power equal to the number of holding periods in a year. For the three-month bill this becomes,

$$
\begin{aligned}
y_C &= (P_T/P_O)^n - 1 \\
&= (1/.982)^4 - 1 \\
&= .0753 \text{ or, } 7.53\%
\end{aligned}
\tag{5.11}
$$

where y_C = compound annualized yield
   n = number of periods in a year

A final concept that is useful is the *bond equivalent yield*. This yield acknowledges compounding and also ignores the artificial convention of the 360-day year.[5]

$$
y_{BE} = (P_T/P_O)^{365/T} - 1
\tag{5.12}
$$

This is perhaps the most accurate depiction of return, but care should be used with very short maturities; for a single-day instrument, this means that the ratio in Equation 5.12 is raised to the 365th power. Even minor deviations from equilibrium can telescope into absurd results. For example, suppose that an overnight repurchase agreement has a simple return of 0.5 percent. This is certainly high, having a simple annualized yield of 182.5 percent, but using the compounding formula it becomes 520.0 percent. Care should obviously be taken in extrapolating investment returns beyond the period that can be guaranteed.

5.3.2   Coupon-Bearing Instruments

Coupon-bearing instruments, like T-notes and T-bonds, are typically described by their annual coupon interest rate, their time to maturity, the number of payments per year (almost always two), and their current price. Comparing instruments with different maturities requires more difficult conversions than those translating between simple and compound interest for bills.

The complications arise from the treatment of intermediate coupon payments. Are the funds considered available for reinvestment, and if so at what rate? It is reasonable to assume that the coupons will be reinvested, but unless a hedge has been established, the returns earned on reinvestments will be uncertain. Guidelines have been established to lead to equations for the price or yield to maturity, but care must be taken to remember that the underlying assumptions can change over time.

The first convention is that the coupon is expressed in terms of an annual return, and if there is more than a single coupon per year, each is the simple interest counterpart to the annual rate. For example, a \$1 million, 9 percent coupon instrument with semiannual payments would return \$45,000 to the investor every six months. Like the T-bill examples, it is common practice to use simple interest for periods under one year.

Accounting for the reinvestment of interest, however, generally includes compounding, but the simplest case is of a bond that has just paid its next-to-last semiannual coupon payment. On that day, its remaining simple return is a variant of Equation 5.1.

$$r = (P_T + C - P_O)/P_O \tag{5.13}$$

where C is the value of the final coupon paid at maturity. This example is direct but obviously does not have any compounding complications included.

For a bond with multiple *semiannual* payments remaining, which has just paid a coupon, the easiest equation relates the bond's price and coupon. The compounded yield to maturity, y_C, translates into $y_C/2$ on a semiannual basis.

$$P_O = \frac{P_T}{(1 + y_C/2)^N} + \sum_{k=1}^{N} C/(1 + y_C/2)^k \tag{5.14}$$

where N is the number of remaining coupons. This can be viewed as the discounted present value of the terminal value of the bond plus the appropriately discounted stream of remaining coupons. The equation for the price *between* two coupon payment dates is only slightly more complicated.

$$P_O = \frac{P_T}{(1 + y_C/2)^{N-s}} + \left[\sum_{k=1}^{N} C/(1 + y_C/2)^{k-s} \right] - A \tag{5.15}$$

where *A* is the accrued interest, and *s* is the *fraction* of a coupon period since the last coupon was paid.

Accrued interest enters Equation 5.15 since, whenever a bond is sold between coupon payments, the buyer must compensate the seller for the interest earned to date but not yet received. The buyer will ultimately receive the entire coupon for the period no matter how long the instrument was held and should receive interest only for the actual ownership period. These accrued interest payments are calculated linearly according to the number of days since the last payment. The other adjustment in the equation allows for fractional-period discounting to reflect the fact that there may not be a whole number of coupon periods remaining.

Equations 5.14 and 5.15 are expressed in terms of the current price of the bond. Of more interest when comparing instruments of different maturities is the solution for y_C. Given the complicated discounting, such a solution is derivable only through iterative methods like Newton's Method, which are best left to computers or sophisticated calculators.[6]

A final caution is in order before leaving the discussion of coupon-bearing securities. Just as it was important to recognize the cash market conventions in place for discount instruments (e.g., 360 days in a year), it is just as important to identify the rules of the game for coupon debt. There are a number of conventions concerning fractional coupon periods, and it is a case of *caveat emptor*. Any two published yield figures should be checked to insure that they were calculated on a comparable basis.

5.3.3   The Term Structure of Interest Rates

Once the annualized yields have been calculated for instruments of different maturities, considerable information can be inferred about interest rates through time. What the market's expectation for one-year rates are going to be six months from now (the implicit forward rates) are derivable from information on hand today. This is particularly relevant when evaluating the likely effectiveness of an anticipatory hedge or when combining a "strip" of Eurodollar contracts to cover an interest-rate exposure spanning many quarters.

For these calculations a simple notation will be introduced. Let $_i r_j$ represent the nonannualized (i.e., simple) return on a debt instrument issued in month i and maturing in month j. For example, $_0 r_{12}$ would be the return on a one-year instrument issued today, and $_3 r_6$ would be the return on a three-month bill to be issued three months from now.

When comparing interest rates across maturities, it is important to include only instruments of the same quality. Placing three-month T-bills alongside six-month commercial paper leaves two open and unanswerable questions. It is impossible to identify the distinct contributions of time in one dimension and quality in the other. If the interest rate of three-month paper was added, both contributions could be readily identified.

Published every day in the major financial press is a list of available Treasury instruments of varying maturities. These give an array of $_0r_1$, $_0r_2$, $_0r_3$, $_0r_6$, $_0r_{12}$, and so on. In fact, because of the wide variety of government debt available on the secondary market, the yield curve points are much closer together than the discrete monthly scheme depicted here, but the principles developed are applicable to any degree of fineness in the periodicity.

The algebra of the term structure of the interest rates is developed from the concept of choice, and the discipline imposed on the marketplace by arbitrage. Look at the simplest case of an investor evaluating a six-month T-bill available today, yielding $_0r_6$. An alternative investment stream would be to buy a three-month bill yielding $_0r_3$ and take the proceeds (capital and interest) and reinvest it at the then prevailing three-month rate. This rate is not known today with certainty, but we shall see that it is hedgeable.

What interest rate, $_3r_6$, would make the investor indifferent between the two choices? Equation 5.16 equates the streams from each alternative.

$$(1 + {}_0r_6) = (1 + {}_0r_3)(1 + {}_3r_6) \tag{5.16}$$

Solving this equation for $_3r_6$,

$$_3r_6 = [(1 + {}_0r_6)/(1 + {}_0r_3)] - 1 \tag{5.17}$$

For example, if the three-month bill today is returning 2.0 percent and the six-month 4.5 percent (remember these returns are *not* annualized), the implicit three-month forward rate, $_3r_6$, equals 2.45 percent. The six-month yield will always be greater than the sum of the two three-month yields because of compounding.

The yields published each day in the paper have been annualized. To do the calculations described here it is necessary to "deannualize" the rates using the techniques from the earlier part of this section. Once the rates are adjusted for their maturities, there is nothing complicated about the term structure calculations.

Calculations like Equations 5.16 and 5.17 can be constructed for any pair of maturities along the yield curve. As more maturities are compared, an array of implied forward rates is constructed.

The only limitations come from the pairs having a common starting *or* ending point. If you were told that a one-year bill, $_0r_{12}$, was 10 percent and "the middle" six-month forward, $_3r_9$, was 5.2 percent, you would be unable to sketch out the yield curve. There are an infinite number of pairs of first quarter spot three-month rates, $_0r_3$, and forward fourth quarter rates, $_9r_{12}$, that would be consistent with the initial pattern. You should be able to show that if $_0r_3$ equaled 0.0 percent, $_9r_{12}$ would be 4.56 percent, *and conversely*. The likelihood in a real market is that the actual $_0r_3$ and $_9r_{12}$ would be closer together, but without one of the rates starting or ending at the same time as the other, it is impossible to pin down the exact values.

This algebra can be built up across many periods.

$$(1 + {_0}r_{12}) = (1 + {_0}r_3)(1 + {_3}r_6)(1 + {_6}r_9)(1 + {_9}r_{12}) \qquad (5.18)$$

Equation 5.18 represents a "strip" of quarterly investments being tied together to equate a single annual investment. If we knew only ${_0}r_3$ and ${_0}r_{12}$ today, it would be impossible to solve for all of the implied forward rates, but if there was information available on ${_0}r_6$ and ${_0}r_9$, all of the calculations would have a unique solution.

The importance of a common time basis cannot be underestimated. A very popular hedge that is discussed in detail below combines many quarters of Eurodollar futures to hedge against commercial debt that spans two or three years. (The combines futures are called a strip.) Eurodollar futures are quoted on an index basis in terms of simple annual interest. The commercial debt may be in terms of semiannual coupons. The bottom line is that the hedge will not be accurate unless both investment streams are examined in terms of their dollar returns. It is necessary to pare down broad terms like *yield* to their basic essence and use the techniques developed in this section. In that way there will be no ambiguity about total return or risk.

5.4   SHORT-TERM INTEREST RATE TRADING

The CME Eurodollar futures and options dominate the short end of the yield curve, and CBOT T-bond instruments hold sway over the long. The reasons for this stem from the distinctly different risks that exist at each end. These risks are sufficiently different to warrant their own discussions despite the similarities shared by all interest rate instruments. In the section that follows, various approaches to short maturity trading are presented, followed by a separate section on longer term instruments.

5.4.1   Inventory Hedging with T-Bill Futures

U.S. government securities dealers are constantly confronted with inventory risk. As bills are bought at auction, there is the chance that yields will go up (prices decline) before the inventory can be liquidated. The strategy is to go short the appropriate T-bill future or futures in an amount comparable to the face value of the bills held. The following example will demonstrate the most basic short-term hedge.

Suppose that a government securities dealer is holding an inventory of $100 million (face value) of the current 13-week T-bill. The bills have 90 days to maturity, and they are trading at a current discount of 5.40. This means that their current price is \$98,650,000 (= \$1,000,000,000[1 − .054(90/360)]). To hedge this exposure would require going short 100 T-bill futures.

Choosing the appropriate contracts depends on the anticipated period of coverage and the maturities available. Suppose that this dealer is confident that the inventory will be placed within a few days, so the objective is the shortest possible coverage. Furthermore, assume that there is a T-bill futures contract maturing within a month. This contract, which calls for the delivery of T-bills with 13 weeks left to maturity closely parallels the instrument held in the inventory. Let the near contract be priced at 94.50.

The relationship of the price of the futures to the current price of the spot represents the basis, which the hedger must find stable over the planning horizon if the program is to be effective. A simple way of looking at the problem is that today the cash price reflects $_0r_3$, and next month's futures is the market's view of $_1r_4$.[7] If the hedge is maintained for a month until the futures contract expires, there will be a serious mismatch between the cash and futures. The inventory will contain bills with two months to maturity ($_0r_2$), while the delivery obligation calls for three-month bills ($_0r_3$). The objective of the hedge should be short-term coverage to minimize the basis risk that will become increasingly acute through time.

Assume that in two days the bill inventory is placed at a price of 94.48, for a total return of \$98,620,000. This represents a loss on the inventory of \$30,000. Suppose that, simultaneously to this cash sale, the futures are bought back at 94.38. This 12-point gain will return a \$30,000 profit (\$1 million ∗ 100 ∗ .0012 ∗ (90/360)). In this simple example, the hedge worked perfectly. All of the cash market losses were replaced by futures profits, because the basis was completely stable for the two-day period. If the futures price had dropped only to 94.39, the basis narrowing from 10 to 9 points, there would have been a \$2,500 shortfall in the coverage. If it had fallen to 94.36, or a basis of 12 points, there would have been a \$5,000 profit. The important point is that as long as the basis variation is less than the cash price variation, the overall risk of the inventory position is reduced. The reader should confirm that if yields had fallen in the two-day period, any cash market windfall would be reduced by futures market losses.

How would the example be modified if the same prices were used but the bills in the inventory had 45 days to maturity instead of 90? In this case, the value of the inventory would have started at \$99,325,000 (\$100 million [1 − .054(45/360)]) and dropped to \$99,310,000 with the 12-point increase in price. Hedging with \$100 million in T-bill futures would have still provided a profit of \$30,000 (assuming a constant basis), so there is a serious mismatch against the \$15,000 cash loss. In this case it is a happy mismatch, producing a windfall, but if yields had fallen, the increase in the cash value of the inventory would not have covered the futures market losses.

To set up the appropriate hedge, the first step is to identify the expected price change in the futures for a given change in the cash. For the short-term hedge anticipated here, it is not unreasonable to expect one-for-one parallel shifts. The next step is to compare what a one-point change translates into for both the cash and futures. For the 45-day cash bill, a one-point change means $12.50, and for the T-bill futures it is $25.00. Therefore, the optimal hedge will be one T-bill futures contract for every $2 million in cash 45-day bills. In the example above, 50 contracts would provide for a very precise short-term fit.

The basis relationships described above, encompassing price and dollar changes, are fundamental to all futures hedging. Any discussion of hedging that relies on a constant price basis or a constant one-to-one matching between cash and futures should be examined closely to reveal its limitations if the restrictive assumptions are relaxed.

The simple inventory hedging example also holds some insights for the position trader. A change of the discount from 5.50 to 5.38 for the T-bill futures in two days is not extraordinarily large or small. On a per contract basis, it results in a price change of $300 (12 points ∗ $25 per point). This amount in comparison to the face value of $1 million is modest, but it is an accurate reflection of the risk. Anyone speculating on the direction of short-term interest rates should understand that the *percentage volatility* on a day-to-day basis is small, so futures markets have traditionally made the base value of the contract large. This combination provides for an effective trading vehicle for all classes of traders.

5.4.2   Eurodollar Anticipatory Hedging

A frequently employed hedging strategy in corporate circles is anticipatory hedging. A firm may know that the interest rate it typically faces equals LIBOR or some basis relative to LIBOR, like 50 points over. The firm may also know that it will require $100 million in short-term financing to cover the first quarter of next year. There is no question whether funds will be available, the only question is at what price?

The firm in July may see the array of Eurodollar futures prices illustrated in Table 5.1. Looking at the first December contract, which prices 90-day instruments, the annualized yield is 8.49 percent. If this price of funds fits the firm's strategic outlook, it may prefer to lock in that rate rather than speculate that rates will decline in the interim. This is the fundamental choice that must always be made in anticipatory hedging.

Many financial officers not accustomed to hedging stop at this point and argue, "Isn't an anticipatory hedge just a bet that rates will be higher? Isn't this just politely presented speculation?" Taken in isolation, the answer would appear to be yes, but such decisions are never made in a vacuum.

In evaluating whether 8.49 percent is an acceptable cost of funds, a financial officer would need to assess the return expected for those funds. If the $100 million will be put into short-term inventory financing where the products have been contracted for at a fixed price, and the expected yield is 12.0 percent on this activity, it is a situation where most of the variables except the cost of funds have been determined. In such a world, the officer must decide whether to fix the cost

Table 5.1
Hypothetical Eurodollar Prices

Month	Year	Price	Yield
Sept.	0	91.58	8.42
Dec.	0	91.51	8.49
March	1	91.45	8.55
June	1	91.40	8.60
Sept.	1	91.35	8.65
Dec.	1	91.31	8.69

of funds and lock in a sure, if unspectacular, return, or remain unhedged and face the prospect of a windfall if rates should decline, or a loss if the cost of funding should rise. Unless superior interest rate forecasting is counted on as a major contributor to earnings, the hedge allows the firm to concentrate on the activities it does best. A more detailed discussion of this topic is included in Section 7.7, but the bottom line is that if the long-term success of the company depends on effective inventory management, ignoring the futures market puts the firm in an unnecessary speculative posture.

The mechanics of the hedge are direct, but there are details that should be observed. Let the expectation of the firm's cost of funds be 50 points over LIBOR and the term of the loan be one-quarter (91 days). Based on today's December Eurodollar quote from Table 5.1, the total interest due on the $100 million would be $2,272,472 (= $100 million * .0899 * (91/360)). The appropriate number of contracts in the hedge is not the naive guess of 100 to match the face value of the loan but 101. This adjustment comes from the fact that each point increase in LIBOR moves the $1 million futures contract $25.00, while it moves the cost of the loan $25.28 (do not forget that 91st day's interest). The extra contract beyond the face value equivalence covers as closely as possible the extra day's cost of funds.

Table 5.2 gives the outcome of the hedge under rising and falling price scenarios. Under almost any outcome, the net cost of funds is virtually the same. Here the variation in cash market interest expense could vary by almost $400,000 while the hedged interest expense varied by only $400.

The assumption about the basis made in this example is that the firm would be able to borrow at 50 points over LIBOR. If between the time the hedge was

Table 5.2
Borrowing Costs of $100 Million at 50 Points over LIBOR

	Case		
	a	b	c
Euro$ futures today	91.51	91.51	91.51
Position	short 101	short 101	short 101
Final futures settlement	92.00	91.50	90.50
Cash market rate	8.50%	9.00%	10.00%
Total interest expense	2,148,611	2,275,000	2,527,777
Futures P/L	(123,725)	2,525	255,025
Net interest expense	2,272,336	2,272,475	2,272,752

placed and maturity the firm's credit rating deteriorated to 75 points over, the cash interest expense would have gone up approximately $63,194, and this risk would have been unhedgeable in the futures market. Similarly, any improvement in the credit rating of the firm would have generated savings. Like all such situations, the firm has substituted a problem that includes level and basis risk for one having only the basis risk component.

5.4.3   Tails

When the hedging situation begins to span any significant length of time, the real-world problem of financing futures positions rears its head. In Table 5.2, case c resulted in profits accruing to the account, while case a had a significant deficit. These changes to the position's value did not necessarily occur on the day before final settlement, and in a mark-to-market world, deficits need to be financed and profits should be invested. Treating this situation involves *tailing* a position.

In the preceding section's example, a hedge was established in July and held until the December Eurodollars futures expired. If the ultimate outcome had been case a with a $124,000 futures loss as rates declined, the timing of that loss and its financing could diminish the ultimate effectiveness of the hedge. Any loss would have to be financed continuously through the maturity of the futures. Part of the $100 million borrowed at that time could be used to retire the margin financing, but this implicitly raises the cost of the borrowed funds since the same originally agreed-upon amount must be paid back 91 days later. The net effect is that the margin financing represents an additional obligation that extends past the futures expiration through the period covered by the Eurodollar cash instrument.

Suppose that the $124,000 futures loss occurred three months before the expiration of the futures and that the borrowing rate for this purpose is the same as for the original loan, 50 points over LIBOR. At that rate the additional expense would be about $5,300, which is enough to raise the total financing costs of the project 11 basis points.

If funds for financing a hedge were available at zero cost, the subject of tails would never come up. It is because there are positive interest rates that an adjustment is necessary. As interest rates rise, profits from gaining futures contracts are augmented by the additional interest they earn. Conversely, losing positions become more costly to finance. If no adjustment to the position is made, the trader will be "overhedged," with any profits from the futures side exceeding the corresponding cash losses and any futures losses exceeding the cash gains. The proper adjustment is to reduce the number of contracts from the naive perfect match. As interest rates climb, the adjustment becomes more significant.

The tail should be opposite the basic hedge position by some fraction to compensate for the potential effect of financing. A simple tail formula, described fully by Ira Kawaller (1986), is:

$$c = -Crt/360 \qquad\qquad (5.19)$$

where c = number of contracts in the tail
   C = base number of contracts
   r = financing (investing) rate for negative (positive) variation margin flows (in terms of 360-day year)
   t = number of financing days

The negative sign indicates that if the original hedge was long, the tail would be short, and conversely. In the example, right before the price changed, the tail would be four contracts long.[8]

The net result in the simple example, when the futures price changed, the loss would be on 97 contracts rather than 101. This six-month financing cost for the variation margin payments would make up the additional interest expense. Table 5.3 presents the alternatives.

In alternative outcome a, if the hedge position had not been tailed back to 97 lots, the total interest expense would have exceeded the target by about $5,300. In the profitable futures case c, the untailed position would have reduced the interest expense by almost $12,500. In both examples, tailing is shown to add precision to the hedge.

Two general points about tailing should be emphasized. First, tails are not

Table 5.3
"Tailing" the Futures Hedge from Table 5.2

	Case	
	<u>a</u>	<u>c</u>
1. Target interest expense	2,272,470	2,272,470
2. Cash market interest cost	2,148,611	2,527,777
3. Futures profit/(loss)	(118,825)	244,925
4. Financing cost of P/L*	5,078	(12,382)
5. net interest cost**	2,272,514	2,270,470

* ( ) indicates interest earned on variation margin gains

** 2 - 3 + 4

unique to Eurodollar hedges. The financing of variation margin is a fact of life for all futures. In most examples in this book, a tail will not be considered because it adds nothing unique to understanding the question at hand. Second, tailing is not a once-and-for-all adjustment. As Equation 5.19 indicates, as the time to maturity shrinks, so does the tail. The tail should be systematically reduced over the life of the strategy to be completely effective. By this logic, one could easily dispense with a tail strategy altogether for hedges lasting a few days or weeks. The extra precision must be weighed against the higher commission and hassle costs of the continuous adjustments.

5.4.4   Strips and Stacks

Most futures contracts have their open interest concentrated in the first one or two contracts, with considerably smaller open interest in the back months. The CME Eurodollar contract is an exception to this pattern, having sizable open positions in the near months but also offering good liquidity in contracts extending out three years. The back-month activity can be attributed almost exclusively to the practices of stripping and stacking, and it has produced a pattern of open interest that is striking in comparison to more traditional contracts.

Figure 5.1 presents a chart of September 1, 1988, open interest by contract month for the CME Eurodollar future and the CBOT T-bond future. The total open positions were 553,224 and 471,596 lots, respectively, both huge numbers by industry standards. The first feature from the chart is the higher open interest in the December '88 contracts than for the spot month. By September 1 many

Figure 5.1
Eurodollar and T-Bond Futures Open Interest

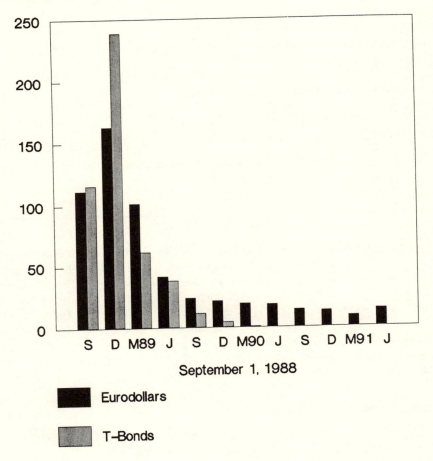

thousands of lots

Eurodollars

T–Bonds

September 1, 1988

hedgers have rolled their spot September positions into December to avoid the possibility of any basis fluctuations that might be associated with the expiration. This is a prudent strategy for hedgers not holding positions to expiration and is typical of contracts like these where commercial traders dominate.

The back-month Eurodollars tell an interesting story. Although not nearly as large as the first three months, which each have more than 100,000 contracts open, the back months all have several thousand contracts. The last eight contracts, spanning the second and third years, have 24.1 percent of the total open position. By contrast, contracts past the first year in the T-bond futures represent only 3.1 percent of the total position. The market participants in Eurodollars have expressed their demand for the ability to span many quarters by supporting contract months, which in most instruments would never be listed.

Stripping Eurodollars is different from a traditional multimonth strategy like spreading in that all of the positions are either short or long (Ira Kawaller, 1988). A strip of the first four months secures the interest rate over a year, and the first eight contracts produce two-year coverage. Strips may also be constructed using only forward months. In July the entire funding rate for the next calendar year can be constructed with a strip consisting of the next December, March, June, and September contracts.

The mechanics of a strip rely on the principles of interest and time discussed in Section 5.3.3. A decision to borrow or lend for one year can be evaluated in terms of a single act to fix the rate for the entire period or a series of quarterly investments and reinvestments.

Table 5.1 presented an array of hypothetical Eurodollar prices. An investment fund facing those prices in July might have $100 million in short-term deposits maturing late in December. At that point the funds will be reinvested for the coming year.

The first thing that should be done is to analyze what a strip of Eurodollars, representing a quarterly rollover strategy, would yield. Assume for simplicity that the fund will receive LIBOR for its funds, although in all likelihood it would receive a few points less. Assuming quarterly intervals of 91, 91, 91, and 92 days, the steps would unfold as presented in Table 5.4.

The total return, if the forecast LIBOR rates were to actually come about,

Table 5.4
Interest Return on a Quarterly Strip

Quarter 1	$100,000,000 * (.0849*(91/360))
	= 2,146,083
Quarter 2	$102,146,083 * (.0855*(91/360))
	= 2,207,632
Quarter 3	$104,353,715 * (.0860*(91/360))
	= 2,268,534
Quarter 4	$106,622,249 * (.0865*(92/360))
	= 2,356,944

would grow to \$108,979,193. This return could have been found from the following equation:

$$(_1r_{12}) = (1 + (.0849)(91/360)) * (1 + (.0855)(91/360)) * \qquad (5.20)$$
$$(1 + (.0860)(91/360)) * (1 + (.0865)(92/360))$$

$$= 1.0898$$

The conclusion is that the projected strip of quarterly investments, with compounding, will return 8.98 percent. Assume that this rate is sufficiently attractive so the fund does not want to speculate on cash rates for the balance of the year. Any alternatives available in July, like a guaranteed investment contract (GIC), spanning the next calendar year should offer a comparable risk-adjusted rate. If the alternatives do not match the strip-derived rate it is a preferable strategy to hedge with futures and lock in the coverage.

The construction of the strip hedge is direct but involves management of capital and interest each quarter. The initial hedge in the December contract would involve buying 101 contracts (do not forget that 91st day). For the subsequent quarters the positions would be 103, 106, and 109, rounding to the nearest whole contract for the March, June, and September contracts, respectively. As in previous hedging examples, alternative cash market outcomes can be demonstrated to produce near constant hedged returns. The mechanics of such simulations should by now be under the command of the reader.

It would appear that such a distant strip hedge would be a prime candidate for tailing, and indeed it is so if it is the intention of the fund to hold the hedge until its ultimate maturity. However, there is no reason to believe automatically that this will be the case. Suppose that a month after the hedge is established, a safe GIC paying 20 points over LIBOR became available for the period in question. The fund might completely liquidate the hedge, with any change in the base LIBOR rate being covered by gains or losses in the hedge, and take advantage of this favorable basis relationship. If such a strategy of short-term protection was anticipated, a tail may not have been worth the trouble of the active management required. Moreover, if there was a high probability that the hedge was going to be lifted quickly, constructing a full tail could leave the position significantly underhedged.

As this manuscript was in preparation, the CME was anticipating adding years four and five to the array of Eurodollar contract months. The demand is expected to come from strippers who seek protection beyond the three years currently available. This coverage begins to get very close to terms covered by the note futures contracts, particularly the new five-year note futures. One can question why any trader would want to trade a complicated strip of instruments spanning five years, when a certain number of a single futures is available to cover the maturity. The answer, as always, comes down to basis risk and liquidity.

The LIBOR reflects this private debt risk better. Basis risk is not zero, but it is much smaller than that faced with T-note futures hedges. The other advantage is the liquidity and flexibility offered by Eurodollar futures. As important as this midmaturity private debt market is, it is still only a part of a larger, more complicated world. It may not be big enough to support its own contract, and so the business gets placed very efficiently in Eurodollars. Drawing on liquidity built by a myriad of different commercial participants, the strip hedger takes an imperfect contract and molds it to its particular requirements.

What happens if the span of the Eurodollar futures is not long enough to cover the risk of the cash exposure? The strategy of stacking addresses this problem.

Suppose that the prices in Table 5.1 represented the full array of contracts available but that the hedger in the previous strip example wanted two years of coverage instead of just one. The first step in solving this problem is to construct "shadow prices" representing what the futures prices would be if the full array of contracts had been available. Table 5.5 extends Table 5.1 to include those shadow prices. The basis for these estimated prices is the cash market yield curve. From the term structure relationships you can show that:

$$(1 + {}_{15}r_{18}) = (1 + {}_0r_{18})/(1 + {}_0r_{15}) \qquad (5.21)$$

That is, the expected 3-month rate of interest 15 months from now is completely determined by today's 18- and 15-month rates. Similar equations may be constructed for any future quarterly value.

Table 5.5
Hypothetical Eurodollar Prices Extended to Include Contracts That Will Be Listed in the Future

Month	Year	Price	Yield
Sept	0	91.58	8.42
Dec	0	91.51	8.49
Mar	1	91.45	8.55
June	1	91.40	8.60
Sept	1	91.35	8.65
Dec	1	91.31	8.69
Mar*	2	91.27	8.73
June*	2	91.23	8.77
Sept*	2	91.19	8.81

*contracts not listed at time of hedge

The expected capital and interest for each quarter can be calculated as it was for the strip example. For the additional December contract, the optimal hedge would be long 111 contracts, and the position would continue to grow across the remaining months: 113, 115, and 119 in the hypothetical contracts. In fact, since the year 2 contracts do not exist, these 347 contracts would be *stacked* on top of the existing December 1 contract positions until the new contracts were listed.

Each quarter as the next new contract is listed, part of the stack is broken off and rolled into a newly listed contract (Table 5.6). The optimal number of contracts for the original month are left, and the balance rolled forward via a spread contract. This process is continued until the months completely covering the hedge period are listed, and then the hedge is entirely in place.

The success of stacking and rolling depends on only one factor, the stability of the intermonth spreads. If new contracts are rolled into at a spread different from that prevailing in the Table 5.5 shadow prices, there will be a basis risk to the hedge. The closer the actual spreads are to that originally predicted, the more efficient the hedge.

The risks from the strategy come from wild swings in the yield curve. For the buyer in the example, the worst thing that could happen would be for the yield curve to invert. If the projected yield spread went from 4 points under to 8 points over, the hedge would have lost 12 points independent of the price level. Fortunately for Eurodollars, over much of their life the back-month spreads have

Table 5.6
Rolling a Stacked Hedge

Quarter	Contract	Hedge Amount	Optimal Contracts	Q1	Q2	Q3	Q4
1	Dec 0	$100.00 Mil.	101	101	101	101**	101**
2	Mar 1	$102.15 "	103	103	103	103	103**
3	June 1	$104.35 "	106	106	106	106	106
4	Sept 1	$106.62 "	109	109	109	109	109
5	Dec 1	$108.98 "	111	458	111	111	111
6	Mar 2*	$111.37 "	113	–	347	113	113
7	June 2*	$113.83 "	115	–	–	234	115
8	Sept 2*	$116.35 "	119	–	–	–	119

* contracts not listed at time of hedge
** contracts which would have expired in the example

been remarkably well behaved, and stacking has been effective. Figure 5.1 shows the evidence of stacking. The most distant contract has 64 percent higher open interest than the penultimate contract month.

5.4.5 Caps and Collars

In each of the previous short-rate examples, the goal was to fix a rate at some point in the future. For the trader who has an opinion on the market and wants to act on it, a futures hedge may not be the best solution.

A bank may offer to its borrowing customer the following terms: $10 million will be available to you in June six months from now. You will repay the obligation in 91 days, and the rate will be 50 points over LIBOR, the LIBOR rate being fixed versus the June Eurodollar future at any time of your choice between now and the borrowing date. Under no circumstances will the rate exceed 10.5 percent.

This complicated offer may look like a free lunch to the borrower. If he thinks rates are going up, he can fix the price now. If the contrary opinion prevails, the price fixing can be postponed, but even if the borrower is wrong, the maximum rate of 10.5 percent forms a cap on the loan's cost.

To the bank the transaction is a combination of a basis commitment (50 points over LIBOR) and a short put. If yields go up rapidly (prices fall), the bank is committed to supplying funds at a maximum cost of 10.5 percent even if the cost of their funds is higher. Figure 5.2 depicts the choices in terms of the interest rate paid.

The bank can do this by buying a put on a Eurodollar future for a maturity closely corresponding to the six-month commitment date. Suppose that the June 90.00 put is trading at 20 points. If the bank evaluates the creditworthiness of the customer at 25 points over LIBOR, offering the funds at 50 points over with a cap provides enough cushion to finance the purchase of the put and tuck away a little extra. The cap loan is really a basis trade with an embedded option. The price of the option is captured in the size of the basis.

What happens after three months if rates have indeed fallen and the borrower decides to fix the contract rate? Now the bank has no use for the put but must instead be able to acquire funds at the current value of the June futures price. The bank could sell the June futures to lock in its cost of funds and sell back the put. Even if prices had dropped and three months had expired, there would still be some value left in the put transaction that would be an extra profit in the deal. By fixing the basis at 50 points the bank has sold a six-month option. If the customer wants to fix prices early and forego the balance of the option value, there is no reason for the bank to ignore and throw away the remaining time value. Once these steps are over, the borrower's cost of funds are fixed and the bank is fully hedged.

The establishment of the hedge by the bank could also be done in less than two steps. Recalling the arbitrage relationships in Section 3.5.3, adding a short call to

Figure 5.2
Borrowing with a Cap

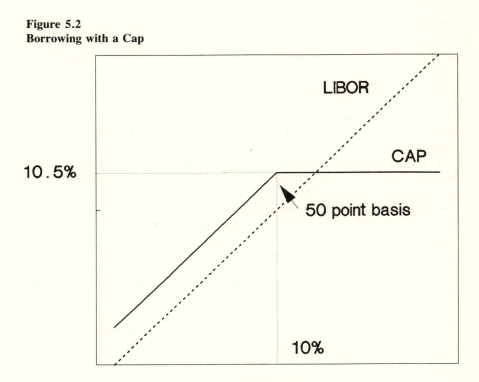

a long put (same strike) produces a synthetic short future. Selling the June 90.00 call while holding the long 90.00 put would still capture the remaining time value and lock in the futures price just as effectively as the two-step approach. Even if the buyer of the call exercises the option early, the bank will still be protected since it will be assigned a short futures position upon exercise.

The borrower facing this choice should not think of the cap loan as a free lunch but instead should evaluate it in terms of its component costs. If it can find another bank that will lend to it at 18 points over LIBOR with the same price fixing arrangement but no cap, it should take this deal and buy its own Eurodollar option. If the option costs 20 points, the net savings would immediately be 12 points over the basis including the cap. Furthermore, if the borrower fixes before the option expires, the put can be sold for whatever value it has left, further increasing the savings.

Operationally, every borrower should evaluate the terms of cap loans in this way to insure that they are priced competitively. But there still may be practical considerations that drive the borrower into a cap loan rather than constructing the pieces of the hedge separately. As irrational as it may sound, some financial officers may not have explicit authority to buy options. Option premiums are expensive and are viewed doubly so after the fact if the insurance provided was not needed. Burying an option premium, even an expensive one, into a basis hides the reality a bit, and the borrower can be given credit for negotiating a cap guarantee from the bank. No economist would condone such an uneconomic activity, but the reality of many firms is that their ignorance in policy about options and futures often comes at a heavy price.

The borrower in the cap example may have the authority to trade options directly but may find the cost too high relative to the expectation about future rates. Suppose that the June Eurodollar futures is priced at 91.00, implying a 9.00 percent rate. Capping that rate at 10.00 percent would require the purchase of the out-of-the-money 90.00 put, for, say, 20 points. If the borrower's opinion about rates suggested a low probability that rates would fall below 7.5 percent, a subsidy plan to the hedge can be developed.

In addition to buying the 90.00 put, a 92.50 call could be sold. If the call premium was 8 points, the net expense would be 12 points. The array of outcomes expressed in rates is given in Figure 5.3. Between rates of 7.5 and 10.0

Figure 5.3
Borrowing with a Collar

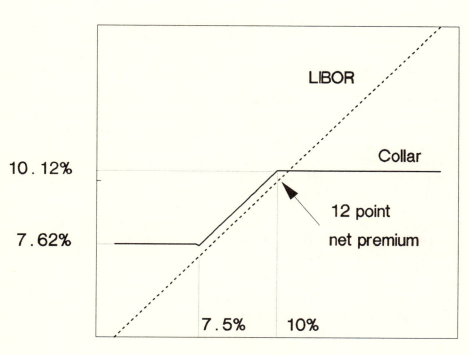

percent, the borrowing costs fluctuate freely, but beyond either extreme they are locked at the limits plus the 12 point premium.

Collars may be adjusted to fit any width band desired. As the strike prices move closer together, the range of fluctuations is restricted until at the limit with equal strikes the equivalent of a futures lock is formed. The effectiveness of the collar strategy comes from the reduction of the variance at modest expense, but it should be applied only when there is a market opinion that rates may decline. Without that probability, there is no reason to allow any variance, and the rate should be fixed with futures.

Caps and collars have been described in terms of single contracts, but there is no reason to so limit the discussion. If protection is needed for a six- or nine-month period, a strategy combining the principles of caps and collars with those of strips can work well. There is an active OTC market in medium-term caps and collars, and it is made possible by the existence of liquid Eurodollar options on futures extending several quarters.

5.5 LONG-TERM INSTRUMENTS

In the United States, trading interest-rate instruments past the maturities covered by Eurodollar futures has generally meant CBOT T-bonds. The exchanges that have T-note contracts or other shorter term vehicles would like to change this situation, but the overwhelming superiority of the bond contract in the first decade of its existence suggests that it will not be displaced easily. In all of the examples that follow, T-bond futures and options are used, but if the underlying instrument that the reader is considering might have a lower basis risk with a T-note contract, the techniques described below are still valid if applied to note futures.

Before strategies are discussed, the pricing of the T-bond futures should be understood. Unlike the Eurodollar futures contract, which is cash settled, T-bond futures call for delivery of an 8 percent coupon, U.S. Treasury bond with at least 15 years to maturity or, if callable, at least 15 years to the earliest call date. The nominal value of the contract is $100,000. This does not mean that the deliverer can provide only 8 percent coupon bonds, just that all bonds delivered will be converted back to this hypothetical 8 percent standard.

For each of the deliverable bonds, the CBOT publishes a conversion factor applicable to a particular contract. These factors are a function of the coupon and the time to maturity, the object being to normalize a disparate variety of instruments to a common standard.

Comparing two instruments demonstrates the process. Consider the $9\frac{7}{8}$ percent Treasuries maturing November 15, 2015, and the $10\frac{5}{8}$ percent bonds maturing August 15, 2015. The latter bonds pay $10,625 in interest each year, the former $9,875. The high-coupon bond should be worth more, and this is reflected in the conversion rates. Placing these coupons and an 8 percent yield into Equation 5.15, keeping in mind the time remaining to maturity and the accrued interest, gives the price of the bond normalized to an 8 percent yield. Divide this price by $100,000 and you get the conversion rates. This calculation is done for every deliverable bond for every contract date to get the conversion factors.[9]

Once the conversion factors are known, the invoice price on the futures delivery is directly available:

$$PI = \$1,000 * F * CF \qquad (5.22)$$

where PI = "principle invoice"
F = futures settlement price
CF = conversion factor

This covers only the principle amount. The accrued interest would also be paid.

The March 1988 final settlement price was 91–22 (91 $\frac{22}{32}$). This means that the principle invoice for the two bonds in question would be:

$$9\tfrac{7}{8}, \quad 11/15/2015$$
$$PI = \$1,000 * 91.6875 * 1.2073$$
$$= \$110,694.32$$
$$10\tfrac{5}{8}, \quad 08/15/2015$$
$$PI = \$1,000 * 91.6875 * 1.2892$$
$$= \$118,203.52$$

It is not surprising that the higher coupon bond is priced above the lower, since the greater coupon is worth considerably more.

For anyone contemplating participating in the delivery process, such a calculation would be performed for every bond available for delivery. Usually, more than 30 bonds are available for delivery at any time. Once their converted invoice prices are calculated they are compared to the current cash value. Anyone wanting to deliver will find the bond in the cash market that is cheapest to deliver. For example, if the 9 $\frac{7}{8}$ coupon bond could be bought at $111,000 and the 10 $\frac{5}{8}$ bond at $118,400, the costs of delivering the two bonds would be $306 and $197, respectively. The 10 $\frac{5}{8}$ coupon bond would be the more likely delivery instrument since it is less costly. Note that accrued interest does not affect the decision because it affects both the cash purchase and futures delivery equally.

The concept of cheapest to deliver is also important throughout the life of the instrument. Since only one bond is likely to be "cheapest" to deliver, the market tracks the cash prices versus the implied principle invoice value closely. The futures market will be priced against the bond expected to be cheapest to deliver at expiration. As interest rates shift, the expected delivery bond can change also. This feature increases basis risk by making it less certain what influences the market will be reflecting.

Another interesting feature of the CBOT T-bond contract is that the last trading day is seven business days before the last business day of the contract month, whereas the last delivery day falls on the last business day of the month. What this does is provide the short an option. Suppose that a short holds 100 contracts worth of the cheapest-to-deliver bond on the last trading day against 100 short lots of futures. It would seem appropriate to make delivery promptly and move on the next transaction. In fact, since the short is perfectly hedged against price risk, it pays to wait. There is always the possibility that conditions will change sufficiently to make another bond cheapest to deliver against the contract. If that happens, the short would sell the current inventory in the cash market at the suddenly favorable cash price and buy the new "cheapest" bond for delivery. In this way the shift in basis is captured as an extra profit.

If such a shift among deliverable bonds does not occur, the short is no worse off delivering the inventory. The deliverer either gains with a shift or does not lose without one. This is a classic option risk profile, and it remains only to determine how the premium is paid. Not surprisingly, it is embedded in the final basis between the futures price at expiration and the cheapest-to-deliver bond on that day.[10]

The basis risk on bonds is a fascinating subject that few but professional traders are expert in. The tricks the basis can play form tremendous trading opportunities for the knowledgeable but should be carefully apprised by the more routine trader. As delivery approaches, unpredictable elements in the basis sometimes accelerate, and prudent hedgers have learned that in T-bond futures, like most delivery contracts, it is wise to roll hedges forward well in advance of expiration and leave the deliveries to the experts. The open interest chart in Figure 5.1 showed how prevalent such rollovers can be with even three weeks of trading remaining.

5.5.1   Basic Principles of Bond Hedging

As has been previously shown, debt instruments come in a variety of coupons, maturities, and qualities. The success of the CBOT T-bond contract, which prices the cheapest-to-deliver Treasury based on a hypothetical 8 percent, 20-year instrument, suggests just how broadly the applications can be drawn. Tying a 30-year, $12\frac{1}{2}$ percent coupon bond to the futures simply involves the careful breakdown of the price and yield behavior of the two instruments. Once the comovement is identified, setting up an appropriate hedge is direct. Holders of inventories of cash bonds could be concerned about higher rates and an erosion of value. Short T-bond futures are the answer. For traders anticipating the purchase of bonds some time in the future, long anticipatory hedges are the answer. Whether long or short, the hedging effectiveness depends on the accurate evaluation of the cash and futures instruments.

The sophistication that has evolved in the 1980s relating cash instruments to bond futures and options has been impressive. The first examples given are based on the wisdom that prevailed in the early part of the decade. Much of it is still valid, but experience has shown that the residual basis risk can be costly, and so more refined techniques involving duration and convexity have evolved. The common theme throughout the examples is to know how the cash instrument behaves. With that knowledge, very effective risk management programs can be constructed.

The earliest hedging technique was one-for-one dollar matching. Cash bonds would be matched in terms of nominal value, with $100,000 in face value hedged with one contract. Anyone holding $1 million in 20-year bonds yielding 8 percent found this an effective approach. Unfortunately, the population of such hedgers was minuscule. The dollar value of a 30-year, 14 percent coupon does not move one-for-one with the T-bond contract. To address this, a refinement calculates a hedge ratio based on the current *cash* prices. This approach is a big improvement over nominal dollar matching, but it still has major deficiencies when confronted with a significant move in rates. A more precise approach was called for and quickly developed.

Regression analysis is used to establish the historical link between the price of the cash bond in question (or portfolio) and the T-bond future. The approach relies on the availability of a time series of cash market data, which for Treasury securities is not a difficult problem. The data should be grouped according to the perspective of the potential hedge. If the risk to be managed spans a month, monthly data should be used. If the trade will only last a day or two, monthly data are of considerably less use. Indeed, to the extent it would present a misleading picture of the potential reduction in basis risk, monthly data might be worse than useless. It is also important that the cash and futures data be synchronous. A regression of the following form should be run over a set of data the researcher thinks is relevant.

$$DCP_t = a + bDFP_t + u_t \qquad (5.23)$$

where DCP_t = change in the cash price, period t
 $\quad\quad DFP_t$ = change in the futures price, period t
 $\quad\quad a$ = regression intercept term
 $\quad\quad b$ = slope of the regression
 $\quad\quad u_t$ = error term

If the data frequency is monthly, the regression period might span several years. If daily or weekly data are employed, shorter data periods may be equally effective. Here, as in the estimation of volatility for option studies, a careful researcher will be suspicious if the regression results are terribly sensitive to the sample period chosen.

The regression is expressed in terms of price changes because that is what is most important to match. The hedger wants to know if the price of T-bond futures changes $10, how much should one expect the cash bond to change? If the answer is $15, the estimate of b, the slope, in Equation 5.23 will be 1.5, and that will be the hedge ratio based on the historical comovement of the instruments. For every $200,000 in cash bonds, the matching position is three futures.

The regression approach is very effective for small changes in yields, because most often the transference between futures and cash is nearly linear for such a range. Alden Toevs and David Jacob (1986) discussed how, as yield changes expand, linear models can provide only an approximation to the behavior in the neighborhood of the current rate. They discussed adding nonlinear terms to an equation like Equation 5.23 to capture any curvature. In such models the optimal hedge ratio becomes dependent on the current level of price. Positions must be monitored and adjustments made periodically as the hedge ratio changes.

A problem arises when the comparison is being made between some cash bonds, like corporate securities, and T-bond futures. The problem can be the paucity of market data on the cash instrument. When there is insufficient data on which to base a regression analysis, it is necessary to estimate the hedge ratio from the characteristics of the bond.

There are two components to this approach. One must first look to see what the expected yield change of the cash bond is with respect to the yield of the underlying asset of the futures and then factor in the "price sensitivity" (Kopprasch, 1981; Figlewski, 1986). The trader hypothesizes that if the yield on the cash instrument moves X, the yield on the futures should move Y. With these respective changes in yields, the resultant price changes can be determined and compared to find a hedge ratio.

With parallel shifts in the yield curve, yield sensitivity reflects the expectation that a 10-basis-point move in the cash market yield will be accompanied by a 10-point move in the futures yield; X equals Y. For many bonds this is a reasonable expectation given historical performance, but it should not always be automatically assumed. This ratio can be determined through regression analysis, or it can reflect an anticipation of how the yield curve will change through time. For cash instruments with different times to maturity from that of the futures contract, a trader with a market opinion on the slope of the yield curve could express it in a controlled way through this variable.

Suppose that, for simplicity in the first example, the yield sensitivity equals 1. Yield curve shifts will be parallel over the relevant range. The cash bond in question is the May 2004, 12 $\frac{3}{8}$ coupon, currently priced at 129 $\frac{16}{32}$, and the comparison is made to the hypothetical 20-year, 8 percent coupon bond behind the T-bond future. Let the respective cash market yields be 8.84 and 8.96 percent.

The first step calculates the price change that results for the cash bond if the yield changes by a small amount, 0.10. Equation 5.15 is solved for the two yields 8.79 and 8.89 percent, which bracket the current yield. The price with the low yield is $130,034.40 and with the higher yield, $129,020.50, a change of $1,013.90. The same equation is then solved for the 20-year, 8 percent coupon bond at yields of 8.91 and 9.01 percent. The price change in this case equals $853.11 ($90,827.20 − $89,974.09). The hedge ratio equals:

$$h = DCP/DFP \qquad (5.24)$$

which in this case equals 1.19. The optimal hedge occurs when the number of futures contracts, C, equals:

$$C = h * (\$C/\$F) \qquad (5.25)$$

where $\$C$ = the face value of the cash position
$\$F$ = the face value of the futures

If the portfolio of bonds in question had a $20 million face value, the optimal hedge would be 238 contracts (= 1.19 * $20 million/$100,000).

To improve the hedge, instead of comparing the cash bond to the hypothetical 20-year, 8 percent coupon, the cheapest-to-deliver bond would be examined. If such a comparison were made the hedge ratio would have to be adjusted by the CBOT conversion factor for that cash bond. The hedge ratio would become:

$$h = (DCP/DCheapP) * \text{Conversion factor} \qquad (5.26)$$

where $DCheapP$ = Change in the price of the cheapest-to-deliver bond. For anyone following the T-bond futures closely, this extra step should be an easy, but important, refinement.

What would a hedge look like for an 11 $\frac{5}{8}$ percent coupon bond with six years remaining, currently yielding 8.52 percent, where the trader believes that the yield curve will become more volatile on the short end over the expected life of the trade? That is, no matter which direction rates take, the expectation is that the yield of the bond with six years remaining will move 25 percent more than the base T-bond.

The relative yield factor is 1.25, reflecting the trader's expectation. The price factor is calculated in the same way as the previous example. In this case a 10-basis-point yield change around the current value produces a $503.60 change in the value of the cash bond. This is to be expected since the price of instruments with less time to maturity are less sensitive to a given yield change than are longer term securities. The $503.60 change divided by the previously determined $853.11 change in the futures' bond, produces a ratio of 0.59. This price ratio is multiplied by the yield factor, 1.25, to give the hedge ratio, which equals 0.74.

Suppose that the trader had $20 million, face value, in these instruments. The optimal number of short futures to protect them would be 148 (= ($20 million/$100,000) * .74). If the relative yield effect had been assumed to be 1.00 instead of 1.25, the number of futures would have been 118.

To see the difference in the effectiveness of the hedge with different relative yield factors, consider the outcome presented in Table 5.7.

In Table 5.7 futures prices are presented as a percentage of par with minimum increments of $\frac{1}{32}$ of a percent (90–13 stands for 90 $\frac{13}{32}$ and $\frac{1}{32}$ = $31.25 per

Table 5.7
Hedging $20 Million in 11⅜ Percent Bonds (with Six Years to Maturity)

A.   Relative Yield Factor = 1.25

Futures position = 148 contracts short

	Original		Subsequent		Gain/(Loss)
	Price	Yield	Price	Yield	
Cash	114.35	8.52%	108.40	9.82%	(1.262 million)
Futures	90-13	8.96%	82-5	10.00%	1.221 million
			net gain/(loss)		(41 thousand)

B.   Relative Yield Factor = 1.00

Futures position = 118 contracts short

	Original		Subsequent		Gain/(Loss)
	Price	Yield	Price	Yield	
Cash	114.35	8.52%	108.40	9.82%	(1.262 million)
Futures	90-13	8.96%	82-5	10.00%	.974 million
			net gain/(loss)		(288 thousand)

contract). Users of these markets should be equally comfortable with either decimal presentations of price or the traditional futures method.

The yield shift considered worked out very close to the original expectation of a 1.25 ratio. The cash instrument's yield went up 130 basis points, and the futures gained 104. If the hedge had incorporated this expectation (case a), the cash market loss to the inventory of over $1.25 million would have been reduced to a loss of 41,000. If the traditional one-for-one yield ratio had been used (case b), the coverage would have been good, but the net loss would have been almost $300,000.

This example gave a happy conclusion to action based on market opinion, but its message was broader. Shifts in the slope of the yield curve are commonplace and difficult to predict, but that does not abrogate the responsibility of the manager to make decisions in this area. Hedges that blindly rely on parallel shifts are bound to have slippage in their effectiveness. If good information about the slope of the yield curve is available, it should be incorporated, and the entire management team should be aware of the implications of the decision.

In the example, if the rates had gone up, but in a parallel fashion, case b would have been the superior hedge. The extra short futures position would have produced a windfall profit in case a, but if rates had fallen in a parallel fashion, case a would have generated losses relative to case b. All such outcomes should be analyzed before a position is established.

5.5.2   Covered Writing of T-Bond Call Options

One of the most popular strategies involving T-bond options is a program of covered writing by funds holding large inventories of Treasury instruments. Used as a mechanism to enhance yields by selling time, the fund managers who do this are expressing a view that rates will be relatively stable with a slight bias toward weakly lower rates.

The intuition of the strategy is appealing. By selling at-the-money or out-of-the-money calls against the portfolio, option premiums representing pure time value are generated. If yields go up, prices fall, and the collected premiums offer some cushion against the capital losses that result. With flat yields, the premiums are pure income enhancement, and if yields slump sufficiently so that prices climb through the call strike level, the bonds will be called away from the owner but at a profit in terms of the underlying bond's price and the time value collected.

Deciding which call strikes to write depends on the market opinion covering the period of the option. If the writer is bullish, the strikes will be higher, because there is no desire to have the options called away too soon, limiting capital gains. Those with a flat price outlook should write the at- or just out-of-the-money calls to maximize the collection of premium. If the bondholder is a strong bear, this is the wrong strategy.

To see these features more clearly, Figure 5.4 shows what happens when a short call is combined with a long cash position. Recalling the synthetic futures and options positions in Table 3-1, adding a short call to a long future is the equivalent to being short a naked put at the same strike price. If prices go up, the gain is limited to the premium received, and if prices tumble, the loss will be point-for-point once the premium is exhausted.

The risk profile of the cash bond portfolio against which calls have been written is not significantly different from the synthetic futures option. The key comparison is between the lines representing long cash and the synthetic short put. For a bond fund that has the first risk profile by its very charter, the shift to the second can be very attractive under a variety of expected market scenarios.

Deciding how many options to sell is a problem very similar to that described in finding the optimal futures hedge in the preceding section. If prices climb and the option on futures is exercised, the writer is assigned one short futures contract at that strike price. If that possibility occurs, the writer will want to be sure that

Figure 5.4
Covered Call Writing

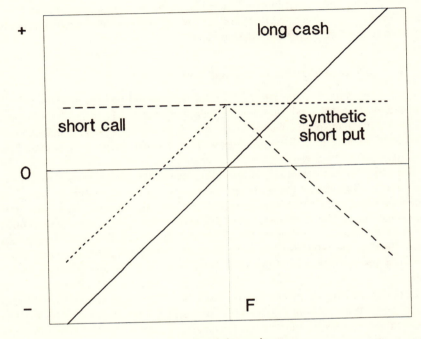

profit/loss

underlying price

the number of short futures accurately reflects the dollar exposure of the cash instruments. Solving for the optimal futures hedge gives the correct number of calls to be written against any given portfolio. Deciding which strike price to write is a matter of market expectation. Critics of covered call writing argue that if the options are priced fairly, there is no long-run gain from any writing strategy. Gains from selling "time" will eventually be offset by the foregone profits when the bonds are called away. In the long run, this may all be true, but the persistent activities of a group of covered call writers suggests otherwise.

These call writers do not in all likelihood mechanically write calls. Instead, they are given the right to employ such strategies, and whether or not to write and at what strike prices, is part of their management decision-making responsibility. Covered call writing is just another tool at their disposal. Just as they exercise their market opinion in deciding which bonds to add to their portfolio, they can employ covered writing when it best fits their market perspective. If their judgement is correct, or if the options are priced a little above fair value, covered writing will enhance yields, and in any case, it will certainly lower the variance of the return.

5.5.3   Duration

The time dimension of bonds is most easily thought of as term to maturity, but this is a slippery characterization. A five-year zero-coupon instrument is a decidedly different creature from a five-year, 7 percent coupon, or a five-year, 12 percent coupon. Frederick Macaulay was dissatisfied with term to maturity as a useful measure of time, seeking instead a concept that would unify instruments with the common characteristic. *Duration* was developed by Macaulay (1938) as a standardized measure expressed in terms of the maturity of a zero-coupon bond of comparable risk. The five-year zero in this paragraph has a duration of five years, but each of the two coupon instruments has a shorter duration because part of the return is received before maturity. Duration captures the timing of the payment streams and weights them according to their importance to the overall return.

The problem is best seen by recognizing that a coupon bond is the exact analogue to a portfolio of zeros maturing at different times. Start with a $1,000 face value, three-year instrument with a 9 percent semiannual coupon. This can be thought of as a portfolio of six zeros, the first five maturing in six-month intervals and paying $45, plus a final $1,045 zero returning the original capital and the final coupon at the end of three years.

No matter what the current yield is, a zero coupon bond has a duration equal to its maturity time. To find the duration of the "portfolio," the weighted average of the individual durations is calculated, where the weights are the shares of the individual discounted zero coupon bonds in the entire portfolio.

Table 5.8 gives the duration of the three-year, 9 percent coupon bond when it is priced at par.[11] The table also demonstrates the analogy to a series of zero coupon bonds. If one was to buy a zero paying $45 in six months, it would cost $43.062 at current yields. The prices of the remaining zeros in the portfolio are in column 3. If one bought the entire group, the portfolio would be worth $1,000, and the respective share in the portfolio of each component is in column 4. These are the weights that are multiplied by the time spans (equal to the duration of the zeros) in a sum to get the total duration.

Since the total duration is a weighted average of the individual components' durations, the largest of which is 3.0 years, it is not surprising that the value is 2.7 years. The early coupon payments push forward the effective time of the instrument.

A general formula to calculate duration incorporates the following steps:

1. Discount each payment by the relevant discount factor.
2. Calculate the share of the total return represented by each discounted payment. These are the weights.

3. Multiply each time of payment by its weight.
4. Sum all components in step 3.

$$D = \frac{C_1}{(1 + r_1)^{t_1}} \frac{t_1}{P_0} + \frac{C_2}{(1 + r_2)^{t_2}} \frac{t_2}{P_0} + \cdots \qquad (5.27)$$

$$+ \frac{C_{n-1}}{(1 + r_{n-1})^{t_{n-1}}} \frac{t_{n-1}}{P_0} + \frac{(C_n + F)}{(1 + r_n)^{t_n}} \frac{t_n}{P_0}$$

where C_i = ith coupon paid
        r_i = annualized discount factor spanning the ith payment
        t_i = time of ith payment in fraction of a year
     P_0 = current price of bond
     F = face value of bond

In the table, it was assumed that interest rates were constant, that the yield curve was flat at the current rate. A more precise measure of duration allows for each coupon's discount factor to reflect the slope of the yield curve. In many cases the changes in the result are modest, but with the ease with which modern

Table 5.8
Duration of a Three-Year, $1,000, 9 Percent Coupon Bond

(1)	(2)	(3) Discounted Cash Flow	(4) Price Weight	(5) Price-Weighted Maturity
T	Payment			
.5	$45	$43.062	.043*	.022**
1.0	45	41.208	.041	.041
1.5	45	39.433	.039	.059
2.0	45	37.735	.038	.075
2.5	45	36.110	.036	.090
3.0	1045	802.451	.802	2.407
		$1000.000	1.000	2.695

    *   = $43.062/$1000

    ** = .043 * .5

spreadsheet programs can produce tables like 5.8, it is a good practice to include the refinement.

Duration is an additive concept. Just as the coupon bond's duration was found to be a weighted average of individual zeros, the duration of any bond portfolio can be expressed as a weighted average of the durations of the component bonds. The weights are once again the share of the bond in the total portfolio. This is a very convenient feature since it allows for the rapid recalculation of the total duration whenever bonds are added or subtracted from the total portfolio.

The three factors determining duration are: (1) the size of the cash flows, (2) the timing of those flows, and (3) the current yield curve. For most coupon bonds the first two elements are fixed, leaving duration to be a function of current rates. As the yield curve shifts up, the duration of a bond falls because of the heavier discounting impacting the more distant payment streams.

The impact of interest rate changes on the duration of a bond can be small for short-term bonds. In the three-year bond example, if the interest rate doubled, duration would only fall from 2.695 to 2.654. For such instruments the simple duration measure is a remarkably robust characteristic, but care must be taken with longer term bonds. Suppose that the 9 percent semiannual coupon bond matured in 10.0 years instead of 3.0. Priced at par its duration is 6.80 years. If the yield doubled, the bond's duration would fall to 5.78, a loss of an entire year. In a changing rate environment, the duration of the bonds in a portfolio must be monitored closely.

To give a flavor of how the interaction of coupon, yield, and maturity combine to influence duration, Table 5.9 gives the duration of a variety of bonds. For each of the three maturities examined (3, 10, and 20 years), yields and coupons are varied around par values. The power of distant discounting is demonstrated clearly with the case of a 9 percent, 20-year bond. At par its duration is less than half its maturity.

Duration's most direct use is as an approximate guide to how much a bond's price will change for a given yield change. It is the *elasticity* of a bond's price with respect to yield.

$$DP/P = -D * dr/(1 + r) \tag{5.28}$$

or

$$dP = -D * P * dr/(1 + r)$$

An example from Table 5.9 will demonstrate the elasticity concept. Start with the ten-year, 9 percent coupon bond priced at par. Let the yield move from 9.2025 to 9.3025 percent. The change in r (dr) is 0.001, and $dr/(1 + r) =$ 0.000916. Multiply this value by $P(= \$1,000)$ and $-D(= 6.80)$, giving a value of \$6.23. The new price of the bond is expected to be \$993.77. Actually running

Table 5.9
Duration of Different Bonds

Time	Coupon	Current Yield		
		6.09%	9.2025%	12.36%
	6%	2.79*	2.78	2.77
3 year	9%	2.71	2.70*	2.68
	12%	2.64	2.62	2.61*
	6%	7.66*	7.35	7.01
10 year	9%	7.13	6.80*	6.45
	12%	6.77	6.43	6.08*
	6%	11.90*	10.44	9.04
20 year	9%	10.98	9.62*	8.35
	12%	10.44	9.15	7.97*

*   Duration of a bond priced at par.

the new yield through the bond pricing formula gives a value of $993.80, extremely close to the predicted.

If the yield change is larger, Equation 5.28 begins to break down, since it is technically accurate only for infinitessimally small changes in r. If the yield on the ten-year, 9 percent coupon bond jumped from 9.2025 to 12.36 percent, the expected decline in price would have been $196.61 ($= -6.80 * 1,000 * dr(1 + r)$). The actual loss would have been $172.05, below that which was predicted, because, as can be seen in the table, duration declined as the yield increased.

If duration was a constant, the trade-off between changes in interest rates and price would be constant as well. Such a situation is depicted in Figure 5.5 as a straight line, the slope of which is determined by D. The true price relationship is given by the dashed line, the slope of which at any point would be the newly calculated duration. This curvature is a primary element in the concept of immunization.

Figure 5.5
Curvature in Duration

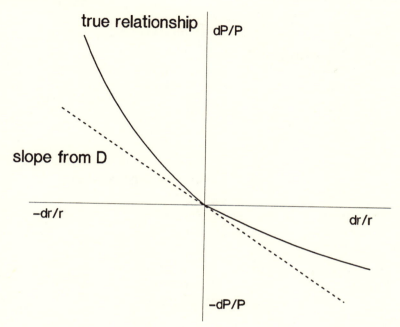

5.5.4   Immunization

A bond portfolio is said to be *immunized* over a target holding period when interest rate changes do not alter the target yield. If the holding period is five years, a five-year zero coupon bond will offer an immunized return equal to its current yield. A six-year zero presents a holding-period risk since the price of the bond at the end of the holding period may be too low to meet the initial investment objective. If a four-year zero is used, a reinvestment is required at maturity. If rates have fallen, this reinvestment may fall short of the target as well. Only with perfect matching is the return guaranteed.

By matching the duration of the asset and the liability, any wedge between the two can be secured. Suppose that the asset is the 10.0-year, 9 percent coupon bond currently priced at par. Its duration is 6.8 years. The ideal funding of the asset would come from the issuance of a 6.8-year zero coupon bond. Assume for the moment that it is also priced at par to yield 8.5 percent. The wedge in rates could reflect the quality difference between the borrower, who may be an individual or small firm, and the lender.

Once the coupon-bond asset is matched with the zero bond liability, the immediate risk picture looks like Figure 5.6. Changes in rates affect the zero

Figure 5.6
Locking In a Differential

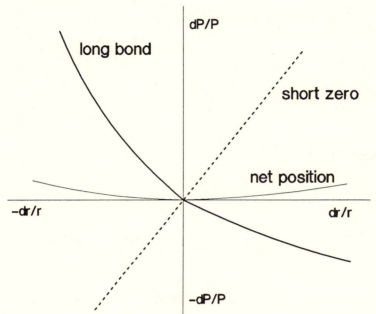

linearly and the coupon bond with a curvature. The net effect is that when rates rise, the coupon bond loses less in value than the zero, and when rates fall, the coupon bond gains more than the zero. Not only is the yield spread protected by this duration matching, but it is enhanced if the rates should move in either direction. Table 5.10 shows the changes in values for the two instruments assuming that the yield on the zero is always 70.25 basis points lower than the coupon bond to reflect the quality difference.

The curvature in the coupon bond is called *convexity,* and as a general rule you want your portfolio to be long convexity. If the asset has more curvature than the liability, the result will be like that shown in Figure 5.6.

If duration matching of assets and liabilities was as simple as this example, volume in the T-bond futures contract would be a fraction of its actual size. Complications come from the structure of the cash market. The 10.0-year, 9 percent coupon bonds may be commonplace, but zeros with a maturity of exactly 6.8 years are not. Placing such an odd issue may result in giving up part of the rate spread.

Another complication comes from the dynamic nature of the process. Suppose that a year passes and rates are completely unchanged. The zero now has a duration of 5.8 years, but the coupon bond's duration has fallen only to 6.3. This should have been foreseen since the duration of the coupon instrument must

Table 5.10
Prices of 9 Percent Coupon and Zero Coupon Bonds of Identical Duration

Yield of Coupon Bond	Price of Coupon Bond	Price of Zero	Difference
3%	$1517	$1492	$25
5%	1317	1308	9
7%	1151	1150	1
9.2025%	1000	1000	0
11%	896	894	2
13%	798	792	6
15%	715	702	13

decline to zero more slowly, spanning the entire decade. The asset may still hold a convexity advantage, but this pales in comparison to the very significant duration exposure caused by the evolving mismatch. To keep immunized, the portfolio would have to be rebalanced periodically. The temporal nature of rebalancing fits in very well with the use of T-bond futures.

Whenever there is a duration mismatch, or gap, between assets and liabilities, futures can be used to cover the exposure. Let the asset be a 20.00-year, 12 percent coupon bond, and the funding for that asset be provided by a 10.00-year, 12 percent coupon bond. If they are both currently at par, the durations of the two bonds are 10.44 years and 6.77 years, respectively. Let the funding be for $10 million.

The position is in peril because if yields increase, the losses on the 20-year bond will exceed those on the 10-year instrument. If it is a permanent shift up, when the first 10 years pass, the capital will have to be refinanced at a much higher cost.

To close this duration gap, equal to an exposure of a long 3.67 year zero bond, the owner of the portfolio should go short T-bond futures. Equation 5.28 gives the foundation for deciding how many contracts to sell.

$$dP_{20} = -D_{20} * P_{20} * dr/(1 + r) \qquad (5.29)$$

$$dP_{10} = -D_{10} * P_{10} * dr/(1 + r)$$

$$dP_F = -D_F * P_F * dr/(1 + r)$$

where P_{20} is the price of the 20-year bonds, P_{10} is the 10-year bonds, and P_F is the price of the futures contracts. D_i is the duration of the respective instruments. Since the portfolio will be long the 20-year bond and short the 10-year and the futures, the goal should be to find the number of futures so that the following equation holds.

$$dP_{20} = dP_{10} + dP_F \qquad (5.30)$$

To solve Equation 5.30, the duration of the cheapest-to-deliver bond on the futures and its delivery conversion factor must be known. The necessary steps are:

1. Compute the current "effective" price of the future. This equals today's futures price times the conversion factor for the cheapest-to-deliver bond.
2. Compute an implied yield to maturity for this cheapest-to-deliver bond from the expected delivery date of the futures contract.
3. Compute the cheapest-to-deliver bond's duration at delivery using the yield calculated in step two.

These steps result in the duration of the deliverable bond on the delivery date calculated at today's price. Rewriting Equation 5.30 in terms of the right hand side of Equation 5.29 gives:

$$D_{20} * P_{20} = D_{10} * P_{10} + D_F * P_F \qquad (5.31)$$

or

$$D_F * P_F = D_{20} * P_{20} - D_{10} * P_{10}$$

The interest rate terms all drop out because they are assumed to be equal. The allowances for nonparallel shifts would include an adjustment factor. Let the duration of the cheapest-to-deliver T-bond be eight years. Then Equation 5.31 becomes:

$$8 * P_F = 10.44 * (\$10 \text{ million}) - 6.77 * (\$10 \text{ million}) \qquad (5.32)$$

$$P_F = \$4,587,500$$

This is the short dollar exposure in the futures required to immunize the portfolio. If the current price is 92.00, or \$92,000 per contract, 50 contracts $(4,587,500/92,000 = 49.9)$ should be sold short to complete the immunization.

As time passes, or yields shift, the duration of the portfolio changes, necessitating a restructuring of the hedge. If the net duration gets longer, more T-bonds should be sold. As the duration gap exposure gets smaller, the hedge may be unwound. The advantage of the T-bond futures market is the tremendous liquidity that makes regular rebalancing an economically viable activity. Without these futures, such precise control over interest rate exposure would be impossible.

The reader should be aware that the examples presented here sometimes rely on simplifying assumptions, like flat yield curves and parallel shifts, to simplify the algebra. Much more detailed models have been developed, but these refined approaches are attacking interest rate risk management at a level of precision well beyond the fundamentals presented here. Fifteen years ago none of these hedging techniques was known, and today the number of knowledgeable practitioners is still small. The basics of duration hedging should be in the tool kit of every financial manager dealing with unmatched assets and liabilities. Moving beyond the basics should be the goal of anyone whose livelihood depends on extreme precision in capturing the price characteristics.

The vast majority of bond problems can be attacked effectively with the techniques presented above. The key point remains, as in all hedging problems, to understand inside-out the price behavior of the cash instrument to be hedged. In that way an effective futures hedge can be constructed and dynamically managed through time. Some interest rate instruments have posed special problems over the years and deserve expanded treatment. Mortgage-backed securities have proved particularly complex, but the general rules still apply. The next section presents the unique cash market behavior of these instruments.

5.6 HEDGING MORTGAGE INSTRUMENTS

In the 1950s and 1960s mortgage lending was a relatively easy affair. Savings and loan institutions used funds from short-term deposits to fund long-term fixed-rate mortgages. As long as the yield curve was upward sloping and stable, this prescription produced a healthy, growing industry. The 1970s, however, produced a rude shock to those firms that had counted on this steady stream of cheap short-term funds. It became painfully evident that the old risk management techniques, such as they were, would not suffice in the modern world.

Since the beginning of trading in interest rate futures contracts, exchanges and practitioners have recognized the difficult risk management problems posed by mortgage instruments. Quality differences and a resulting basis risk between mortgage instruments and T-bonds suggested that a specialized contract was possible, but the CBOT has struggled through several incarnations of a GNMA contract without lasting success. The pricing characteristics of the underlying securities never seemed to mesh well enough with whichever futures contract was trading to make any of them viable. The potential hedger is left with T-bond futures to meet any long-term requirements.

If basis risk was the only problem, mortgages would be no different from corporate bonds. A more fundamental issue is the problem of prepayment. As yields fall, two things are likely to happen. If housing activity is stimulated by falling rates, current borrowers are more likely to sell their existing homes and cash out the old mortgages. For those who do not move, there is the increased likelihood of refinancing. The problem this poses to the lender is that just as the mortgage's value is going up, it evaporates from the portfolio. When rates climb, there is a reduced probability of refunding.

The net result of this "prepayment problem" is that mortgage lenders are not only providing funds, but they are in a risk position where their potential downside is large, while the up side of the distribution is truncated. This is very much like the exposure provided by a short option, and evaluating that option is one of the most difficult problems in interest rate management.

A final problem has to do with the volatility of the yield curve. Nonparallel shifts in the yield curve can produce extreme volatility in the overall portfolio, sometimes inverting short rates over long. In such instances the traditional hedging techniques that rely on parallel shifts can be of limited use.

Solving these problems involves some of the most creative and thoughtful practitioners in the industry, because the stakes are huge. Individual institutions now face more interest rate risk than they would have ever thought possible in the 1960s. The cash market and futures and options market solutions to these issues are still evolving, but early examples have shown tremendous promise. All of the ideas share a common theme. Know the behavior of your portfolio under a wide range of possible outcomes and plan to allow for any eventuality. Understanding the risk profile of the instruments in question is key.

5.6.1   Mortgage Duration and Convexity

Savings and loan organizations historically might have had a large fraction of their deposits in instruments maturing in under two years, while the majority of their loans would have been fixed-rate long-term mortgages. Although this can be enormously profitable with an upward sloping yield curve, from a duration perspective, a significant gap existed that meant a large risk from shifting rates. The ability to close this gap became a top priority after the early 1970s experience.

The objective became one of matching payment and return streams more closely. One way to do this was to secure a larger fraction of necessary funding in long-term CDs rather than short-term deposits. This had the effect of lengthening the duration of the liabilities toward that of the asset. Another approach at the opposite end of the spectrum was to shift to floating-rate mortgages. This changed the effective term of the asset to bring it into closer alignment with the shorter term liabilities. As rates moved through time, the payment on the mortgage would move up or down parallel with the cost of funds. Both of these steps were important in narrowing the gap.

To the extent that the income streams from the mortgages did not exactly match the payments to the deposits, the net duration of the portfolio could be determined and hedged in the interest rate markets, as described in the previous section. Extreme care had to be taken to account for the possibility of nonparallel shifts in the yield curve. This would be covered by allowing a yield ratio to be different from one derived when comparing the expected moves in the cash and futures instruments, but there are limitations to this simple approach.

A bigger problem with mortgages comes from their option characteristics. Figure 5.7 shows the price-interest rate trade-offs for a portfolio of mortgages as compared with traditional coupon bonds with the same duration at the current price. Recall that duration is the slope of the price line at any point, and if duration increases as rates fall, the instrument is said to have positive convexity. The coupon bonds display positive convexity throughout the range of interest rate moves. The mortgages, by comparison, have convexity moving from positive, when rates increase, to strongly negative for the region covering yield declines. As rates fall, mortgages are prepaid, placing an effective ceiling on the degree of price appreciation. As rates increase, there are fewer prepayments, which adds to the ultimate earnings of the mortgage portfolio and eases some of the decline in price from higher yields. The effect, however, is not as dramatic on the up side as with falling rates.

If the mortgages are funded with zero coupon bonds of identical initial duration, the risk profile would be that found in Figure 5.8. Instead of having the

Figure 5.7
The Convexity of a Mortgage

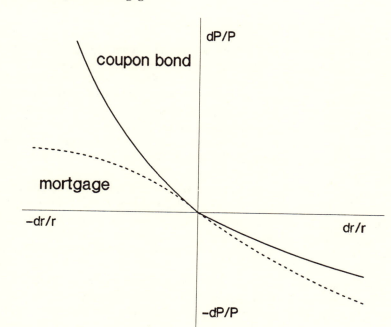

Figure 5.8
Hedging Mortgages with Zeros

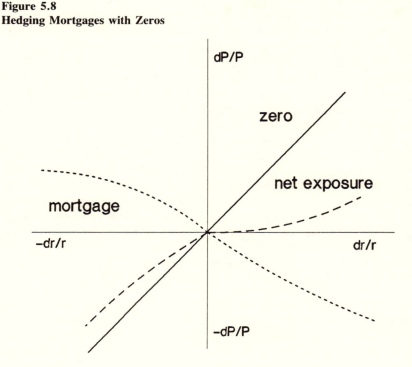

positive spread characterized in Figure 5.6 for an immunized bond, the "duration-hedged" mortgage portfolio shows great risk if rates should fall.

To address this problem it is necessary to match the convexity of the asset and liability. In this case the portfolio is short convexity, so to balance this dimension an appropriate number of call options would be bought. If rates went up, the calls would expire worthless, and some of the net returns of the position would have gone to pay the premium. If rates declined, the additional value of the calls would replace the deficiency in the mortgages because of the inherent negative convexity.

The basics of such hedging are direct, but the execution is difficult because of the highly variable behavior of the price of the mortgages. Great care should be taken in determining the price lines in Figure 5.8. Option models are being employed to price the inherent value of these instruments, but they also may be incomplete when it comes to nonparallel shifts in the yield curve or other structural changes.

One recent approach that shows considerable promise involves multifactor models of price sensitivity (Rudd, 1988). In this technique, the price of the portfolio is compared to that of a standardized basket, like a market index of bonds or the T-bond futures. The price is statistically analyzed to identify the contribution of term structure changes (level and slope), any imbedded options in the bond, any quality related spread factors, and any tax or liquidity effects. By identifying the contributors to an instrument's price, the risk can be identified and offset. Multifactor models are new in this area, but if the statistical properties can be established and verified through experience with a variety of rate environments, they have considerable potential in the evaluation of very complicated risk.

5.6.2   IOs and POs

There have been several specialized products created in the past few years from mortgages. Of particular interest to cash trading desks have been the derivative products called IOs (interest only) and POs (principal only) formed by breaking traditional fixed-rate mortgages into their component parts. If all of the mortgages are held until their expected payment day, POs are simply zero coupon bonds. However, with the probability of mortgage prepayments increasing with falling rates, the return on the PO can arrive with an uncertain timing. POs have positive duration; their value falls when rates go up and conversely.

IOs are fundamentally different, being only the pass-through of interest paid on the pool of mortgages. If rates go up, prepayments of mortgages slow down, and interest payments extend further through time. With declining rates, prepayments accelerate, and the IO stream of payments is cut off at the knees. IOs have negative duration; their value tends to climb with higher rates and conversely.

These instruments are important because they can be added to a mortgage portfolio to balance an undesirable characteristic, *if the pricing of the instrument is understood.* The price lines of IOs and POs are more complex than coupon bonds and can be more volatile separately than the mortgages from which they are derived.

When these instruments were first introduced, some firms would not participate in their trading because the risk characteristics were not well understood. Other firms scoffed at this attitude as they reaped large returns from buying packages of mortgages, breaking them into their IO and PO parts, and reselling them to buyers seeking certain unique characteristics. Any smugness quickly disappeared when a single Merrill Lynch trader generated massive losses totaling tens of millions of dollars from the activity. The mortgages had been purchased, priced incorrectly so that one-half sold out quickly (too quickly some say), and the other lingered in inventory. Either by design or through ignorance, the exposure was not hedged, and the resulting unfavorable yield shift produced headlines throughout the financial world.

The cash mortgage market will continue to evolve and create new products. The lesson of IOs and POs is one of risk control. It is unlikely that the management of Merrill Lynch understood the extent of their exposure in this trading. The complexity of the instruments offers no excuse. If a conscious decision to speculate on a yield shift is made, whatever the outcome is, it should not come as a surprise. Under no circumstances should a firm allow trading decisions to be made without a good grasp of the risk exposure involved.

5.6.3   Savings and Loan Institutions in the 1980s

In 1973–74, before the infant interest rate futures markets had taken their first steps, the yield curve inverted, federal interest rate ceilings chased deposits from S&Ls, and the thrift industry was thrown into a turmoil. After regaining some degree of normalcy in the middle part of the decade, inflation struck again in 1979–80, inverting the yield curve once more and sending many unhedged members of the thrift industry over the brink. Those who survived did so largely because their cash instrument management had improved dramatically in just a few years. A few had begun to use interest rate futures.

By the later half of the 1980s the savings and loan industry was again under attack. Failures were running at a record pace. Federal deposit insurance was being stretched to the limits. It appeared at first glance that the complexity of the new financial instruments had gotten away from the thrifts, causing a crisis of management that was nearly unparalleled in the post–World War II environment. From many quarters came the cry that interest rate hedging techniques needed to be used by broader sectors of the industry to stem the tide.

From the futures and options industry perspective, such suggestions were well directed and could only lead to improved stability in time. Unfortunately, unlike the episodes beginning in 1973 and 1979, the root cause of the problem in the 1980s was not volatility of interest rates. The term structure had remained in a carry for most of the 1980s with the spread between the longest and shortest rates rarely varying more than 100 basis points in a year. Any thrift just borrowing short and lending long over this period would have found one of the rare moments of the 1970s and 1980s when the old techniques would have still worked.

The reality of the thrift crisis of the late 1980s was one of credit quality, and the problems stemmed from poor judgment in the creation of loans. The major losing sectors were energy, farming, and commercial real estate in the Sun Belt. Just ten years earlier each of these sectors had a ''can't miss'' tag on it, and there was no shortage of funds for expansion.

Farmland in the later part of the 1970s was a classic example of the problem. Prime corn/soybean land was selling at a price whereby the gross receipts of the sale of above-average-sized crops would not cover the interest on the mortgage used to acquire it. Farmers who expanded in this period did so by taking the returns from existing parcels to subsidize the purchase of the new land. When confronted with the apparent risk in the purchase price, the reply typically cited past appreciation or relied on a logic that the price of land could not go down since ''they weren't making it anymore.'' Once crop prices fell even slightly, the contraction set in, and paper fortunes were quickly wiped out.

The lenders to the farmers and the energy concerns shared their optimism and were among the first to champion their continued expansion plans. After all, many of the bankers had backgrounds very similar to the people to whom they were lending the funds. By the time the full impact of the cycle hit home, there was nothing left for interest rate management techniques to do. It made no difference that the loans were priced to yield 300 points over the cost of funds. A huge fraction of the loans was nonperforming. With the tools available, many of the failed thrifts could have managed the risks of an inverted yield curve far better than the losses from the bad loans.

The next section suggests that much of the problem resulted from failure to manage real interest rates. The credit worthiness of the firms was too low to withstand a large increase in the *real* obligations when inflation subsided. The borrowers had counted on inflation to be a partner in paying back the loans, but the partnership had been dissolved. The story of the savings and loan industry in the late 1980s is one of an evolution. The industry had built, and was getting comfortable with, increasingly sophisticated techniques and instruments for managing interest rate risk. Unfortunately, this growth had apparently obscured one of the basics. If the quality of the portfolio is terrible, no amount of hedging or trading sophistication will save it. In learning new management techniques, the old and still effective ones should not be discarded.

5.7   REAL AND NOMINAL INTEREST RATES

In all of the examples in this chapter there have been no distinctions drawn between real and nominal interest rates. The rates discussed so far have all been nominal, representing the total dollar return over a given period. Real interest rates are the return above inflation. As a first approximation, the real interest rate equals the nominal rate less the inflation rate for the period. A more precise equation accounting for the effect of inflation on the accrued interest is:

$$(1 + r) = (1 + i)/(1 + \pi)$$

where r = real rate of interest
        i = nominal rate of interest
      π = rate of inflation

In the United States we have been fortunate in having moderate inflation so that the complications of such distinctions can be avoided. With the exception of 1973–74 and 1979–80, inflation in the United States has generally been below 5 percent per year. It is widely assumed that nominal rates reflect the current inflation and that the real return is a fair reflection of how capital should grow through time. This perspective was an easy one to maintain through the 1980s when rates above inflation provided investors a very healthy return.

It would be foolish, however, to ignore real rates on the assumption that nominal rates will always be sufficiently higher to provide an adequate return. In both the 1973–74 and 1979–80 experiences with double-digit inflation, nominal rates failed to rise fast enough to cover an accelerating inflation's impact. Holders of even T-bills lost wealth as inflation outstripped nominal returns.

Other countries' experiences make them view the United States' naive perspective with envious amusement. In 1988 inflation in Brazil was running around 20 percent per month. This translates into a little over 0.5 percent per day.

In such an environment the real return is of paramount importance, and the economy is structured to reflect this. First, contracts that extend for prolonged periods are all indexed. The real return is agreed upon through the bargaining process, and the nominal component is an automatic adjustment. The second feature is the shrinkage of time. Contracts that are not indexed are all for very short periods. The overnight loan market includes private savers, and anyone can get a quote on overnight money on a sum as small as $200 dollars. Try to get that from a New York banker.

Managing nominal rate risk in such a world means managing inflation risk, since it is the largest component of the sum. But such risk management problems are not unique for Brazilians. Other countries, like Great Britain, where the inflation experience has been more modest, have also tried to come to grips with the problem. In Great Britain there are a class of government bonds that have capital indexed periodically to the current rate of inflation. These bonds may have a coupon of 2 to 3 percent, but the bondholders understand that their capital is also augmented at a pace that will keep its purchasing power constant.

The importance of this for investors of all kinds is profound. People save not to acquire huge stacks of worthless paper but instead to provide for future consumption streams for themselves and their children. Nominally denominated assets cannot insure such consumption. There is always the possibility that the government will expand the supply of money, raising prices and unilaterally lowering the real value of their debt outstanding.

The problem is acute for annuity companies that have to fund liabilities that are basically in real terms, with assets that are earning nominal returns. Consider the pension fund stating that a retiree's payments will be a function of the last three year's income, an event that may not be determined for more than a decade. To fund that obligation, the firm takes in payments equal to a fraction of the worker's wage and invests it in a nominal instrument. As long as the investment return exceeds inflation, there will be no problem in meeting the ultimate obligation. If inflation should suddenly accelerate, the plan would be underfunded.

Indexed bonds are certainly an effective way to meet this problem, and retirement funds in the United Kingdom have been active buyers of the government's indexed issues. But this alternative is not open to U.S. funds since the Treasury has chosen not to follow this route. One perspective holds that such instruments are unnecessary since the government has a firm grasp on inflation. A more cynical view would suggest the government is keeping inflation in reserve as an available solution to the debt crisis of the 1980s. No matter what the reason, the failure to have indexed bonds for their portfolio puts pension fund managers in a position of extreme risk with respect to inflation.

One solution that was tried in the 1980s by the Coffee, Sugar & Cocoa

Exchange was the development of inflation futures. Based on the Consumer Price Index (CPI), these futures could be matched with nominal rate instruments to create synthetic real rates of return. Lenders at nominal rates would buy such futures to lock in the current expected rate of inflation and keep the further acceleration of prices from eating into their real return.

The academic reception to the new contract was extremely warm. Milton Friedman (1984) presented a strong theoretical case for their use, and Gary Koppenhaver and Cheng Lee (1987) explored hedging models for banks seeking to cover their inflation exposure. ''Real Immunization'' strategies were proposed to allow pension funds to immunize their real rates of interest as well as the nominal value (Wissner, 1987). In addition to proponents, there were detractors.

Some observers argued that the contract could never work because everyone is hurt by inflation, and no one is helped. In such a world there would be only buyers and no sellers. In fact, such a view misses a very important beneficiary of accelerating inflation, anyone who has borrowed at nominal rates. Farmers in the Midwest and the energy sector in the Southwest were actively encouraged to expand with borrowed funds in the late 1970s and early 1980s. It was not supposed to matter that they were borrowing at near record high nominal rates, pumped up to reflect the day's active inflation. After all, prices of grain, livestock, and oil would continue to go up as well.

Many well-managed companies in these sectors went under a few years later when inflation fell faster than anyone had expected, and these debtors were straddled with obligations that were all too real. A 16 percent nominal loan may not look too bad when inflation is at 12 percent and climbing, but when inflation tumbles to below 4 percent as it did in 1982, the burden can be suffocating. If these borrowers could have transacted at real rates, or could have sold inflation futures, the trauma of the 1980s would not have been nearly as severe.

Floating-rate debt, tied to short-term nominal rates, is an imperfect solution. As inflation fell rapidly from 1980 to 1981, interest rates fell from their historical peaks but leveled off well before inflation bottomed out. Nominal rates actually accelerated in 1983 as the economy moved out of the recession, a recovery accomplished with no acceleration in prices. Floating-rate debt is effective only when short-term rates move responsively to inflation, which historically they have not. Anyone looking to that instrument for an inflation hedge will find considerable basis risk.

The CPI futures at the CSCE were launched in 1985. After an initial flurry of trading that accompanies most new products, activity fell to near dormancy. Observers note that the timing was difficult at best. In 1985 oil prices tumbled from over $25 a barrel to near $10, bringing about the first quarterly decline in prices in more than 20 years. Hedgers wanting to protect themselves against accelerating inflation found themselves giving up a rare windfall to savers that accompanies negative inflation. Although the volatility of inflation was large enough to produce sizable gains and losses in the contract, it was not large enough to catch the public's imagination or to spark great trading interest.

Timing is certainly important in new product launches, but there was also an important element missing. There were no dealers holding "inventories" of inflation waiting to be hedged. Although the exposure to unexpected changes in inflation was, and remains, vast, there was no central marketplace of inflation risk that could be traded against. Individuals could combine nominal rate instruments and CPI futures to create synthetic real rate instruments, but there were no actual real rate bonds against which to form the arbitrage. Once again the role of the arbitrageur in providing much needed liquidity was demonstrated.

The current view for inflation futures in the United States is dim. There is no trading currently, and there are only limited numbers of private indexed debt instruments against which to form the arbitrage. But the idea should not be completely discounted. Inflation futures, very similar to those developed in the United States, are now trading reasonably well in Brazil. If you ask a Brazilian why the U.S. market has not worked, the likely response will be "because you have no volatility." At some point in the future this contract may find a place in the risk management tool kit of Americans. Until that time, firms and individuals with an exposure to changing inflation will have to continue to manage this risk in any indirect fashion available.

NOTES

1. This refers only to default risk. There is ample demonstration that the value of these instruments can vary considerably over time.

2. The T-bill would return $((100/92) - 1) = 8.7$ percent versus 8.0 percent for the Eurodollar. Section 5.3 gives the relevant cash and futures market formulas.

3. The underlying instrument of the option is the T-bond future, so the pricing is identical except that the minimum fluctuation is $\frac{1}{64}$ of a point.

4. Marcelle Arak, Laurie Goodman, and Susan Ross (1986) provided a detailed explanation of the cheapest-to-deliver problem on T-bond futures.

5. If the period in question is a leap year, Equation 5.10 can be modified to capture the 366th day.

6. Marcia Stigum (1981), pp. 136–38 provided a clear exposition of the application of Newton's Method to the multiple coupon bearing instrument problem. Readers interested in their own programming should consult Stigum or any applied calculus book to define the key iterative steps.

7. See Section 5.3.3 for a description of the $_ir_j$ terminology.

8. $-(-100)(.085)(182/360) = 4.34$, which when rounded gives four long contracts.

9. These calculations are very sensitive to the accurate accounting of the delivery dates and accrued interest. It is a wise policy to receive periodically a table of conversion factors from the CBOT Economic Analysis and Planning Department rather than calculate the factors yourself.

10. In addition to the delivery-day option, there is an option imbedded in the time of day for deliveries. Notice of delivery is given several hours after trading closes. If the cash market should suddenly drop after the futures closes, it may pay to acquire the cash instruments and deliver against that day's settlement price. This "wild-card" option seems to be worth a few points to the short.

11. The 9.2025 percent current yield represents the compounding effect from semiannual coupons $(1.045 * 1.045 = 1.092025)$.

CHAPTER 6

Foreign Currency Futures and Options

6.1 BACKGROUND

The first financial futures markets were based on foreign currencies relative to the value of the dollar. It was an opportune beginning because all of the elements necessary for successful trading were present. The base markets were large and growing with the expansion of foreign trade. There was a sophisticated dealer community in place that would become the core of commercial traders. Finally, there was soon to be considerable risk. The Bretton Woods system of coordinated currency action among the major developed nations was crumbling. It was no longer possible to constrain currency values within narrow bands, and the risks associated with variable exchange rates would soon be widely felt.

Some traders were skeptical that the techniques of grain and livestock trading could be transported into an entirely new area like currencies. What was soon learned was that currencies were not that mysterious and that many of the trading characteristics fell into traditional futures patterns. Currencies were bought and sold on a spot and forward basis. Inventories were maintained at a readily identifiable cost. If the markets were in a carry or a backwardation, the same signals were sent as if it had been a corn or coffee market. Traditional futures traders quickly adapted to the new markets.

The most basic feature of currency trading is that the futures are actually interest rate markets. If the spot price is known, and one is told the interest rates in the two countries, the futures price can be determined with certainty. This is due to a principle known as interest rate parity, an arbitrage condition that binds the markets of freely convertible currencies worldwide.

6.2   INTEREST RATE PARITY

Suppose that the spot and one-year forward rates of the deutsche mark versus the dollar was 2DM/$. Either today or next year you could buy 2 million DM for $1 million. Suppose also that the one-year LIBOR for Eurodollars was 7 percent per annum and for Euro DM it was 5 percent. At these prices a risk free arbitrage exists.

Someone holding 2.0 million DM could invest it at the current rate and at the end of one year have 2.1 million DM. The alternative would be to buy $1.0 million today and simultaneously agree to sell $1.07 million for 2.14 million DM. The purchased dollars would be invested at 7 percent to grow to the forwarded amount. Given the two alternatives, the second choice would be the clearly preferred investment avenue, but there is no reason to constrain it to an individual already holding the DM portfolio. A creditworthy arbitrageur could borrow the 2 million DM at 5 percent, could enter into the spot and forward currency transactions, and, after investing the $1.0 million at 7 percent, could yield a 40,000 DM profit at no risk.

If currencies are freely convertible this arbitrage would go on until either or both of the following happened. Interest rates in the two countries would tend to equalize as capital flowed from Germany to the United States. The other alternative would be for the forward DM/$ rate to fall below the spot price as dollars would be actively bought today and sold a year from now. The arbitrage activity would continue until the prices and interest rates adjusted sufficiently to eliminate the risk-free profit.

Interest rate parity occurs when there are no arbitrage opportunities available. It is succinctly expressed in the following equation.

$$F = S[1 + (r_f - r_\$)/(B/T + r_\$)] \tag{6.1}$$

where F = forward foreign currency per dollar rate
S = spot foreign currency per dollar rate
r_f = foreign interest rate
$r_\$$ = dollar interest rate
T = days between forward and spot
B = base number of days for the interest rate

Equation 6.1 assumes that the interest rates for the two currencies are quoted on a common basis. Dollars, DMs, Swiss francs, and yen are quoted in terms of a 360-day year. Sterling and Canadian and Australian dollars have their rates quoted in terms of 365-day years, and an adjustment must be made.

$$F = S[1 + (r_f - r_\$)(B_\$/B_f)/(B_\$/T + r_\$)] \tag{6.2}$$

where $B_\$$ = the base number of days for the dollar interest rate; and B_f = the base number of days for the foreign currency interest rate. If $B_\$$ equals B_f, Equation 6.2 reduces to Equation 6.1.

Whenever the foreign currency interest rate exceeds the dollar interest rate (r_f − $r_\$$ is positive), the forward exchange rate will exceed the spot rate. That is, it will take more units of foreign currency to buy a dollar in the future than it does today. Consequently, by comparing interest rates one can immediately determine whether the forward market should be in a carry or backwardation. Higher dollar interest rates will simply lower exchange rates (backwardation) and conversely, lower dollar interest rates will produce a carry market.[1]

Interest rate parity is one of the most pervasive of all laws in economics. If two countries had identical real interest rates, but one country was inflating at 10 percent per year and the other had no inflation, this would be reflected in nominal interest rates that were 10 percentage points apart. Not surprisingly, the forward rate for the inflating currency would be about 10 percent per year lower in value in the forward market. If the currency was going to be worth less in the country of issue, the foreign exchange market would see to it that it would be received with equal treatment in other nations.

Interest rate parity holds for periods extending from today to some date into the future, but it also holds between any two future dates. The exact analog of the term structure argument from Section 5.3.3 applies equally well to currency rates. The spread between futures contracts expiring two months and five months from the current date will reflect the relative two-month forward rates for three-month money for each country. Given two national yield curves and a spot rate, the futures prices for the currency are precisely defined.

6.3   FIXED VERSUS FLEXIBLE EXCHANGE RATES

The preceding discussion has reflected the world of the 1970s and 1980s where rates have been allowed to move freely in the marketplace. These circumstances have not always been the norm, and there has been active discussion during much of the 1980s on the virtues of getting the floating exchange-rate genie back into the bottle. To see the entire picture it is useful to gain a historical perspective on global exchange-rate policy.

Before the introduction of paper money, precious metals formed the medium of exchange. Since the supply of this form of money was fixed in the short run, ebbs and flows of money across nations were the mirror image of the trade flows. If a country bought more goods than it sold, its share of the total supply of gold and silver fell. It was as simple as that. Trade imbalances could not persist for long because there was a finite supply of money. If a country would deplete its share, the only remedy would be to sell more goods to restock the treasury.

One might think that in such a world there would never be inflation, but such was not the case. With the discovery of the new world and the expropriation of Incan and Aztec gold and silver, the supply of money expanded rapidly. It hit Spain first as more money was chasing the same amount of goods and gradually, but surely, spread throughout Europe as trade flows changed in response to Spanish wealth. Just because gold and silver coinage are more tangible than paper money does not eliminate the fundamental link between the quantity of money in circulation at any given time and the price level.

The next step in the evolution of money was the introduction of paper currency, convertible to gold or silver at fixed rate. This gold standard was a practical alternative to the exclusive use of metals for economies that were growing. Paper in many ways is a much more practical medium of exchange than the metals it stood for, and as long as its value could be maintained versus the traditional mediums, it was widely accepted.

By fixing the value of money in terms of gold, reins were placed on the central banks of the country issuing the currency. If too much paper money was printed, the populace would want to convert back to gold, depleting the national reserve. The object, therefore, became to keep the amount of paper currency in circulation at a constant ratio to the stock of gold at any given time. If a country's trade balance was in a deficit, gold would flow out to pay for the excess purchases, and the supply of paper money would be restricted. This "tight money" policy would slow down the economy and perhaps lower prices at home. These two impacts would curtail demand for foreign products while making domestic goods more attractive to foreigners. The process would continue until the trade balance problem was completely addressed.

The gold standard was a remarkable international system. As long as all nations maintained their currency/gold ratios, flows of goods and capital reflected pure efficiency of the trading partners. Problems arose, however, when the basic ratio was broken. A country playing by the rules had tough choices to make when a deficit trade balance led to precious metal outflows. Contracting the domestic money supply then had the same impact it does today. The home economy slows, unemployment rises, and there is general unrest.

The alternative to playing by the rules when there is a trade deficit is *not* to constrict the domestic supply of money. When the demand for the reserve metal grows, as it will from both domestic and foreign holders of claims against it, the government simply devalues by increasing the price of gold at which it will make conversions. This is the classic application of the golden rule, "He who has the gold, makes the rules."

Devaluations can have a devastating impact on a foreigner's willingness to hold any given currency. Once a fraction of someone's wealth has been expropriated by a devaluation, it is unlikely that they will be eager to hold that asset in the future unless there are assurances that such events cannot happen again. Since it is impossible to receive effective assurances of this type, the currency will be further discounted to reflect the risk of future devaluations. Despite these disadvantages, there are times when the outflow of wealth is so great that a devaluation is the only viable alternative open to a country.

The gold standard left the scene in stages during the period between the world wars. Country after country devalued or restricted convertibility until the idea of a global metal-based currency system was completely antiquated.

The expectation of a post–World War II environment cried out for stability across currencies, and this was found in the Bretton Woods agreement, signed as World War II was drawing to a close. Currency values were pegged to the dollar, which was convertible to gold, for foreigners only, at $35 per ounce. Since the United States led the world in industrial production and military strength, there was little doubt that the dollar would be solid. Interestingly, since one could earn interest on dollar deposits, while gold cost money to hold in terms of storage and insurance, there was very little demand for conversions. The dollar was better than gold. Throughout the 1950s and early 1960s it was non–U.S. currencies that periodically devalued against the dollar when the trade imbalances grew too extreme. Everyone wanted dollars.

The mid-1960s proved you can have too much of a good thing, especially when the subject is paper money. The progress made by the postwar European and Japanese economies began to catch up with the United States. As foreign products became increasingly commonplace in U.S. markets, dollars flowed out, and it no longer was taken as an axiom that the dollar was as good as gold. In the face of mounting conversions by foreigners, President Nixon closed the gold window in 1971. Freely floating exchange rates were not far behind.

Bretton Woods had provided for target values, defended by the major central banks of the free world. If the ranges proved inaccurate, they would be adjusted through periodic devaluations. With the collapse of the agreement, the marketplace emerged as the arena to derive a fair exchange rate for any given currency.

In the years since 1972, there have been many critics of flexible rates. They look at a period like 1982 to 1988, when the dollar went from $1.80 to $1.02, and back to $1.80, against sterling, as a supposed example of "excessive" volatility that hurt economies and distorted trade. Because of this uncertainty, the critics call out for a return to a more controlled environment.

Economists as a group are a fairly bright lot, but that sometimes leads a few in that fraternity to believe they are smarter than the market. Looking backwards after a correction it is easy to state that a currency was overvalued or undervalued. To suggest that there should be controls to eliminate this variance suggests also that there is a workable mechanism to define the appropriate mean.

Leo Melamed, the founder of financial futures in 1972 as chairman of the IMM, has collected a number of essays on the subject of flexible versus fixed exchange rates (Melamed, 1988). Of particular interest are the recent essays by Rudiger Dornbusch and Stanley Fischer, looking back over our long, and not always pleasant, experience with floating rates. They both concluded that there probably is not much hope that a workable system of fixed rates can be achieved. Interestingly, the arguments have not changed much since Milton Friedman's famous article written in 1953 (reprinted in Melamed, 1988) at the height of Bretton Woods.

The main problem stems directly from Equation 6.1, although it may not be immediately evident that this is the case. To have stable exchange rates through time requires interest rates to be equal across the countries. This in turn requires macroeconomic-policy coordination across countries that is likely impossible in sovereign nations. In essence, if the U.S. interest rates got out of line with the rest of the world, domestic macroeconomic policy would have to be adjusted to push the interest rates back in line. Failing that, a devaluation of the currency with the higher interest rates would be inevitable.

What are the prospects of the United States, Germany, or Japan subjugating its domestic economic policies to a goal of steady exchange rates? Not great, in all probability. Anytime there is domestic economic and political hay to be made, it is virtually certain that the exchange rate will be a lower priority.

Furthermore, if a nation pays lip service to an agreement targeting its currency in a certain range and then proceeds to follow a contrary domestic policy, the same kind of capital flows will result that came from trade imbalances under a gold-based system. In today's world of very efficient flows of capital, there is not a country on the globe that has deep enough pockets to support its currency for very long in the face of vast redemptions. No country is unassailable, and none of the major countries will agree to giving fixed exchange rates a priority over domestic policy. In such a world, targeted exchange rates are an impossibility.

There are many economists who point to benefits that would accrue from more stable rates as an argument for international cooperation. With stable rates, firms involved in trade could invest with more certainty of an adequate return. All capital in the economy would be better used. The same arguments can be made for a host of agricultural commodities, but the experience with price controls, buffer stocks, and international trade constraints for basic commodities has been a disaster. Prices may be stable over short periods, but whenever a shock hits supply or demand, the resulting collapse of the agreement produces volatility far in excess of that which an unconstrained market would have experienced. There is no reason to believe a foreign currency agreement to stabilize rates would be any different.

The economists making these arguments for agreements are correct on one element. The world would be a better place with more stable rates. It would also be better off if all governments acted responsibly, but passing legislation to mandate responsible action is not likely to be an effective answer. Far better is the creation of an efficient marketplace, giving continuous signals about the course of events. If currency values are volatile, it is all the more important to have futures and options markets to help manage that risk. Individuals cannot always control the actions of their governments, but with the foreign exchange markets, the populace can control its exposure to those actions.

6.4   DIRECT AND CROSS-RATE HEDGING WITH FUTURES

Foreign currency futures are most often used as direct hedges against an anticipated asset or liability in another currency. The standard example would be the importer of Japanese microchips who has ordered a shipment priced in yen for delivery in six months. The importer has in turn forward priced the chips to various U.S. manufacturers in dollars. If the dollar should decline relative to the yen before shipment and payment, there is great potential for loss in the entire transaction.

To secure the price relationship the importer could borrow dollars today, convert them to yen at the spot rate, and invest the yen at prevailing yen interest rates. With proper planning, the borrowed yen would have grown to an amount large enough to pay for the microchips. The dollar receipts from the manufacturers would have been used to pay back the original loan.

Some importers may maintain credit lines and portfolios of currencies just for this reason, but there are severe inefficiencies in this approach. The biggest problem comes from tying up credit, when what is really needed is insurance against a change in relative prices.

A simpler means of obtaining protection is to fix the exchange rate by use of a bank forward contract or a futures contract. The choice between the two avenues depends on the firm's ability and willingness to maintain the position itself. If the firm is unwilling to monitor the position precisely and finance margin calls, the bank forward market will probably be a better vehicle. The bank will take on many of the details, for a fee, that would have to be assumed directly with a futures trade. The mechanics of either hedge are identical, although the futures hedge will likely be constructed with a much more favorable basis since there will be no bank service charges incorporated into the prices.

The example below assumes that the trade is done in the futures market. Let the contract price of the microchips be ¥1 billion and the futures price be 0.0082\$/¥(= 121.95¥/\$). The expected dollar value of the transaction is therefore \$8.2 million, and suppose that the importer has sold the chips forward to various U.S. manufacturers for \$9.0 million.

To protect the profitability of the transaction, the importer tries to buy an appropriate number of yen futures. Since IMM futures have a base size of 12.5 million yen, the importer would buy 80 contracts to cover the exposure completely. Table 6.1 gives the outcome of the hedge under different price scenarios, stepping the yen price up and down a tenth of a cent per yen.

In this simple example, whether the price went up or down, a fully hedged position produced the same total cost to purchase the ¥1 billion. Note that in the second to last line of the third column, an unhedged position would have produced a loss on the total transaction.

Considerable emphasis has been placed on basis risk and the idea that when a company hedges with futures it is translating price-level risk for basis risk. It may seem odd, therefore, to have an example in which the total cost of the yen purchased is exactly equal in all outcomes, but this is typical for currency hedges. Unlike hedges involving corn, cocoa, or nonstandard stock index portfolios, there is no basis risk in currencies stemming from quality differentials. A yen is a yen is a yen.

Table 6.1
Hedging a ¥1 Billion Long Exposure (All Prices in Dollars)

	A	B	C
Initial price	.008200	.008200	.008200
Final price	.007200	.008200	.009200
Profit/(loss) per contract	(12,500)	0	12,500
No. of contracts	80	80	80
Total p/(l)	(1 million)	0	1 million
Cash cost of ¥1 billion	7.2 million	8.2 million	9.2 million
Net cost	8.2 million	8.2 million	8.2 million

The only risk the importer faces is that the timing of the futures contract does not exactly match that of the cash transaction. During the period of the mismatch, there is the risk that the relative interest rates could shift and diminish the effectiveness of the hedge. If there is a reasonably close fit between the cash and futures transaction, this is a minor problem. Any firm concerned with it, however, could have entered into a customized forward transaction with a bank instead of a futures hedge, but the initial yen price may have been $0.008300/¥ instead of $0.008200/¥ available with the futures.

A slight variation on this example would have the importer selling not to U.S. manufacturers but to Canadian concerns at a fixed price of C$11 million. The importer's concern is now the yen/Canadian dollar forward rate of exchange, but there are no such futures directly available.

The yen/Canadian dollar exchange rate is provincially called from a U.S. perspective a cross-currency rate. International banks routinely offer a full matrix of such rates for their clients, but it is not necessary to go to the bank OTC market if futures are available for both currencies in the equation.

Suppose that the U.S. dollar/Canadian dollar exchange rate reflected in the futures contract corresponding to the timing of the cash contract is 0.80 US$/1.00 C$. The rates of exchange are transitive, so the ¥1 billion can be expected to cost C$10.25 million (¥1 billion * 0.0082 US$/¥ * 1.25 C$/US$). The total risk can be decomposed into two pieces. First, the yen could appreciate relative to the U.S. dollar, and second, the Canadian dollar could fall relative to the U.S. dollar. To get a complete hedge the importer would buy 80 yen contracts and sell 102 Canadian dollar positions.[2]

Table 6.2 shows how an adverse move in the implied ¥/C$ rate can occur in a number of ways. But the combination of long yen futures and short Canadian

Table 6.2
Hedging a ¥1 Billion Long Exposure against C$

a) Exchange Rates

Case	Original US$/¥	US$/C$	C$/¥	Ultimate US$/¥	US$/C$	C$/¥
1.	.00820	.8000	.01025	.00900	.7500	.01200
2.	.00820	.8000	.01025	.01200	1.0000	.01200
3.	.00820	.8000	.01025	.00720	.6000	.01200

b) Futures Outcomes

Case	¥ Futures Position	P/L US$	C$ Futures Position	P/L US$
1.	long 80	.8 mil	short 102	.51 mil
2.	long 80	3.8 mil	short 102	(2.04 mil)
3.	long 80	(1.0 mil)	short 102	2.04 mil

c) Canadian Dollar Cash Outcomes

Case	Futures P/L C$*	Ultimate C$ Cash Cost of ¥1 bil	Net C$ Cost of ¥1 bil
1.	1.747 mil	12.0 mil	10.253 mil
2.	1.760 mil	12.0 mil	10.240 mil
3.	1.733 mil	12.0 mil	10.267 mil

* Futures P/L converted to C$ at prevailing rate.

dollar futures protects the position. The top section of the table shows how ¥/C$ rate of 0.01025 can change to a rate of 0.01200 through a combination of adverse and favorable moves in the US$/¥ and US$/C$ rates. Case 1 has both currencies moving adversely against the U.S. dollar for the importer. In case 2 both currencies appreciated against the dollar, and in case 3 both fell. In each instance the combined effect hurt the importer. Cases could also be easily constructed where an unhedged position would have profited.

The center section of the table gives the U.S. dollar profits and losses that would be realized from each part of the hedge under the different scenarios. The final section converts the combined future profits and losses into Canadian dollars at the rate prevailing when the hedge matured. Under the example here, the cash price of the billion yen at expiration would be 12.0 million Canadian, but when the profits from the hedge are applied, the net cost is very close to the 10.25 million Canadian originally targeted. The difference between the target and the actual is due to the impossibility of holding a fractional number of Canadian dollar futures contracts.

The method of cross-currency hedging is direct and efficient. Because of the efficiency of currency futures based in dollars, the hedger may construct the hedge positions directly or may go to a bank offering cross-currency forwards. The depth of the foreign exchange OTC market is in part due to the efficiency of the futures markets that stand ready to accept unwanted risk on the cash side. When evaluating a cross-currency OTC rate, however, the client should not assume the rate to be efficient but would instead evaluate the returns from a direct futures hedge relative to the bank offer. In that way the costs of the bank services can be carefully evaluated.

6.5   CURRENCY HEDGING WITH OPTIONS

Actual examples of how companies hedge are difficult to come by for obvious reasons, so when glimpses of how actual decisions are made become available, it can be particularly enlightening. In early 1985 Lufthansa purchased $500 million worth of new aircraft, but payment was not due until a year later. Since deutsche marks are Lufthansa's natural currency, there was a full year's exposure to the value of the dollar. This company's decisions regarding this risk were the subject of a CME report (Chicago Mercantile Exchange, 1986).

The situation was not an easy one. For three years the dollar had climbed steadily against all major currencies. There was widespread talk of how the dollar was overvalued and that the major nations would not tolerate further appreciation. Unfortunately, similar bold talk was popular throughout 1984, and anyone who stayed unhedged owing dollars had been killed in terms of local currency.

There were several alternatives available to Lufthansa:

1. Stay unhedged. Speculate that the dollar would fall relative to the deutsche mark in the coming year.
2. Sell deutsche mark futures or forwards out one year, locking in the prevailing rate.
3. Buy at- or out-of-the-money deutsche mark puts. If the dollar continued to appreciate, the puts would provide protection, but if the dollar fell, all that would be lost would be the premiums paid.

From the reports available at the time, it appears Lufthansa split between alternatives 1 and 2. They set the forward rate on half the commitment and left the balance uncovered.

At the time of the sale, the spot rate was about $0.30/DM and the forward rate $0.31/DM, reflecting higher interest rates in the United States than in West Germany. The market expectation was that the $500 million dollars would be worth 1,613 million DM in a year.

The option prices at the time of the sale reflected the high volatility that had been the norm in the currency markets. The $0.30/DM put cost $0.014/DM, and the $.29/DM put was valued at $0.010/DM. This meant that if the airline sought to guarantee that its total cost would have been no more than 1,667 million DM (the 0.30 strike), the total cost would have been about 75 million DM (= (.014/.30) * 1,613 million), or nearly 5 percent of the total value of the deal projected using the current forward rate. The 0.29 put would not have provided any coverage until the value was 1,724 million DM, and that coverage would have cost 54 million DM, or 3 percent of the deal.

These are large numbers, and apparently, they were too large for Lufthansa. According to published reports, their strategy was to fix $250 million in the forward market at a price of 0.31 and let the balance float. One can never know if this was part of a dynamic hedging strategy that would have provided more fixing of prices if the dollar had continued its climb, because throughout 1985, the dollar tumbled. When the year had passed, the exchange rate stood close to $0.45/DM, almost a 50 percent appreciation in the mark.

The outcome of the airline's strategy was to split the difference, $250 million at 0.31 and $250 million at 0.45, for a total expense of 1,362 million DM, well below the original expectation of 1,613 million DM. With perfect hindsight, the optimal choice would have been to be completely uncovered, but this was not obvious at the time the position was established.

What would the hedge strategies have produced? Buying full coverage with the out-of-the-money 0.29 puts would have cost 54 million DM as previously noted. They would have expired grossly out-of-the-money. In fact, they probably would have had virtually no salvage value even with six months remaining. The $500 million would have been covered at the end of the year for 1,111 million DM, which when added to the premium would have produced a total cost of 1,165 million DM, a savings of almost 200 million DM over the strategy actually pursued. The "expensive" options would have proved to be the superior insurance vehicle.

This example points out one of the classic dilemmas posed when considering long options for hedging. How much is a reasonable premium before the event? The firm considering these options should first examine the pricing in terms of the volatility implied. If the market's perception of volatility is greater than that of the hedger, it may be preferable to try to replicate an option with a dynamic hedging strategy and avoid the excessive part of the premium. If, on the other hand, the volatility in the market is lower than the trader's independent assessment, and there is a concern about an adverse move, the market option represents a bargain no matter how high the dollar (or deutsche mark) expense.

The strategy taken was neither fish nor fowl. If the dollar had continued to appreciate, the fixed part of the plan would have proved correct, and the floating point would have been in error. What opinion did Lufthansa express by its action? It seems that its objective was always to be half right, so as to avoid criticism for being more than half wrong.

Even if Lufthansa had no opinion on which direction the dollar was going, the preferable approach would have been to have an opinion on the volatility and tailor the risk profile so as to minimize the exposure given the cost of the options. In that way management would be performing its assigned tasks using all of the information available to it.

Many corporate treasurers, whose companies do not have a hedging mentality, find that it is a great deal easier to get $500 million for airplanes than $30 million for option premiums to protect their value. This is certainly true in many corporations and is the subject of the discussion in Section 7.7. When explicit option premium payments are impossible because of a narrow corporate perspective toward hedging, it may be possible to enter into cap or collar arrangements similar to those discussed for interest rates in Section 5.4.5. If this route is taken, it is still important for the corporate treasurer to evaluate the implicit options to see that fair value is being received from the cap or collar provider.

6.6   SPECULATIVE CURRENCY OPTION STRATEGIES

Many people believe the press reports when a prominent central banker is quoted as saying, "We believe the [*your favorite currency*] has fallen sufficiently, and there is general agreement among the major developed countries that its value should remain in this general vicinity." Other listeners as a general rule do not believe pronouncements of central bankers but have learned that it can be extremely expensive to try to fade them during the occasional moments when they put their money where their mouth is.

What can one do if there is a belief that the market will be neutral over the investment horizon? Retreating to the sidelines is never entirely satisfying, but before the introduction of exchange-traded currency options there was little else available. Options have provided flat market strategies that exploit the phenomenon of time decay, and many have found these strategies particularly attractive in the area of currencies.

Two of the best known of these strategies are the short straddle and short strangle discussed in chapter 3. The short straddle consists of a granted put and granted call, both at-the-money. A short strangle also combines a granted put and a granted call, but this time the strike prices are both out-of-the-money.

Suppose that Swiss francs are trading at 55 cents/SF. If the implied volatility of the market is 10 percent, a 30-day short straddle will generate 1.26 cents in total premiums from the written at-the-money options. This is the maximum return possible from the strategy and occurs only if the underlying futures expires exactly at the strike price. The 1.26 cents in premium collected forms a cushion around the strike price, providing for a profitable trade if the futures price ends up between 53.74 and 56.26. Beyond those boundary points in either direction, the position loses point for point with the futures since one of the options will be exercised, and the loss on the futures would exceed the total premium received.

Strangles can come in all widths, with further out-of-the-money options generating less potential profit but simultaneously posing less risk. Table 6.3 gives the alternative values for strangles one, two, and three strikes out-of-the-money. The maximum profit is earned if the option expires anywhere within the range of strikes spanned by the put and the call. Figure 6.1 gives the diagrammatic view of the profit/loss picture at expiration.

These neutral market strategies are typically entered into as the options approach expiration. The time values are not as large, but the rate of decay is accelerating, and the positions pose less risk than do similar approaches using more distant options. Care should be taken as expiration nears to monitor the gamma risk of the position. If the futures is near one of the two strike prices of a strangle as expiration approaches, there is great loss potential for the position, and defensive positioning is probably called for.

In addition to straddles and strangles, there are other option strategies that may

Table 6.3
Straddle and Strangle Strategies

Swiss Franc = 55 cents/SF

Prices in Cents Per Swiss Franc

Strategy	Strikes Call	Put	Premium* Call	Put	Maximum Profit	Breakeven Low	High
Straddle	55	55	.63	.63	1.26	53.74	56.26
Strangle 1	56	54	.26	.25	.51	53.49	56.51
Strangle 2	57	53	.08	.07	.15	52.85	57.15
Strangle 3	58	52	.02	.01	.03	51.97	58.03

* calculated using 30 days to maturity and 10% volatility

Figure 6.1
Currency Straddles and Strangles

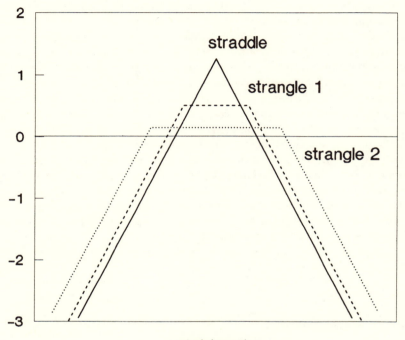

profit/loss

straddle

strangle 1

strangle 2

underlying price

be used to exploit time decay in a neutral market. Unlike the previous strategies, however, there is a slight bullish or bearish bias to the spreads discussed below.

Long calendar spreads are structured by writing a nearby call and buying the same strike price call with a later expiration. In a market that remains flat, time decay will affect both options, but will more rapidly diminish the premium of the granted, nearby option than the value of the long, deferred option. Figure 6.2 shows the objective. As both contracts move toward expiration, the spread expands from S_1 to S_2 creating the profit.

The goal of the calendar spread is best met in neutral markets, and as soon as the short option value gets close to zero, the spread should be liquidated. At that point further profits are limited (the short option can decline only so far), but the potential losses are not. If the short option is near zero, the spreadholder should recognize that in a rapidly declining market, the long option could suffer severely, eventually eliminating the profitability of the spread. Either the position should be liquidated or the risks voluntarily assumed.

Figure 6.2
Time Decay and Calendar Spreads

time value

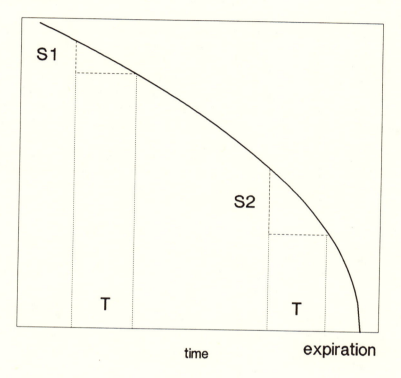

time   expiration

A variation on the calendar spread is the diagonal spread. The trader still writes the nearby option and buys a more distant one, but this time at different strike prices. Diagonal spreads allow for more precision in carry or inverted markets. Suppose that the September Swiss franc futures contract is trading at 55 cents per SF and that the next maturity, December, is at 56 cents. A diagonal spread consisting of one short September 56 call and one long December 57 call captures the same degree of "out-of-the-moneyness" in both. With 60 days until expiration for the September option (150 for the December option) the 56 call could be sold for 0.48 cents and the December 57 call bought for 1.00 cents, a debit of 0.52 cents. Table 6.4 gives possible outcomes with only five days left in the nearby option.

Case a in the table is near the ideal outcome. The spread between the futures has stayed constant, but the level has gone up. Time decay has still weighed heavily on the nearby call, so even as it is now at-the-money, it is worth less than it was originally. The back-month option has increased in value because the impact of time is less the further the option is from expiration. The net effect is that when the spread is liquidated there will be a profit of 0.38 cents. The maximum profit is 0.48 cents (equal to the difference in the strike price less the original net premium paid) whenever the futures spread stays constant, and so this outcome is good.

Case b shows the example if nothing happens except the passage of time. There is a modest profit, which the trader would do well to capture by liquidating the position with the few days left. The reason for this is shown in case c. Suppose that a shock hit the Swiss franc market driving prices sharply lower in the few days before expiration. The September 56 granted call could only fall 0.02 to zero, whereas the decline in the December position would be much greater. A modest profit could be quickly turned into a loss similar to that experienced in case c.

In case d, assumptions are relaxed about the futures spreads. If U.S. interest rates fall to be equal to the Swiss, either case d or e could occur. If U.S. rates fell under the Swiss, case e could come about. In each of these cases, these basis switches adversely produce moderate to large losses. Note that even with the

Table 6.4
Long Diagonal Swiss Franc Option Spread

Case	Sept. Futures	Dec. Futures	Sept 56 Call	Dec 57 Call	Value of Spread*	Profit**
Original with 5 days remaining	55.00	56.00	.48	1.00	(.52)	
a.	56.00	57.00	.26	1.16	(.90)	.38
b.	55.00	56.00	.02	.72	(.70)	.18
c.	54.00	55.00	.00	.41	(.41)	(.11)
d.	55.00	55.00	.02	.41	(.39)	(.13)
e.	56.00	55.00	.26	.41	(.15)	(.37)
f.	58.00	58.00	2.00	1.73	.27	(.79)

    *   short the Sept 56 call, long the Dec 57, debits in parentheses.

   **   (.52)-value of the spread

major bull move in case f, since the carry flattened out, a major loss resulted. The use of the descriptive term *long* must be made cautiously unless the relationship between the two contracts will be stable.

From the simulated outcomes in Table 6.4 it is easy to characterize the calendar or diagonal spread strategy as being very risky if the futures carry or inversion is volatile. That is precisely the reason that this strategy can be effective for currencies. It is almost unheard of for relative interest rates across countries to swing so widely that a carry market would shift to an inversion, or conversely. If yields began to shift it would be a more gradual evolution, likely offering an opportunity for a repositioning of the risk.

6.7 HEDGING OTC OPTIONS FOR FOREIGN EXCHANGE

In the hedging examples in this chapter, references have been made to OTC alternatives to exchange-traded futures and options. Banks can offer forward contracts and OTC options because they have learned to manage the exposures they create for their clients. If some customers are buying while others are selling, the price risks can offset one another and the banks are left with credit risk. But if the price risks do not cancel one another, the bank will seek coverage in other ways.

For OTC options, banks can create profit opportunities by matching their exposure to combinations of exchange options. In the case of a company that needs an August 55 SF call, a bank might calculate the fair value of the option, charge that plus a small premium, and then cover the risk in a comparable September exchange-traded call. This approach is very similar to that of the exchange calendar spreads discussed in the previous section.

A different problem presents itself if the granted OTC option matches the exchange options in terms of maturity but not strike price. If a customer seeks the right to buy 5 million Swiss francs at 55.50 cents per SF, the OTC strike price falls between the available exchange strikes of 55 and 56. The 5 million Swiss franc 55.50 call position may be created synthetically by the bank buying 20 exchange call options with a strike price of 55 and 20 with a strike of 56.[3] The premiums for the two options may be 1.10 and 0.70 cents per SF, respectively.

The banker can turn around after buying these options and sell the OTC 55.50 call at 0.90 and just cover the premium costs. Obviously, there would be some effort made to cover commissions and generate a profit, but for simplicity, assume that 0.90 is the OTC premium. Although the cost of the program is covered, it remains to be demonstrated that the risks correspond favorably.

Figure 6.3 shows the combined risk position. Looking first at the short OTC 55.50 call, the full 0.90 premium would be earned on each option anytime the price is below 55.50 at expiration. Above 55.50 the position loses point for point. On the long call side it is convenient to look at the position on a per contract basis for comparability to the granted option. Since for every two

Figure 6.3
Covering OTC Options

profit/loss

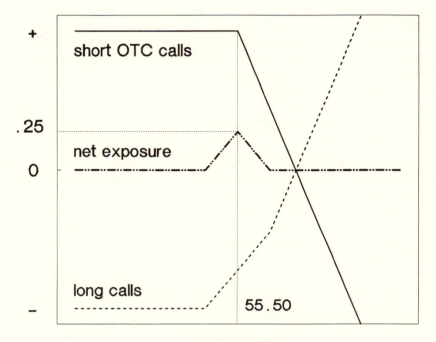

underlying price

granted options one option at each of the 55 and 56 strikes is purchased, a perfect match comes from combining a "half" of each of the exchange instruments. The total loss possible would be 0.90 (.5 ∗ 1.10 + .5 ∗ .70) per contract, if the price is below 55. From 55 to 56 the 55 call starts to return a profit, and above 56 both options are in-the-money.

The net result of this is a perfect matching of risk at prices below 55 and above 56, with no gain or loss to the position.[4] Between 55 and 56, however, an interesting event happens. The purchased 55 strike call begins profiting as soon as the price touches 55, but there is no corresponding liability until 55.50. Profits begin to accumulate on this "half option." At 55.50, the granted option comes into the money, building a liability twice as fast as the profits in the 55 call are growing. The modest profits built from 55 to 55.50 begin to decline. At 56 the second purchased call begins contributing and balance is restored. If the price happens to settle exactly at the strike price of the granted call, a small windfall results.

The basic shape of Figure 6.3 corresponds to that of a long butterfly (Section 3.5.8), with the difference being that the wings of a butterfly are below the break-even line and not on it. This argues that the bank should *not* charge 0.90 for the 55.50 call, exactly between the premiums of the 55 and 56 exchange-traded calls, but should charge *less* if it is seeking only the fair price.

This result is also derivable from the convexity of the option pricing line, which produces declining deltas for calls as the strike price increases. If the 55.50 call was appropriately priced exactly midway between the 55 and 56 strikes, it would imply a constant delta over that entire range. Only if the 55.50 call premium lies below this midpoint are the equilibrium conditions fulfilled.

The bank may appear to be fair to its customer by charging this way. After all it is only just covering its costs. In reality, however, the customer is buying a long butterfly for the bank. Under the right circumstances there will be a tidy profit ($12,500 in the 5 million SF example), and there is absolutely no chance of loss.

Hedging the exposure of granted OTC options includes both dimensions of time and strike price. By understanding how these factors influence an option's price, banks are able to create profit opportunities for themselves while meeting their customers' demands. It is a situation of potential benefits for both sides, but once again, the customer should be aware of the risk and the pricing models to insure that there is appropriate value for the purchased services.

6.8   ALTERNATIVE APPROACHES TO COVERING FORWARD EXCHANGE EXPOSURE

6.8.1   Spot Rate Risk/Relative Interest Rate Risk

The IMM currency futures succeeded after a long learning period because the market broke open an interbank cartel that routinely excluded customers it did not believe qualified. Individuals and small businesses found it extremely difficult to express their market views. Furthermore, the IMM offered cost savings for smaller-sized transactions relative to that available from the banks. Still, after more than 15 years, the futures markets account for only a fraction of total currency transactions.

The forward market for currencies is dominant for a number of institutional reasons. First, the interbank market was well established, closely linked geographically, and extremely liquid before the introduction of the IMM in 1972. The model of multiple grain markets selling different products and linked only with high transportation costs did not apply to currencies. There was no quality or geographic basis risk to speak of because of the homogeneity of the market and the efficiency with which funds could be transferred. When the IMM futures were created, they did not become the center of the market, magnetically drawing information together as the early futures markets in grains had done.

The textbook futures transaction of a dealer hedging open forward commitments is not typical of currency risk management. When a bank offers a forward rate, it may be for anywhere up to a year or two or more into the future. The liquidity of the futures contracts past the nearby month is limited, making the classic hedge uneconomical. The dealer may establish the hedge in the nearby contract and roll the positions forward as liquidity builds in the next month, and certainly some hedges are built this way. More banks, however, break the problem apart into its spot price risk and the relative interest rate risk.

Suppose that a customer comes to a bank when the spot deutsche mark rate is 2.04 DM per dollar and wants to buy 10 million DM forward at a price of 2.00 for delivery in a year. The bank looks at the current 90-day Eurodollar rate and the spectrum of Eurodollar futures and calculates that the 360-day rate is implicitly 7.00 percent.[5] The bank, using Equation 6.1 to solve for r_G (the interest rate on deutsche marks), finds that if DMs can be invested to earn 4.89 percent (on a 360-day basis), the forward rate requested by the customer can be met.

$$2.00 = 2.04[1 + (r_G - .07)/([360/365] + .07)] \qquad (6.3)$$

$$r_G = 4.89\%$$

Believing that this rate objective can be met, the bank books the trade for the client and then begins the process of shedding the risk it has created. The first step is to borrow \$4.67 million for one year. This is the amount, at 7.0 percent interest, that is repayable with the \$5.0 million to be received in one year. The \$4.67 million is immediately converted to DM at the spot rate of 2.04 DM per dollar, returning 9.53 million DM today. If these funds earn 4.89 percent, 10 million DM will be available at maturity to meet the obligation.

The spot rate risk has been eliminated, but the bank still faces the risk that the Eurodollar interest rate will increase *relative* to the Euromark rate. Loans of this type rarely have a fixed interest rate for a full year. More typically, there will be a quarterly rolling over of the funds at the prevailing rates. This is the remaining risk in the transaction. Table 6.5 presents the outcomes under alternate pairs of annual average $r_\$$ and r_G.

There are three components to the net return. The difference in the spot and forward exchange rates produces a return to the bank holding the DMs even if the funds are not invested. In this example the appreciation is \$95 thousand, as the dollar goes from 2.04 to 2.00, and accrues to the holder of the marks under any interest rate outcome because the exchange rate risk has been removed. The other components are the interest paid on the borrowed dollars and the interest earned on the marks. Cases a and b demonstrate that parallel shifts in the interest rates of the two countries produce virtually offsetting changes in the interest paid and received. The asset and liability are equally affected.

In case c the Eurodollar rate increased by 100 basis points, with r_G staying constant, and in d, $r_\$$ stayed constant and return to the DM moved adversely. In either case the net effect is virtually the same. Case e is a catastrophe, with the

Table 6.5
Relative Interest Rate Risk

	DM					
	(all money values in thousands of dollars)					
Case	Appreciation	$r_\$$	Cost	r_G	Interest Income	net*
Target	95	7.00%	(331)	4.89%	236	0
a.	95	8.00%	(379)	5.89%	284	0
b.	95	6.00%	(284)	3.89%	188	-1
c.	95	8.00%	(379)	4.89%	236	-48
d.	95	7.00%	(331)	3.89%	188	-48
e.	95	8.00%	(379)	3.89%	188	-96
f.	95	6.00%	(284)	5.89%	284	96

* = DM appreciation plus net interest

cost of borrowed funds climbing and the return on the asset falling. Finally, the last example shows the interest rates equalizing and a windfall accruing to the banker.

How is this problem to be addressed? Today there are only limited and imperfect mechanisms available. Since relative interest rates are less volatile than the spot exchange rates, it is frequently the case that after the spot transaction occurs, the interest rate part is left uncovered in anticipation that another customer will appear soon with need for the opposite side of the transaction. If such a customer does arrive, the exposure will be eliminated. In the interim, by covering the lion's share of the exposure in the spot market, the bank has reduced its risk to a sometimes acceptable level.

The bank may have a speculative view toward relative rates and choose to hold this position for that purpose. In the example, if the expectation was for the spread to narrow, the forward sale of marks would be an ideal way to take a position. If the opposite expectation was held, the bank would adjust by offering to sell the DM at a higher forward rate to discourage the accumulation of an exposure that was expected to be harmful. The important consideration is that the bank may feel comfortable with a modest speculation in this area because the relative interest rates are not that volatile. There are few banks that would feel that comfortable with an outright exchange rate risk.

During times when there is more uncertainty on interest rates, the bank may not wish to speculate or hope that an offsetting transaction would become available promptly. The risk may be too much to bear. The choices at this stage are limited. Hedging the interest expense with a strip of Eurodollars would fix the cost side, but leave the return side open. If case c in the table was the ultimate outcome, the hedge would be perfect. However, such a position does nothing for the bank if it is r_G that is volatile (case d) and hurts the position if $r_\$$ and r_G are falling together (case b). Placing the Eurodollar strip is an expression of belief that not only will the spread move adversely, but that the greatest part of the move will be attributable to an adverse move in Eurodollars.

6.8.2   Eurorate Differentials

It would seem to be a logical step to hedge r_G in a Euromark contract, but this option is not available because no such contract exists. As popular as the Eurodollar contract is at the CME, there are no viable counterpart contracts for other Eurocurrencies in Europe or Asia. In times of volatile rates, there are no alternatives except to widen the bids and offers on the forward rate in an attempt to cover some of the risk until an internal hedge appears. This is not a good solution for the marketplace.

The CME has tried to attack this problem directly. It has developed but as of this writing has not received CFTC approval for a contract called a Eurorate Differential Contract ("DIFF"). The original proposal calls for three contracts capturing the relative interest rate differential between Eurodollar rates and Euromark, Eurosterling, and Euroyen rates, respectively (DM DIFFs, sterling DIFFs, and yen DIFFs). The pricing of the contract comes from the main part of Equation 6.1, and the terms are structured to parallel the Eurodollar contract.

Like the Eurodollar, the price is an index equaling 100 minus the key rate. In Eurodollars this key rate is the 90-day LIBOR for dollar deposits. For DIFFs the key rate is the *difference* between the same 90-day dollar LIBOR and the 90-day Eurocurrency LIBOR.

$$P = 100 - (r_\$ - r_f) * (90/360) \tag{6.4}$$

where r_f is the Eurocurrency rate for the non-U.S. funds.

From the equation, if the Eurodollar rates exceed those of the other Eurocurrency, the instrument will be priced below 100, but prices above 100 are also possible. It is incorrect to think of 100 as "par" in this case. It is only a starting point for the index.

Like the Eurodollar contract, a 0.01 price change produces a $25 change in the value of the contract. The rough analogy is that this equals the dollar interest payment for each 0.01 percentage point of interest on $1 million for 90 days. In this case, however, it is the 0.01 change in relative interest rates that is important.

Looking back on the example, the bank had a risk that the spread between rates would widen. In terms of equation 6.4, a wider spread would produce a lower price so the appropriate hedge would be to sell DM DIFFs. The risk covered a year, and the futures are structured in terms of 90-day segments, so a strip would be appropriate.

The arithmetic of strip hedging has already been demonstrated, so the detail will not be repeated here. It is sufficient to note that if the annual rates move 100 basis points, the combined change of a strip covering the period will be about $10,000.[6] Five strips, covering the $5 million at risk, would change about $50,000 per 100 point change in the differential. From Table 6.5, the two cases of 100 point adverse moves produced losses of $47,000 and $48,000, amounts that would be very closely offset by a DIFF hedge. In none of the cases in the example was there a relative rate move that could not be covered by such a contract. This is not true for hedges constructed with existing instruments.

Spreads can be constructed between DIFFs and the corresponding Eurodollar contract to create dollar-denominated synthetic Eurocurrency positions. If a trader held a view that Euroyen rates would rise but had no opinion on Eurodollars, the appropriate strategy would be to buy a yen DIFF and sell a Eurodollar future (note that the influence of r_f in Equation 6.4 is positive). As the Euroyen rate went up, it would make no difference what happened to Eurodollars, because that rate's influence on the two contracts in the spread would be offsetting. If the view on the yen rate was correct, the spread position would profit.

The demand for DIFFs has yet to be proven in the marketplace, but fundamentally the contracts address a segment of the banking industry that has a great deal of risk. Furthermore, for reasons that will be discussed in more detail in the next chapter, banks will have a greater incentive to move into such futures because of new bank capital requirements. These regulations require banks to make capital provisions for many off-balance sheet transactions like forward contracts to reflect the risk they represent. Any transactions extending beyond a year are particularly hard hit. Futures positions that are traded on exchanges with daily marking to market are, however, exempt from these charges, in recognition of the minimal credit risk they pose. For this reason the benefits of internal hedging with offsetting forward contracts may fall in the coming years, and more positions will be traded through the exchanges.

6.8.3 Swaps

In a pure forward transaction, there is no exchange of collateral. An agreement is made with the client, and the bank is exposed not only to the spot and relative interest rate risk but also to the chance that the counterparty will not perform. Since there is no collateral, or an organized system of margin, banks must choose their customers carefully. It is precisely this kind of risk that the new bank capital charges are designed to capture.

A creation to circumvent this problem is the swap. Instead of agreeing to an explicit forward rate, and hoping the counterparty will perform, the bank and the client exchange time deposits denominated in different currencies. At the time of the exchange, the timing and amounts of the return of principle and interest have been previously agreed upon. The swap pricing creates an implicit forward rate for the currencies.

In entering a swap agreement, the bank is still exposed to risk. There is the spot rate risk between the time of the agreement and the first exchange. This is usually immediately shed by buying the foreign currency, just as was done in the forward examples. The second risk comes from the interest rate risk if a rollover of the deposits is the responsibility of the bank.

Suppose that a bank enters into a swap arrangement taking in £20 million in 90-day deposits in exchange for $36 million of its own dollar deposits (spot rate = $1.80/£). The parties agree to swap back in 360 days $38.5 million for £22 million (forward rate = $1.75/£). The problem faced by the bank is guaranteeing that the sterling deposits will earn 10 percent for the duration of the swap. The interest rate risk on rolling the dollar deposits is the problem of the client.

There are currently only poor instruments available for hedging this risk, but with the introduction of DIFFs, a spread between the sterling DIFF and the Eurodollar futures should do the trick. Since the risk to the bank is that Eurosterling rates will fall, the DIFF should be sold and the Eurodollar futures bought. This would isolate the particular risk in question and should allow such banks to make much more efficient swap quotes since risk premiums do not have to be incorporated into the bid and offer for the swap.

Swaps have addressed an important risk in the area of foreign exchange transactions, namely, the counterparty risk. By holding a customer's collateral, there is a much greater probability of ultimate performance. This feature has opened the foreign exchange markets to many firms that would not otherwise have qualified for forward transactions. For this reason alone, they have been a major contributor to opening up these markets. However, risk is still there, and the new capital charges will apply to swaps. There is still the need for risk management, and, as usual, the futures markets are working to provide effective tools.

NOTES

1. There are always exceptions. Sterling is not quoted traditionally in terms of sterling per dollar but, instead, dollars per pound. The IMM futures markets are all quoted in terms of dollars per unit of foreign currency too. This inverts the above statements on backwardation and carry markets for cash sterling and all futures and options on futures.

2. The Canadian dollar futures size is 100,000 C$, so an exposure of 10.25 million C$ cannot be perfectly matched. A close fit would be obtained with either 102 or 103 contracts. The choice between the two should be based on the hedger's speculative bias of the C$ versus the US$.

3. The CME Swiss franc contract, options and futures, calls for the delivery of 125,000 SF. 20 contracts corresponds to 2.5 million SF.

4. If the bank had added a markup to the granted call, there would have been a parallel shift up in the combined risk curve to reflect this.

5. There may be a market quote for a one year rate, but it is likely that such a quote would be based on the offering bank doing the strip. There is little reason for a professional international bank to have this service done for them.

6. A likely situation would find the banker covered with 90-day interbank rates for the

first quarter and a strip of DIFFs for the remaining three. If the annual average moved 100 basis points, it would all have to occur in the last three quarters since the first is fixed. An average move of 133 points in each of quarters 2, 3, and 4 would accomplish this total move. Each DIFF contract would change $3,325 (133 * $25), implying that the strip would change about $10,000.

== CHAPTER 7 ==

Regulations, Accounting, and Risk Management

7.1   INTRODUCTION

The quickest and most certain way to date a book about markets is to include specifics on regulations, accounting rules, and taxes. It seems that the only industry growing faster than financial futures and options is the business of changing the tax code. Other areas of regulatory import have shown more stability (some would say inertia), but no text covering general issues can pretend to be topical covering the details. The tax, accounting, and regulatory themes covered below are designed to be a general introduction only, and no claim is made as to their continuing applicability. There is no substitute for sound professional advice from your lawyer and accountant. The final section on risk management and internal controls, however, depends only on common sense and should be timeless.

7.2   HEDGING DEFINED

The single most common division in regulations covering financial futures and options is between speculators and hedgers. Speculators are sometimes grudgingly accepted for the liquidity they provide to the marketplace, but nowhere are they encouraged through regulatory advantages. Hedgers, on the other hand, are widely recognized throughout the rules, and in most cases their futures market participation is structured to be as efficient as possible.

There are two dominant definitions of hedging. The first is provided in Section 1.3(z) of the General Regulations under the Commodity Exchange Act. This definition states that bona fide hedges are positions that "normally represent a substitute for transactions to be made or positions to be taken at a later time in a physical marketing channel, and where they are economically appropriate to the reduction of risks in the conduct and management of a commercial enterprise." The definition goes on to state that the risks could arise from the change in the value of actual or anticipated assets, liabilities, or services of the trader.

An important element of the CFTC definition precludes any position from being a hedge if it cannot be "established *and liquidated* in an orderly manner in accordance with sound commercial practice" (emphasis added). This language was designed to prevent commercial firms from establishing apparent hedge positions and then holding them through a normally uneconomic delivery in order to squeeze the market.

The CFTC regulations go on to enumerate several types of transactions that would automatically be categorized as a hedge, but they also make it clear that many trades not on the enumerated list would qualify for hedge treatment. The net result is that any position that can be matched to a risk in the balance sheet will in all likelihood qualify for CFTC hedge treatment if it is traded in an orderly fashion. Blake Imel and his associates (1985) traced the evolution of the CFTC hedge definition from its roots when it was only required to cover agricultural instruments to a time covering a broad range of financial futures. The basic principles have not changed significantly throughout the years, but today there are a number of commercial activities that use futures and options that are not linked directly to a cash market instrument. These trading strategies include the creation of synthetic cash market instruments that are not expected to be a "temporary substitute" for the actual position. Such strategies are logical steps in the use of futures and options, but their application may have been restricted by rules allowing only bona fide hedges. This subject is particularly important in the area of speculative position limits, which is discussed in the next section.

The CFTC definition is important for many regulations, but it is by no means the universal standard. Most exchanges use it whenever their own rules call for a distinction between speculators and hedgers (e.g., position limit rules, margin rules). Other bodies adopt definitions more in keeping with their notion of hedging, which may be more or less restrictive than the CFTC's rule.

The Financial Accounting Standards Board (FASB) Statement No. 80 (SFAS 80) defines the appropriate accounting standards for financial futures (not including foreign currency futures, which are covered in SFAS 52). The SFAS 80 definition requires four criteria to be met before a futures position can be considered a bona fide hedge:

1. The futures contract relates to a hedged item. Hedged items may include existing assets, liabilities, and firm commitments or anticipated transactions.
2. The futures contract must be designated as a hedge for either an individual item or a group of items at the time the position is established.
3. The hedged item must expose the firm to either interest rate or price risk.

4. It is probable that there is a high correlation between the futures contract and the hedged item. (Jarnagin and Booker, 1985)

SFAS 80 is deliberately silent on how high is a "high" correlation. The firm must be able to demonstrate that any hedge it claims has an adequate expected correlation to meet the criterion.

Hedges against anticipated transactions must identify the significant terms, including the maturity, of the anticipated cash action. The anticipated transaction need not be carried out, but there must have been a high likelihood of it occurring. A different transaction may not be substituted without the loss of hedge status for the futures (Arthur Andersen, 1985).

The FASB hedging definition is not based on the CFTC view of the world, but there are no apparent contradictions. As Imel and his colleagues pointed out (1985, p. 56), it is possible that the CFTC definition could be consulted in interpreting certain situations not covered explicitly in SFAS 80, but to date the CFTC staff has not been asked for such interpretations.

An important element in either definition is the implicit recognition of cross-hedging as a viable form of risk management. Throughout the text, examples have been given of specialized portfolios of stocks being hedged against the S&P 500 or short-term commercial debt being hedged in the Eurodollar contract. In all of these examples the futures was not the exact counterpart to the cash instrument. If the hedge definitions did not recognize these trades as bona fide, there would be numerous regulatory hurdles impeding their effective use. These regulations are discussed in subsequent sections.

7.3   EXCHANGE REGULATIONS

Exchanges want to make trading their contracts as easy as possible, but they also understand that if the trading and financial integrity of the markets cannot be insured, the likelihood of long-term success is small. To that end these self-regulatory bodies have developed a group of rules to oversee trading practices, financial standards, and the fair and open functioning of the markets. Typically, exchanges have departments of compliance, audits, and market surveillance to cover the three areas.

The exchanges' regulatory umbrella covers only its members, but there are times that data requests to those members may reach the customer level. If a nonmember believes that a request for information is onerous, there are no direct sanctions that an exchange may apply to for noncompliance. The quid pro quo, however, is that the member firms carrying the account may be disciplined, and the ultimate sanction is the liquidation of the position. Typically, when an exchange seeks information about an account or a trade, it does not do so in a flippant fashion or in an attempt to make work. It is trying to gather pieces to a complex puzzle to determine if the financial and trading sanctity of the market will be maintained.

Most steps the exchanges take in the areas of financial and market surveillance would be done whether or not there was a government regulator peering over their shoulders. One area of exchange regulation, however, was forced upon the exchanges by the 1982 Amendments to the Commodity Exchange Act. These amendments said that each designated board of trade must place into its rules limits to positions held by speculative accounts. Bona fide hedgers were not to be restricted by these position limits, but there had to be a mechanism to monitor the positions of commercial firms to verify that their positions were hedges.

The speculative position limit rules stemming from the 1982 amendments had their origin in federal spec limits in grains, oilseeds, and cotton. Some members in Congress were shocked to learn that silver during its rapid price increase in 1979–80 had no statutory limits on how large a position any speculator could hold. Although they wanted such limits in place universally, there was no inclination on the part of the CFTC to formulate and enforce these rules as they were required to do in the domestic agricultural products.

The exchanges all argued that speculative limits were an ineffective tool to manage positions and would prove burdensome to commercial firms who would have to apply for exemptive relief if they sought to take on hedges larger than the limits. All of this turned out to be true, but it did not dissuade the drafters of the amendment creating spec limits.

Commercial firms that want to take on hedge positions greater than the speculative limits must apply in advance to the exchange, typically to the market-surveillance department. The evidence in support of the application would include a description of the cash market activity forming the basis of the hedge. If the information is found complete, an expanded limit specific to the firm will be set. If these limits are found to restrict the hedging capacity of the firm, they can be expanded further.

To enforce these position limit rules, exchanges collect from the clearing firms position data by account. Every account above a certain minimum level must be identified. In that way the exchange can aggregate accounts of a common owner over all of its clearing members to form the total position. It is this total position that is subject to the limits.

If the 1982 amendments mandating these limits had not passed, it is doubtful that exchanges would have chosen to operate in this way. Large positions would be monitored to make sure that an account or group of accounts was not gaining an undue influence over the position, but the mountains of daily data that are piled up would probably not be collected. The CFTC's view of the world is that you cannot be too careful, whereas the exchanges would probably weigh the benefits of this activity more carefully against the costs.

Exchange self-regulation is working best when it appears invisible. To an average customer, the best situation occurs when fills are received promptly at a reasonable price, expirations are characterized by a careful convergence of cash and futures, and there are no financial incidents that threaten the customer's capital. If all of these conditions hold, the exchange regulatory mechanism will have little need to reach out to that customer, and all parties will be pleased.

7.4 ACCOUNTING FOR FINANCIAL FUTURES

Accounting standards for all financial futures except for currency futures are provided in SFAS 80. Currency futures and forwards are covered in SFAS 52. The major difference between the two treatments is that SFAS 80 recognizes anticipatory hedges and SFAS 52 does not. To be treated as a hedge, a foreign currency future must be against a current asset, liability, or firm commitment. This inconsistency is minor but should be recognized.

The basic accounting principles are made easy because of the mark-to-market system used to evaluate and margin futures. For futures that are entered into for speculation, unrealized gains and losses, as well as realized gains and losses, should be included in the current income statement. Similar procedures are used for hedge positions against cash instruments that are carried at market value. Only when the hedges are against cash instruments that are not carried at market value are the gains or losses deferred.

The principles rely on symmetric treatment of the cash and futures instruments. If the gains on the futures offset the losses on cash, it is only proper that they be recognized in the same period as the cash market instrument's outcome. The steps that must be followed to qualify for this treatment involve verification of the matching of the cash and futures instruments. In particular, disclosure must be made identifying the instruments being hedged and the method of accounting for the futures contracts.

Accepted options accounting standards have not been set by the FASB in a formal statement of financial accounting. Instead, the industry has developed a set of consistent treatments that should be used as a guide. In 1985 the Accounting Standards Executive Committee of the American Institute of Certified Public Accountants approved a paper entitled ''Accounting for Options.'' This has been submitted to the FASB for consideration, but as of March 1989, the board had not acted on it. In the absence of a formal standard, there may be alternative approaches available. Major accounting firms frequently publish brochures outlining their views (e.g., Arthur Andersen, 1986), but the user should carefully consult with his or her own accountant for guidance in this area.

The treatment of options on futures closely parallels the standards set for futures. If the options are not hedges, they are to be marked to market and treated in current income. If they are hedges, but the hedged item is carried at market value, mark-to-market treatment is also used. Settlement prices for all exchange options are used to meet this mark-to-market standard. If the options are OTC, it may be difficult to get accurate prices for this purpose. In such cases an accepted standard pricing model may be used as a basis for the daily evaluation.

For hedges against items not carried at the market, the accounting becomes more complicated. The first distinction is between purchased and written options. Purchased options qualify for hedge treatment if the option position reduces some price or interest rate risk of the hedge item. The option must also be designated as a hedge at the time it is purchased. As with the futures definition of a hedge, there must be the anticipation of a reasonable correlation between the cash instrument and the *underlying instrument* of the option. This allows for the possibility of cross-hedging with options.

Written options are more difficult. They must meet the criteria required of purchased options, but some firms believe that the written option must also be deep in-the-money or be matched in delta-equivalent groups to qualify as a hedge. The rationale for this view is that such options on futures behave basically like the futures and can therefore be matched against a cash instrument. The treatment that applies for short options depends greatly on the degree of protection afforded versus the income generated from the premiums. If the intention of the option was to provide price protection and was so identified, hedge accounting treatment of the option may be allowed. If, however, the intention was to generate income, the premium should be marked to the market since there is no underlying hedge item.

There are some accountants who hold that other short options can qualify for hedge treatment, and at the opposite extreme are those who believe that no written option should qualify. These are open questions since the final standards have not been set. For a firm using short straddles and strangles as mechanisms for managing inventory risk, the final resolution of these issues is of great importance.

Options also pose differences caused by the distinction between time and intrinsic value, which *may* be split in the accounting of purchased options used for hedging. Since time value erodes over the life of the option independently of the value of the underlying instrument, it may be thought of as an insurance cost. This cost, treated separately from the intrinsic value, can be amortized over the life of the instrument. Hedge accounting as discussed for futures should be applied to the intrinsic portion of the option. If the hedge item is valued at the market, so should the intrinsic value. If gains and losses on the hedge item are included in income as they arise, the intrinsic value should be matched to that realization.

Short options do not have this insurance payment characteristic, and the time and intrinsic values should not be split under any circumstances. Suppose that an option is written as protection against a decline in a cash instrument. The protection is limited to the size of the collected premium, which includes both time and intrinsic values. For this reason they should not be split.

Combination positions with options pose interesting cases that are usually recognized in logical ways. Synthetic futures positions created by the combination of long and short options should be treated identically as regular futures. An option spread where the premium paid exceeds that of the premium received can be treated like a long option, with the net time value amortized over the life of the option and the net intrinsic value matched to the hedge item. Net credit spreads are treated like simple short options.

In the previous interest rate and currency chapters, examples were given of caps and collars. These positions can be constructed explicitly by the hedger using exchange-traded options, or cash transactions incorporating these option features may be purchased in the OTC market. Any fees paid for a cap should be treated as the premium of a long option. The time value may be amortized, and any reimbursement payments that occur are the equivalent of intrinsic value and should be included in the cost of the ultimate purchase. The OTC collars should be similarly treated as option spreads.

Financial futures and options are relatively young instruments, and the accounting practices covering their use have evolved quickly and in most cases logically. The major area of uncertainty is the treatment of written options, but as experience grows with all option products the standards will become clearer. Consistency of treatment and completeness of documentation will certainly continue to be the foundation of any treatment.

7.5   TAX TREATMENT OF FUTURES AND OPTIONS

The tax code's rapid evolvement over the 1980s reached every corner of modern commerce, and financial futures and options were no exception. When it comes to taxes, the treatment afforded hedge and speculative positions are widely different. The hedge accounting rules discussed in the previous section reflect the tax treatment. Anything that is marked to market is treated as current income, and anything afforded hedge considerations can be deferred to the period when the hedge item is considered for tax purposes. Speculative trades have not had such a consistent pattern.

The tax treatment of speculative futures had three major phases in the 1980s. Before the Economic Recovery Act of 1981, futures positions were treated like capital assets. Gains or losses were realized upon the liquidation of the position, and those held for more than six months qualified for long-term capital gains treatment. Such characteristics enabled some large-wealth individuals to defer payments of unrelated capital gains by using a strategy known as "tax straddling." Relatively risk-free offsetting spread positions would typically be established. As the underlying market moved, one spread would have a gain, another a loss. The losing straddle would be realized by rolling it into another spread. In that way a loss in the current year could be generated and the offsetting gain preserved until the next tax year. With a bit of planning, it could be translated into a long-term gain qualifying for lower tax rates. This practice was challenged successfully in the courts by the IRS, but it was more effectively eliminated by the revised treatment of futures in the 1981 Act.

The Economic Recovery Act of 1981 carved out a separate and unique set of rules for futures. It said that all futures contracts had to be marked to market at year end so that any gains or losses could be accounted for in the current year.

This destroyed the possibility of rolling gains from year to year and ended the concept of tax straddling. There were genuine hardships created by this change, so as partial compensation, futures gains and losses were deemed to be 60 percent long term and 40 percent short term, *no matter what the actual holding period was*. With the maximum marginal rate for individuals at 50 percent, this produced a tax rate of 32 percent for futures (0.40 at a short-term rate of 50 percent and 0.60 at the long-term rate of 20 percent).

Options on futures were not part of the equation until 1982, at which time the appropriate tax treatment had not been determined. Some argued that they should be treated like stock options, but it was quickly realized that this would reopen a crack for a new breed of tax straddles to crawl in. ''Section 1256'' contracts joined the vocabulary shortly thereafter. Section 1256 of the Internal Revenue Code defines a group of contracts that require marking to market and year-end evaluation. These contracts include ''regulated futures contracts'' (exchange-traded, marked-to-market futures), foreign currency futures or forwards, non-equity options on futures or broad-based designated indexes like the OEX, and dealer options. All Section 1256 contracts would qualify for the same treatment previously afforded futures.

The only wrinkle to this fabric came from mixed straddles, which were positions that contained both Section 1256 contracts and other instruments that were afforded regular capital gains treatment. In these cases, if the mixed straddle was appropriately identified at its inception, the Section 1256 contracts in it would be afforded the same treatment as the other instruments. This view paralleled that of hedge treatment of Section 1256 contracts in keeping the offsetting positions on a common footing.

The Tax Reform Act of 1986 indirectly changed the treatment given to these contracts without ever explicitly mentioning them. By eliminating the distinction between rates on long- and short-term capital gains, the 60/40 rule for futures became superfluous. It is worthy of note, however, that the 60/40 treatment for Section 1256 contracts was not eliminated, so if a wedge ever again develops between the long- and short-term rates, futures and their options will have unique rates.

There are four classes of traders for tax purposes: brokers, commercial hedgers, traders, and investors. A broker acts as an agent and earns commission income that is completely separate from trading gains and losses, which are typically taxed identical to the positions of an investor. As we have seen, commercial hedgers match their positions against cash market obligations and use standard accounting principles to reflect this. Income and losses from hedging are ordinary income. Traders are different from investors in the intensity of their effort. Individuals whose livelihoods depend almost entirely on trading profits can deduct certain expenses to arrive at an adjusted gross income that are not allowed to investors. Investors' expenses are limited by the rules governing itemized deductions.

The old phrase, ''The more things change, the more they stay the same,'' does not apply to taxes. The decade of the 1980s saw constant major and minor tinkering to all elements of the tax code, and futures and options were certainly affected. There is no reason to expect any more consistency in the future. What can be hoped is that a modicum of consistency is maintained so that investors and hedgers can concentrate on the markets rather than try to navigate through a series of decision-distorting tax rates.

7.6   SPECIFIC INDUSTRY REGULATIONS

In addition to Exchange and CFTC regulations, the general tax code, and broad accounting standards, there are certain industries like mutual funds, commercial banks, and insurance companies that have particular crosses to bear. The depth of the individual regulation varies from industry to industry, but virtually everything beyond the broad brush strokes is too detailed for this chapter. What follows is an outline of key topics by industry that shape decisions about the use of futures and options by a particular group. The topics are more completely treated in a series of CME "White Papers" (1986, 1987a, 1987b, 1987c, 1987d, 1987e). Like the tax code and accounting standards, developments in this area can occur quickly and should be monitored closely.

7.6.1   Mutual Funds

Mutual funds must be registered with the SEC according to the Securities Act of 1933 and the Investment Company Act of 1940. Part of the requirements of such funds is the preparation and distribution of a prospectus that identifies the fund's objectives, the manner of trying to reach the objectives, and the risks. In the prospectus the fund would identify that it intends to trade futures and options and in what capacity. If a fund has never before traded futures and options it must first obtain shareholder approval before amending its registration and new prospectus. It must also receive clearance from the SEC and the CFTC.

One of the biggest obstacles in the path of mutual funds to using futures and options was the prohibition in the 1940 Act against mutual funds issuing "senior securities." This was designed to prevent the funds from issuing debt more senior than the claim of the shareholders and thus expose that group to risk. The SEC traditionally maintained that by opening a margin account, a fund would be creating the possibility of senior claims. To protect themselves against possible violations of the 1940 Act, certain funds have sought "no action" letters from the SEC stating that if they engage in such trading they will not be pursued by the SEC. Relief has typically been conditional on the fund agreeing that all such futures and options will be used for hedging purposes. Sometimes firms have stipulated limits of their total assets that could be covered by futures. Since the positions are designed to reduce the risk of the portfolio, the SEC has generally granted the relief.

The custody of margin funds is a classic example of the conflicting regulatory reach. The Commodity Exchange Act and the CFTC Regulations stipulate that all customer funds at an FCM be segregated and accounted for separately. Moreover, the FCM must have access to those funds on demand. The 1940 Act, however, states that a fund's securities and investments must be placed in the custody of a bank, a member of a national securities exchange, or the fund itself.

To meet the requirements of both laws, funds and FCMs have set up custodial accounts at third-party banks. The CFTC allows this arrangement under the condition that an FCM has the absolute right to liquidate open positions in an account in deficit or draw down funds under certain circumstances. The SEC goes along with the arrangement if the custodian releases funds to the FCM only if the fund has failed to honor its commitments to the FCM, and the fund sweeps excess funds from the account regularly. It is not clear whether third-party custodial accounts insulate a fund's shareholders as intended by the 1940 Act, but it is true that the statutes have created an extra, very expensive, layer of steps for FCMs and their customer funds.

There are special federal tax treatments that apply to regulated investment companies (RICs). In particular, if certain conditions are met, a fund will not be subject to federal income tax on the investment income and capital gains it distributes to its shareholders. To qualify as a regulated investment company:

1. At least 90 percent of the fund's gross income must come from dividends, interest, payments for securities loans, gains from the sale of stock or other securities, and gains from options and futures.
2. Less than 30 percent of its gross income must be derived from the sale of stock or securities held for less than three months.
3. A fund must diversify its holdings along prescribed lines.

The second item on the list caused many funds to shy away from futures and options as a short-term substitute for cash positions, since such trading activity could jeopardize the fund's status as an RIC. The Tax Reform Act of 1986 had in it an important milestone, amending point 2 to allow gains and losses from clearly identified hedge transactions to be netted.

7.6.2   Pension Plans

The Employee Retirement Income Security Act of 1974 (ERISA) spells out the fiduciary responsibilities covering the vast majority of private employee benefit plans. A fiduciary to a pension plan is anyone who:

1. Exercises authority or control over a plan's management or the disposition of its assets
2. Gives investment advice (for compensation) concerning the plan's property
3. Has any discretionary authority in the administration of the plan

In 1982 the Labor Department, which oversees the administration of ERISA, determined that margin funds at an FCM are not plan assets and therefore the FCM would not be deemed a fiduciary to the plan merely because it holds margin funds.

The primary responsibility of a fiduciary is to act in a prudent fashion in regard to the plan's portfolio, in the exclusive interest of the plan's participants and beneficiaries. In issuing its prudent investor regulations in 1979, the Labor Department appeared to endorse an approach to investing that evaluated the entire portfolio rather than looking at the individual components. Before that, some fiduciaries had feared that they would be judged imprudent if they had highly leveraged futures and options in their portfolio, even if the net result was a reduction of risk.

The view now is that futures and options are neither inherently prudent or imprudent, the standard being the role they play in the entire portfolio. Some have gone further to argue that fiduciaries who do not hedge when it is possible to do so are acting imprudently. The acceptance of these instruments is not yet so wide that this extreme view holds much sway, but it is true that more funds are becoming knowledgeable about the risk reduction possibilities of hedging.

7.6.3   Savings and Loan Associations

The Federal Home Loan Bank Board (FHLBB) regulates all federal savings and loan associations. In the early 1980s this regulator recognized that interest rate options and futures could be an effective tool in managing interest rate risk and authorized their associations and those insured by the Federal Savings and Loan Insurance Corporation (FSLIC) to hedge with these instruments. State-chartered associations insured by the FSLIC are also subject to state approval.

Futures transactions in these instruments are allowed to reduce the firm's "net interest rate exposure," which can be viewed as the volatility of earnings caused by a mismatch of interest-sensitive assets and liabilities. Macrohedging is allowed, eliminating the need to identify individual cash instruments as the basis for the hedge contracts. Savings and loans are restricted in the contracts they may trade to a set corresponding to their permitted cash investments. Exchange-traded futures and options on T-bills, T-bonds, and Eurodollars are all allowed, but the firm may not trade agricultural products, metals, or currencies.

Since savings and loans are typically at risk from rising rates raising the cost of their deposits higher than their returns on the mortgages, short positions in interest rate futures are most widely recognized. The FHLBB has produced an enumerated list of strategies that may be used, and other nonenumerated approaches may be acceptable. The list includes short positions:

1.   To protect against risks resulting from forward commitments to originate or purchase mortgages

2.   To protect the value of the portfolio

3. To fix liability cost

4. To protect against risks resulting from a maturity imbalance between assets and liabilities

Long positions are severely restricted to a few instances in which they offset short positions or cover the commitment to sell mortgages forward at a fixed price. These long hedges are further limited to those instances when the forward commitments exceed 10 percent of the firm's long-term assets with fixed interest rates. There is clearly an apprehension that long positions may be misused for short-term speculation. Interestingly, the FHLBB does not allow spreading of futures contracts, since it views that activity as an attempt for profit that may create interest rate exposure rather than hedge it.

Options may generally be traded as long as they are exchange traded and approved by the CFTC or SEC or options generated by a member of the Association of Primary Dealers in United States Securities. There is no requirement that the options be used to reduce interest rate risk.

Long options may be taken on without limit, on the assumption that the size of the premium will discourage excessive use. Short *covered* calls are also not limited. Short puts are another story, being subject to limits based on a sliding scale of assets and net worth. As traditional as the FHLBB's view on futures is, their stance on options is a curious mixture of traditional and laissez-faire.

7.6.4 Commercial Banks

Numerous regulatory bodies have their fingers in the pie when it comes to commercial banks. The comptroller of the currency has primary regulatory responsibility for nationally chartered banks. For bank holding companies or state member banks, the Federal Reserve has that role. Insured, state-chartered, non-member banks are the domain of the Federal Deposit Insurance Corporation, and various state regulators cover noninsured state banks. What follows emphasizes the allowable activities of national banks and holding companies. For guidance on the other types of commercial banking activities, the respective regulators should be contacted.

The comptroller of the currency noted in Banking Circular No. 79 (1983) that national banks may use financial futures under their broad authority to exercise "all incidental powers" that are necessary to carry on the business of banking. The circular goes on to note that the contracts may be used to reduce interest rate risk arising from their portfolio or from asset-liability mismatches. It also mentioned that futures as part of the dealer–bank permitted trading activities should conform to safe and sound banking practices.

The guidelines given to bank holding companies in this area by the Federal Reserve Board include:

1. The establishment of written guidelines by the holding company to insure that financial futures and options are being used in a safe and sound manner

2. Internal controls and audit programs

3. That all open positions should be reviewed and market values determined at least monthly

4. A prohibition on speculative practices

5. Written notification within ten days to the District Federal Reserve Bank once financial futures or options trading is begun

With the exception of point 3, the treatment is fairly noncontroversial, recognizing the hedging potential of the contracts. Point 3 is surprising only because any firm trading these positions should monitor the trading positions much more often than monthly.

Possibly the most important development in banking regulations during the latter half of the 1980s was the development of revised capital adequacy rules. An overview of the plan can be found in Federal Reserve Bank of New York (1987). Internationally, the accounting treatment of bank capital can vary widely from nation to nation. This, combined with the rapid evolution of "off-balance sheet" items like interest rate and currency swaps and forwards, had led to a broad dissatisfaction with the completeness of the capital adequacy rules. In multinational negotiations, 12 major developed counties agreed in the summer of 1988 to minimum standards that would be fully operational by 1992.[1]

Widely recognized as an important step to strengthen international banking, these standards defined capital uniformly, weighted bank assets by their degree of risk, and set minimum capital levels for banks to maintain. From the futures and options perspective, the most important element was the capital haircuts required for off-balance sheet items. For the first time, there will be capital charges against OTC products like interest rate and currency forwards and swaps. The charges on instruments extending beyond a year are particularly severe, reflecting the additional risk that the long-dated contracts pose.

Notable in this new treatment is the explicit recognition that exchange-traded futures and options that require daily mark-to-market variation payments will not be subject to any capital charges. This is a strong positive recognition of the minimal risk of these contracts as compared to the counterparty risk posed by OTC instruments. The net effect is that there will be an incentive to move off-balance sheet items onto the floor of an exchange, as the banks try to structure their portfolios to minimize any negative impact on their capital. As the demand for financial futures grows, the exchanges will have to be attuned to the needs of this section of the financial community to enhance their products' appeal. There is a significant chance that open interest will begin to build in the back months for long-term positions or that strategies like stacking will become more widely used.

7.6.5 Insurance Companies

The approach to regulation of insurance companies is every state for itself. As of 1987, 35 states and the District of Columbia allowed trading in futures and options in some form, whereas the remaining 15 either had outright prohibitions or had not allowed any of their companies specific permission to trade. Among the states that allow trading, there are a wide variety of approaches. Most states allow trading for hedging only, and frequently a cap is placed on the percentage of assets that may be devoted to such trading.

Because of the importance of New York's regulations to a broad class of insurers, they deserve a closer look. The rules allow only hedging in futures, options, and options on futures to reduce interest rate and foreign exchange risk. According to New York state rules, only anticipatory hedging is permitted because authorized hedging transactions must offset price changes in eligible investments intended to be sold or acquired. A hedge may not be held for more than one year, and the timing of the hedge must closely match the timing of the cash transaction. There are strict limitations on the cost of the hedge relative to the firm's admitted assets.

The peculiar features of the New York rules when compared with the guidelines covering banks, pension funds, and mutual funds are not unique to that state. Quirks and inconsistencies abound, and the nation's exchanges are working hard to bring about more consistent standards. Until that happens, insurance companies will in all but a handful of states continue to be severely hampered in their efforts to manage risk with options and futures.

7.7   INTERNAL RISK MANAGEMENT AND CONTROL

The previous sections of this chapter have emphasized external regulations, accounting procedures, and tax laws. Any complete treatment of futures and options trading cannot ignore these effects, since they may make the difference between deciding to hedge or not. But once the outside environment is defined, the decision to trade must be made in the best possible internal environment. Hedging is not something that can be turned on and off like a light bulb, one day being good, the next day being something to be avoided. Hedging decisions must be part of the complete decision-making framework. Firms that have a history of success using futures and options to manage their risks have developed a tradition of complete integration. Futures and options are not matched against cash positions as an afterthought or add on. To develop an effective plan requires knowledge and control.

7.7.1   Ex Ante and Ex Post Hedging

A firm that has never used derivative instruments before suddenly decides to see what hedging is all about. Why? Typically, such a shift in view is a response to a negative event. Interest or exchange rates shifted suddenly, turning a promising enterprise into a big loser. The incentives are even higher to shift gears if a competitor did not show a loss because it had been hedged. The attitude is that "if only I had done that, things would have been great."

Although bitter experience is sometimes an effective way to get a point across, the view expressed above is one of the worst possible reasons to think about trading futures and options. An attitude that emphasizes looking back, or ex post evaluation, will sooner or later damn the hedge approach because it will lead to the statement "if only I hadn't done that . . ."

Given the relative youth of financial futures and options, there are few firms that are genuinely expert in this trade. Banks and securities dealers are among the best operations because of their long-standing trading orientation. Among manufacturing firms, agricultural and food-oriented companies stand out because their familiarity with traditional futures has been remarkably transportable into the new arena. These firms all share a common characteristic: they look forward. If a trade makes sense it does so before the first position is established. Ex ante evaluation requires confidence and agreement in the decision. If an "unhedged" outcome would have produced large gains, the original strategy is not condemned, because the firm understands that today's home run might be tomorrow's pop up with the bases loaded.

The fundamental decision that has to be made does not concern which tools to use and how. A firm must decide if it is willing to speculate in an area that is within its power to control. But speculation is a matter of degree. A company that has no wish to leave its fate in the hands of an uncertain interest rate level may make a very conscious decision regarding the relative price of the cash instrument and the futures or option it trades against. The firm must decide what areas it has an advantage in and in what ways should it control those factors where there is no advantage.

Thomas Fitzgerald (1986), in a candid talk entitled "How Corporations Use Futures," described the preparation that goes into trading decisions at Hershey Foods Corporation (HFC), a firm that has long taken a professional approach to the markets it is involved in. His examples all relied on the cocoa market since that is probably the most basic trading that HFC engages in, but everything about the decision process is perfectly generic. Fitzgerald, who moved through the commodity purchasing side of the HFC to become its corporate treasurer, knows well that the same process used in making cocoa trading decisions also applies to actions in financial futures.

Fitzgerald's comments described only the HFC, but they could have been made about any of HFC's major competitors in the chocolate business. M & M Mars, Cadbury, or any other major chocolatier would not have persisted in that business without a similar command of trading and risk management. The firms in the industry may not always make the same decisions because of varying market opinions, but the process arriving at those decisions looks very similar across the firms.

The first decision concerns the firm's objectives. The HFC has decided that its prime objective is to be competitive selling chocolate products, which means that speculation on the price of cocoa or another cost that can be extremely detrimental to the long-run success of the company should be avoided. The board and senior management are of a like mind as to what direction the firm should take and the tools best suited to the task.

This view does not mean that the company operates without regard to price or that it follows a mechanical strategy designed to drive the variance of factor costs to zero despite the total impact. Fitzgerald outlined four steps that the HFC follows to formulate its trading decisions:

1. The development of a business plan
2. An assessment of risk tolerance
3. An assessment of the competitive situation
4. An evaluation of the market

The business plan includes profit objectives, production decisions, cash flow questions, and any marketing factors that need to be considered. This strategic plan defines the targets in a realistic manner. For a company like HFC in which the cost of raw materials is a large fraction of total sales, variability in the price of commodities is an important component in the development of a strategy. As market volatility increases, the importance climbs even more.

The HFC has a planning horizon spanning several years. One approach to risk would be to fix the price of cocoa with forward commitments spanning the entire horizon. This would eliminate price volatility but would prove disastrous if cash prices tumbled after the supplies were priced. The HFC's competitors would have it at a significant price advantage for the duration of the hedge. What they do instead is estimate their commodity costs several quarters out and establish targets that would achieve certain levels of profitability. These targets are revised as market conditions unfold or business conditions change. They keep one eye on the market and one eye on the business plan. Importantly, the coordination between the market and the business plan is done by a high-ranking committee on a weekly basis.

The company must evaluate its tolerance to risk. Public companies might be more risk averse than privately held firms for a variety of reasons. Other factors will enter this decision as well. Full exposure to prices may be too much risk, but complete cover probably generates too little. The HFC views itself as flexible relative to its market expectation and business plan. The futures market is used as a mechanism for achieving the plan when appropriate, not as a total risk avoidance device.

A firm's competitive situation is important in developing pricing strategies and evaluating the need for risk reduction. A strong competitive pressure may allow little tolerance for risk, or it may push the firm to become more aggressive in its strategies. A firm's own business plan should concentrate on its own strengths, while being aware of the competition.

Finally, pricing decisions must be made. As the market events mesh with the business plan, opportunities develop to buy the needed raw materials. There may be a good cash price in Ghana to act on, or the futures may be priced to make an anticipatory hedge appropriate. An options strategy may arise that fits into the plan and offers an additional profit opportunity. If the game plan has been developed appropriately, there will be chances across the markets to implement it. If adjustments are required they can be made, but the evaluation of the trading effectiveness is always made against the business plan and not against some hypothetical after the fact strategy.

The above program works at the HFC and countless other firms that understand and appreciate the role of the options and futures markets in meeting their total goals. Implicitly behind this program is a system of control to insure that there are no unplanned deviations from the game plan. The extent of possible control is discussed in the next section.

7.7.2   Internal Control

The steps leading to a trading decision were described above and, importantly, included top-level understanding of the targets and the mechanics needed to get there. A trader who wants to incorporate a new option strategy into the plan should in all likelihood have to convince the firm's senior management and board that the proposal fits into all of the firm's targets and risk tolerances. This is the ideal, but it is sometimes not the reality.

Too often in the rapidly evolving world of financial futures and options there is a schism between the traders and the ultimate decision makers. There are the traders who know, or think they know, how the strategies work and managers who might be overwhelmed by the technical expertise of the traders and so fall back on the ex post bottom line as an evaluation tool. Such cases are ripe for catastrophe.

There are many stories of prize money managers who are written up for their high returns one year, and in the next year, when the losses pile up, their clients are shocked that they were ever exposed to such risk. The example of IOs and POs at Merrill Lynch seemed certainly to fall into this category, unless the management explicitly recognized that they were exposing the firm to tens of millions of dollars in risk. Internal control starts with knowledge and ends with having the appropriate monitoring tools.

Going back to the trader with a new options strategy to try, the appropriate first step is internal education. As this book has hopefully demonstrated, there is nothing that mysterious about evaluating the risks and rewards of cash, futures, or options positions. Anyone who cannot present the basics without relying on pages of advanced math should be encouraged to try the approach first with his or her own capital.

The problem is that the incentives and costs are not symmetric in these cases. If the trader uses the new idea and it loses the firm a great deal of money, he or she will in all likelihood get fired. The loss may be extreme, but it is limited. If the strategy works, the trader gets recognition, bonuses from the profits, and maybe an offer from a competing firm, all representing a considerable upside potential. The firm, on the other hand, sees more limited profit opportunities but faces the full force of the loss should that outcome occur. The trader is essentially long an option, and the firm is short. Absent a significant payment to cover the risks, there would seem to be no reason why a firm would want to allow itself to be in this position, but, unfortunately, cases too often appear.

Any firm involved with trading of futures and options should have a clear understanding of the risks and rewards of the position before trading is authorized. These risks must be monitored regularly, and that is when modern sophistication can play a prominent role. The technology exists to evaluate the current position on a virtually real-time basis any time the markets are open. More importantly, however, as events are changing, option models can simulate further changes in prices and volatilities to measure the impact on the portfolio.

If the model captures the essence of the risk/return of the instrument in question, the firm can do much more than check overnight to see what the profits and losses are. It is now possible to build real-time simulators to identify potential trouble spots before they occur. With such controls, strategies can be developed to initiate rebalancing trades to reduce the probability of disaster.

The ultimate control rests with the firm. Depending on the thirst for profit or the desire for stability, traders can be kept on a loose leash or under rigid control. Strategy decisions should always be made beforehand, and the investment in monitoring compliance with the strategy should be commensurate with the a priori need for risk control.

7.7.3   Final Comments

Firms managed risks from equity price changes, currency movements, and interest rates for hundreds of years before the invention of financial futures in the 1970s. The contracts came into being not because they were indispensable to the management of risk, but because they were extremely efficient in solving certain dimensions of the problem. Careful firms were slow to adopt these trading techniques, but this should be seen as a sign of the firms' careful approach to risk that had probably served them reasonably well for decades. Responsible traders do not just wake up one morning and say, "I think this is a good day to start trading futures."

Progress in trading has seen a steady climb. This is reflected in trading volumes for these products that seem never to quit expanding, except for the occasional after-crash pause now and then. The trading populations will likely continue to grow as more domestic firms learn the advantages and the markets become increasingly internationalized. The base keeps expanding, and care must be taken to insure it is solid growth.

The most promising note comes from the experience that has been gained in widely varied trading environments. As traders move up in the ranks of management, trading in options and futures will no longer be thought of as special or extra activities. Instead, it will be incorporated rightfully into the main flow of activities and decisions. It can also be expected that as financial futures and options traders gain more experience, they will be better prepared the next time there is a severe shock to any of the markets. Developing better, more informed business plans and having improved market skills should provide for even broader risk management opportunities in the future.

NOTE

1. Belgium, Canada, France, Italy, Japan, Luxembourg, the Netherlands, Sweden, Switzerland, United Kingdom, United States, and West Germany.

Glossary

AMERICAN OPTION. An option that may be exercised at any time before expiration.

ANTICIPATORY HEDGE. A futures or option position that is taken on to protect the value on an anticipated purchase or sale at a later date, in the cash market.

ARBITRAGE. The nearly simultaneous purchase and sale of equivalent commodities with the desired effect of gaining a profit. This action brings two prices closer in line.

ASK. The price at which an individual is willing to sell. Also known as the offer price.

AT-THE-MONEY. An option that has its exercise price equal to the underlying price.

BACKWARDATION. An array of prices that has the forward or futures contracts priced lower than the spot price. Also known as inverted or reverse carry. Opposite of contango.

BASIS. The difference between the prices of two instruments differentiated by space, time or quality.

BEAR MARKET. A market in which prices are falling.

BEAR SPREAD. A combination of a long and short futures, a long and short call, or a long and short put, such that the position is expected to profit with declining prices.

BID. The price at which an individual is willing to buy.

BID/ASK SPREAD. The difference between the prevailing bid and ask prices. (*See* Prevailing Bid/Ask.)

BINOMIAL MODEL. A model that assumes the next outcome can be one of only two possibilities.

BOX. A combination of a long call and short put at one strike price plus a short call and long put at another price. This is a long synthetic futures plus a short synthetic futures.

BUCKET SHOP. An enterprise where customer orders are matched against other customers or the house position instead of being sent to the floor of an exchange for execution and clearance. Illegal in the United States.

BULL MARKET. A market in which prices are increasing.

BULL SPREAD. A combination of long and short futures, a long and short call, or a long and short put, such that the position is expected to profit from increasing prices.

BUTTERFLY SPREAD. A combination of options, either all calls or all puts, that involves a long option at one strike price, short two options at a higher strike, and another long option at yet a higher strike. The difference between the first two strikes should equal the difference between the second and third.

CALENDAR SPREAD. A combination of a short and long call, or short and long put, that is based on different option months. The strike prices of the two options may be the same or different.

CALL. An option that gives its holder the right to buy the underlying instrument.

CARRY. *See* Contango.

CASH AND CARRY. A combination of a long cash position and a short futures position designed to profit from a price basis greater than the cost of carry.

CASH MARKET. The market for immediate sale or purchase of an instrument. Also known as the spot market.

CASH SETTLEMENT. The form of final futures or options settlement that involves a payment of cash rather than ultimate delivery of the underlying instrument.

CHEAPEST TO DELIVER. The cash market instrument meeting the delivery specifications of a futures contract that can be delivered at least cost to the short.

CLEARING HOUSE. The entity organized to match and process trades of buyers and sellers on a futures or options exchange(s). Usually either an independent corporation or a division of an exchange(s).

CLEARING MEMBER. A firm that is a member of a clearing house.

COMMISSION. A fee paid for the execution of a trade.

CONDOR SPREAD. A combination of options, either all calls or all puts, covering four strike prices: long options at each of the first and fourth strikes and short options at each of the second and third strikes. The strike prices should be at equal intervals.

CONTANGO. An array of prices that has the forward or futures contracts priced higher than the spot price. Also known as a carry. Opposite of backwardation.

CONTINUOUS. The property of a function that has no gaps.

CONVERSION. A spread position consisting of a short futures contract plus a long call and a short put with the same strike price.

CONVERSION FACTOR. A constant calculated by the CBOT for each deliverable T-bond or T-note that converts the cash instrument into the hypothetical par delivery bond or note.

COST OF CARRY. The expense of holding a product from one time to another. Typically, the cost of carry will include storage and financial costs.

COUPON. The regularly scheduled, periodic interest paid on a bond.

COVERED CALL. A position where the writer of a call also holds a long position in the underlying instrument.

CROSS-RATE. From the U.S. perspective, a cross-rate is any exchange rate between two non–U.S. currencies.

DAILY SETTLEMENT. The process of establishing the trading day's final price. Used as a foundation for marking positions to market.

DAY TRADER. Any futures or options trader who establishes and unwinds all positions during each trading session.

DEEP-IN-THE-MONEY. An option that, if exercised, would have intrinsic value and has a premium at or near that intrinsic value.

DEEP-OUT-OF-MONEY. An option that has a premium very near zero.

DELIVERY. The process by which the short of a futures contract meets all obligations through the actual sale of the underlying instrument to the long. In options, delivery is known as exercise.

DELTA. The amount an option premium is expected to change given a small change in the underlying instrument's price.

DISCRETE. The property of a function that is composed of individual outcomes that do not occur continuously.

DURATION. The weighted average maturity of a bond. The duration of a coupon bond gives the effective maturity of the instrument, with its price sensitivity equal to that of a zero coupon bond maturing at a time equal to the duration.

EARLY EXERCISE. The exercise of an American option before its expiration date.

ELASTICITY. The responsiveness of one variable with respect to another. Always a ratio of the percentage changes of the two variables.

EUROCURRENCY DEPOSITS. Time deposits at major London banks, denominated in dollars, yen, deutsche marks, Swiss francs, and so on.

EUROPEAN OPTION. An option that may be exercised only at the expiration time.

EXCHANGE RATE. The price of one nation's currency in terms of another.

EXERCISE. The act of converting an option into the underlying instruments. (*See* Delivery.)

EXERCISE PRICE. The price at which the owner of an option may buy, in the case of a call, or sell, in the case of a put, the underlying instrument. Also known as a strike price or striking price.

EXPIRATION. The date that any given option or future ceases to exist.

FACE VALUE. The original principal amount of a loan.

FLAT BOOK. A portfolio that is neither long nor short.

FLOOR BROKER. Anyone who executes customer orders on the floor of an exchange.

FLOOR TRADER. Anyone who trades for his own account on the floor of an exchange, also known as a local. Can include scalpers, day traders, and position traders.

FORWARD CONTRACT. Any contract that calls for performance at some time in the future. Usually describes an agreement not made on an exchange.

FORWARD RATE. Typically, an interest rate or currency exchange rate to be effective at some time in the future.

FUTURES COMMISSION MERCHANT (FCM). A firm that transacts futures business for public customers.

FUTURES CONTRACT. A contract to buy or sell a standardized product at some point in the future. In the United States, the only legal futures contracts are those traded on designated exchanges.

FUTURES-STYLE MARGINS. A system of margins for options in which both the buyer and the seller post risk margins, and the positions are marked to market daily.

GOLD POINTS. The bounds within which the price of two related markets may fluctuate without creating an opportunity for arbitrage.

HEDGE. A position using futures and/or options that is opposite to an actual or anticipated cash market exposure.

HEDGE RATIO. The number of futures or options contracts that precisely matches the offset positions.

HISTORICAL VOLATILITY. The standard deviation of the percentage changes of the price changes for an instrument, calculated over a given period.

IMMUNIZATION. The process by which the value of a bond portfolio is insulated against changes in interest rates.

IMPLIED VOLATILITY. A calculated figure of volatility that is derived from a single price and interest rate configuration. (*See* Historical Volatility.)

LIBOR. The London Interbank Offered Rate. This is the interest rate for Eurodollar time deposits at major London banks.

LONG. A position that is the purchase of a futures, option, or cash instrument. Long can also mean the individual holding such positions.

MAINTENANCE MARGIN. The minimum amount of money that must be kept in an account to secure a futures or options position. The amount varies from contract to contract.

MARGINS. Funds deposited by a position holder to guarantee the performance of the contract.

MARKET ON CLOSE ORDER. An order to buy or sell a futures or options contract within the closing range of prices for the day.

MARKET ORDER. An order to buy or sell a futures or options contract without specifying a price. A market sell order should be done without delay at the current bid; a market buy order should be filled at the current offer.

MARK-TO-MARKET. The process of debiting losses and crediting gains for margin accounts on a daily basis. Calculations are based on the settlement price. (*See* Daily Settlement.)

NAKED OPTION. A short call or put written by someone with no cash, futures, or options position that would move in the opposite direction as the short option.

OFFSETTING POSITION. A transaction in cash, futures, or options that is the economic opposite of an existing position. Someone short a futures contract can take on an offsetting or liquidating position by going long the same contract.

OPEN INTEREST. The number of futures or options contracts outstanding at any time. This will include all contracts not yet offset (futures and options), exercised (options), delivered on (futures), or cash settled (futures and options).

OPTION. A contract conveying the right to buy (call) or sell (put) an instrument or index value at a predetermined price for a fixed period.

OUT-OF-THE-MONEY. An option that has a strike price that is higher (call) or lower (put) than the current underlying price, making it uneconomical to choose to exercise the option.

OVER-THE-COUNTER MARKET (OTC). Transactions in cash and forward transactions made by dealers and brokers away from the organized exchanges.

PIT. The physical location, frequently multitiered, in which futures and options trades occur at organized exchanges. In some markets, this area is known as a ring.

PORTFOLIO INSURANCE. A strategy combining cash, futures, and options orders designed to put a lower bound on the value of a group of stocks.

POSITION LIMIT. The maximum number of contracts an individual may hold in any given contract, either alone or acting in concert with other investors.

POSITION TRADER. A futures or options trader who speculates on the intermediate or long-term price level of the underlying commodity.

PREVAILING BID/ASK. The highest bid and the lowest offer in the market at any time. Also known as prevailing bid/offer.

PREVAILING BID/OFFER. *See* Prevailing Bid/Ask.

PRIVILEGE. A term synonymous with option; largely absent from modern usage.

PROGRAM TRADING. A broad group of trading strategies that have the common feature of real-time computer evaluation of trading opportunities to guide decisions.

PUT. An option that gives its holder the right to sell the underlying instrument.

REPURCHASE AGREEMENT. A transaction in which an asset is sold, and simultaneously, an agreement is made to buy it back at some time in the future. The difference in the purchase and sale prices reflects the opportunity cost of holding the asset over the time period.

REVERSE CONVERSION. A spread position consisting of a long futures contract plus a short call and a long put with the same strike price.

RHO. The amount an option premium is expected to change given a small change in the interest rate.

SCALPER. A local floor trader who provides liquidity by offering to buy or sell in a futures or options pit. Typically, a scalper will hold an open position for a very short time.

SEAT. The symbolic term for a membership on a futures, options, or securities exchange.

SETTLEMENT PRICE. Final daily price reflecting the closing range in futures and options markets, used by the clearing house in determining daily mark-to-market payments.

SHORT. A position that involves the sale of a futures, option, or cash instrument. Short can also mean the individual holding such positions.

SPECULATION. The activity of trading on anticipated price changes that are not offsetting to the commercial activity of the individual or firm.

SPOT MARKET. The market for the immediate sale or purchase of an asset.

SPOT PRICE. The price prevailing in the spot market for an asset.

SPREAD. A combination of long and short positions in options or futures that typically reduce the risk when compared to the outright positions.

STOCK INDEX. A simple or weighted average of stock prices built to reflect the performance of the entire group of stocks.

STRADDLE. A combination consisting of one put and one call, either both long or both short, at the same strike price and with the same underlying instrument.

STRANGLE. A combination consisting of one put and one call, either both long or both short, with the same underlying instrument but with the put strike price lower than the call strike price.

STRIKE PRICE. *See* Exercise Price. Also known as striking price.

STRIP. A combination of all long or all short Eurodollar or T-bill futures or options spanning several contract quarters. Used to create the synthetic equivalent of a longer maturity contract.

SYNTHETIC CALL. A combination of a long futures plus a long put is a synthetic long call. A combination of a short futures plus a short put is a synthetic short call.

SYNTHETIC FUTURES. A combination of long call and a short put at the same strike price is a synthetic long futures. A combination of a short call and a long put at the same strike price is a synthetic short futures.

SYNTHETIC PUT. A combination of a long call and a short futures is a synthetic long put. A combination of a long futures and a short call is a synthetic short put.

TERM STRUCTURE OF INTEREST RATES. The relationship of interest rates across similar quality debt instruments of varying maturities.

TICK. The minimum price change allowed for an option or a futures contract.

TIME VALUE. The value of an option above its intrinsic value. Time value declines as maturity approaches, all other things being held the same.

VARIATION MARGIN. The account adjustments to reflect profits or losses calculated from the daily marking-to-market.

VEGA. The amount an option premium is expected to change given a small change in the volatility of the underlying instrument's price.

VOLATILITY. The measure of the degree of price change expected for an asset. (*See* Historical Volatility.)

ZERO COUPON BOND. A bond that makes no explicit interest payments during its life but trades at a discount to its face value.

References

Arak, Marcelle, Laurie S. Goodman, and Susan Ross (1986). "The Cheapest to Deliver Bond on the Treasury Bond Futures Contract," in Frank J. Fabozzi, ed., *Advances in Futures and Options Research,* vol. 1, part B, pp. 49–74. JAI Press, Greenwich, CT.

Arthur Andersen & Co. (1985). "Accounting for Interest Rate Futures." Working Paper.
———— (1986). "Accounting for Options." Working Paper.

Banerjee, Anirudoha, and Robert Weaver (1987). "Does Futures Trading Destabilize Cash Prices? Evidence for U.S. Live Beef Cattle." Staff Paper No. 138. Agricultural Economics and Rural Sociology Department, Pennsylvania State University, University Park, Pennsylvania.

Bear, Robert M. (1986). "Introduction to Futures Contracts," in Frank J. Fabozzi and Frank G. Zarb, eds., *Handbook of Financial Markets,* pp. 635–55. Dow-Jones Irwin, Homewood, IL.

Black, Fischer (1976). "The Pricing of Commodity Contracts," *Journal of Financial Economics* 3 (January–March): 167–79.

Black, Fischer, and Myron Scholes (1973). "The Pricing of Options and Corporate Liabilities," *Journal of Political Economy* 81 (May–June): 637–59.

Bookstaber, Richard M. (1981). *Option Pricing and Strategies in Investing.* Addison-Wesley, Reading, MA.

Bookstaber, Richard, and Roger Clarke (1984). "Option Portfolio Strategies: Measurement and Evaluation," *Journal of Business* 57, no. 4:469–92.

Brady Commission (1988). *Report of the Presidential Task Force on Market Mechanisms,* January. Washington, DC.

Carasik, Karen S. (1981). "Exchange-Traded Clearinghouse (Offset) Options," *Journal of Futures Markets* 1:539–41.

Chicago Mercantile Exchange (1986). "Lufthansa: A Case Study in Options," *Market Perspectives,* September.

———— (1987a). "Futures and Options Trading for Commercial Banks: The Regulatory Environment," CME White Paper Series Number 5.

———— (1987b). "Futures and Options Trading for Insurance Companies: The Regulatory Environment," CME White Paper Series Number 4.

———— (1987c). "Futures and Options Trading for Mutual Funds: The Regulatory Environment," CME White Paper Series Number 1.

———— (1987d). "Futures and Options Trading for Pension Plans: The Regulatory Environment," CME White Paper Series Number 2.

———— (1987e). "Futures and Options Trading for Savings and Loan Associations: The Regulatory Environment," CME White Paper Series Number 3.

Commodity Futures Trading Commission (1987a). "Interim Report on Stock Index Futures and Cash Market Activity during October 1987," November. Washington, DC.

———— (1987b). "A Review of Stock Index Futures Trading on January 23, 1987," July. Washington, DC. Report.

———— (1988a). "Final Report on Stock Index Futures and Cash Market Activity during October 1987," January. Washington, DC.

———— (1988b). "Follow-up Report on Financial Oversight of Stock Index Futures Markets during October 1987," January. Washington, DC.

Comptroller of the Currency (1983), Banking Circular No. 79. Washington, DC.

Cox, John C., and Mark Rubinstein (1985). *Options Markets.* Prentice Hall, Englewood Cliffs, NJ.

Cox, John C., Stephen A. Ross, and Mark Rubinstein (1979). "Option Pricing: A Simplified Approach," *Journal of Financial Economics* 7 (September): 229–63.

Draper, Dennis W. (1985). "The Small Public Trader in Futures Markets," in Anne E. Peck, ed., *Futures Markets: Regulatory Issues,* pp. 211–70. American Enterprise Institute, Washington, DC.

Edwards, Franklin R. (1987). "Does Futures Trading Increase Stock Market Volatility?" November. Mimeo.

Federal Reserve Bank of New York (1987). "The Risk-Based Capital Agreement: A Further Step towards Policy Convergence," *Quarterly Review* 12, no. 4:25–34.

Figlewski, Stephen (1986). *Hedging with Financial Futures for Institutional Investors.* Ballinger, Cambridge, MA.

Fitzgerald, Thomas (1986). "How Corporations Use Futures," Speech given to the National Association of Business Economists. May 21, 1989. Chicago.

Friedman, Milton (1953). "The Case for Flexible Exchange Rates," in *Essays in Positive Economics.* University of Chicago Press, Chicago, IL.

———— (1984). "Financial Futures Markets and Tabular Standards," *Journal of Political Economy* 92, no. 1:165–67.

Geske, Robert (1979). "A Note on an Analytical Formula for Unprotected American Call Options on Stocks with Known Dividends," *Journal of Financial Economics* 7 (December): 375–80.

Geske, Robert, and Richard Roll (1984). "On Valuing American Call Options with the Black-Scholes European Formula," *Journal of Finance* 39 (June): 1271–78.

Gray, Roger W. (1963). "Onions Revisited," *Journal of Farm Economics* 45, no. 2:273–76.

Imel, Blake, Ronald Hobson, and Paula Tosini (1985). "The CFTC's Hedging Definition—Development and Current Issues." Commodity Futures Trading Commission, Washington DC. Report.

Jarnagin, Bill D., and Jon A. Booker (1985). *Financial Accounting Standards,* 7th ed. Commerce Clearing House, Chicago.

Johnson, Philip McBride (1985). "Federal Regulation in Securities and Futures Markets," in Anne E. Peck, ed., *Futures Markets: Their Economic Role,* pp. 291–323. American Enterprise Institute, Washington, DC.

Katzenbach, Nicholas (1987). *An Overview of Program Trading and Its Impact on Current Market Practices.* New York Stock Exchange, New York. Report.

Kaufman, Perry (1984). *Handbook of Futures Markets.* Wiley, New York.

Kawaller, Ira (1986). "Hedging with Futures Contracts: Going the Extra Mile," *Journal of Cash Management,* July/August, pp. 34–36.

——— (1987). "Debunking the Myth of the Risk-Free Return," *Journal of Futures Markets* 7, no. 3:327–31.

——— (1988). "A Primer on Eurodollar Strips," *Financial Managers' Statement,* March/April, pp. 72–75.

Koppenhaver, Gary D., and Cheng F. Lee (1987). "Alternative Instruments for Hedging Inflation Risk in the Banking Industry," SM-87-5, January. Federal Reserve Bank of Chicago. Report.

Kopprasch, Robert W. (1981). *An Introduction to Financial Futures on Treasury Securities.* Salomon Brothers, New York.

Macaulay, F. R. (1938). "Some Theoretical Problems Suggested by the Movements of Interest Rates, Bond Yields, and Stock Prices Since 1856." National Bureau of Economic Research, New York. Report.

Melamed, Leo, ed. (1988). *The Merits of Flexible Exchange Rates.* George Mason University Press, Fairfax, VA.

Merton, Robert C. (1973). "Theory of Rational Option Pricing," *Bell Journal of Economics and Management Science* 4 (Spring): 141–83.

Rockwell, Charles S. (1967). "Normal Backwardation, Forecasting, and the Returns to Commodity Futures Traders," *Food Research Institute Studies,* Supplement to vol. 7.

Roll, Richard (1988). "The International Crash of 1987," UCLA Report #9-88. John E. Anderson Graduate School of Management, Los Angeles, CA.

Rudd, Andrew (1988). "Duration, Convexity, and Multiple Factor Models," *Investment Management Review,* September–October, pp. 58–64.

Securities and Exchange Commission (1987). "The Role of Index-Related Trading in the Market Decline on September 11 and 12, 1986," March. Washington, DC.

Stigum, Marcia (1981). *Money Market Calculations.* Dow-Jones Irwin, Homewood, IL.

Toevs, Alden L., and David P. Jacob (1986). "Hedging with Financial Futures," in Robert B. Platt, ed., *Controlling Interest Rate Risk,* pp. 62–116. Wiley, New York.

United States House of Representatives (1988). "Report on the Regulation of Futures Margins," Committee on Banking, Finance and Urban Affairs, Subcommittee on Domestic Monetary Policy, August. Washington, DC.

Whaley, Robert E. (1986). "Valuation of American Futures Options: Theory and Empirical Tests," *Journal of Finance* 41, no. 1:127–50.

Williams, Jeffrey (1986). *The Economic Function of Futures Markets*. Cambridge University Press, Cambridge, UK.

Wissner, Leonard H. (1987). "How to Protect against a Bear Bond Market," *Pension World,* January, pp. 40–44.

Working Group on Financial Markets (1988). "Interim Report of the Working Group on Financial Markets," May. Washington, DC.

Index

About the Author

TODD E. PETZEL is Vice President, Research at the Chicago Mercantile Exchange.

ISBN 0-89930-152-5

EAN

HARDCOVER BAR CODE